ENCYCLOPAEDIA OF INDIAN GOVERNMENT: PROGRAMMES AND POLICIES

ENCYCLOPAEDIA
OF
INDIAN GOVERNMENT:
PROGRAMMES AND POLICIES

Vol. 9

Water and Energy Resources

Edited by

Satish Tiwari

ANMOL PUBLICATIONS PVT. LTD.

NEW DELHI - 110 002 (INDIA)

ANMOL PUBLICATIONS PVT. LTD.
4374/4B, Ansari Road, Daryaganj
New Delhi - 110 002

Encyclopaedia of Indian Government: Programmes and Policies

First Edition, 2000
ISBN 81-261-0515-1 (Set)

PRINTED IN INDIA

Published by J.L. Kumar for Anmol Publications Pvt. Ltd., New Delhi - 110 002 and Printed at Mehra Offset Press, Delhi.

Contents

Preface — *vii*

1. Water Resources: Programmes and Policies — 1
2. Energy and Environment Sectors — 41
3. National Water Development Agency — 137
4. Commission Board and Research Station — 143
5. Research and Development Organisations — 230
6. Water Resources Authority Advisory Board — 291

Preface

Encyclopaedia of Indian Government: Programmes and Policies contains authoritative information on about fifty departmental policies and their future developmental programmes.

Organised to be completed in 40 volumes, this gigantic work covers Agriculture; Atomic Energy; Chemicals and Fertilizers; Coal; Commerce; Communication; Culture; Defence; Education; Environment and Forests; External Affairs; Finance; Food & Consumer Affairs; Food Processing Industries; Health and Family Welfare; Home Affairs and Internal Security; Human Resources; Industry; Information and Broadcasting; Labour; Law, Justice and Company Affairs; Non-conventional Energy Sources; Ocean Development; Parliamentary Affairs; Personnel, Public Grievances and Pensions; Petroleum and Natural Gas; Planning and Programme Implementation; Planning and Statistics; Posts and Telegraphs; Power; Rural Development; Science and Technology; Social Justice and Empowerment; Space; States Affairs; Steel; Steel and Mines; Sugar and Edible Oils; Surface Transport; Textiles; Tourism; Urban Development; Water Resources; Women and Child development etc.

Based on the information derived from authoritative sources, this work contains authentic facts and figures. I am deeply beholden to all the scholars whose writings are cited or substantially made use of in the present work. I am also thankful to Anmol Publications Pvt. Ltd. for undertaking publication of this encyclopaedia. I am solely responsible for shortcomings in presentation of matter.

Encyclopaedic in nature, this will prove a dependable reference work for scholars and academics besides those appearing for different competitive examinations.

—Satish Tiwari

1

Water Resources: Programmes and Policies

The Ministry of Water Resources is responsible for laying down policy guidelines and programmes for the development and of country's water resources. The Ministry is responsible for the. following functions

(a) Overall planning, policy formulation, coordination and guidance in the sector of water resources as a whole.

(b) Technical guidance, scrutiny, clearance and monitoring of the irrigation, flood control and multipurpose projects (major/medium) of the States.

(c) Infrastructural, technical and research support for sectoral development at the State level.

(d) Providing special central financial assistance for specific projects and assistance in obtaining external assistance from the World Bank and the other agencies.

(e) Overall policy formulation, planning and guidance in respect of minor irrigation and command area development, and also the administration and monitoring of the centrally sponsored schemes in these areas.

(f) Overall planning for the development of ground water resources, establishment of utilisable resources and formulation of policies of exploitation, overseeing of and support to the State level activities in ground water development Formulation of the national water development perspective and determination of the water balance of different basins/ sub-basins for possible inter-basin transfers.

(h) Coordination, mediation and facilitation in regard to the resolution of differences or disputes relating to interstate rivers and overseeing of the implementation of interstate projects.

(i) Operation of the central network for flood forecasting and warning on interstate rivers, the provision of central assistance for some State schemes in special cases and preparation of flood control master plans for the Ganga and the Brahmaputra.

(j) Negotiations With the neighbouring countries, like Bangladesh, Nepal and Pakistan. in regard to river waters, water resources development projects and the operation of the Indus Water Treaty.

Ministry of water resources

The Prime Minister is holding the charge of the Ministry of Water Resources since March, 1998. Shri Som Pal assumed charge of Minister of State of Water Resources in addition to Minister of State of Agriculture from 3.2.1999. Shri Mata Prasad remained the Secretary in the Ministry of Water Resources up to 23.4.1998. Shri Z. Hasan took over as Secretary in the Ministry of Water Resources from 29.6.1998.

The work of the Ministry is divided among the following wings:

- Administration
- Finance
- Policy and planning
- Project and minor irrigation
- Eastern rivers

— Indus
— Command area development
— Water management

Each Wing is headed by an officer of the level of Joint Secretary. The functions of these wings are as follows:-

Administration wing

The Administration Wing is responsible for cadre management of the Central Water Engineering (Group 'A') Service, cadre management of CSS/ CSCS/ CSSS posts in the Ministry as well as its attached offices, matters concerning personnel in Central Ground Water Board, matters relating to All India Service officers in the Ministry, training of officers and staff, all matters relating to ground water development, annual report and annual action plan of the Ministry, Parliamentary Consultative Committee, Implementation of Official Language Act, vigilance, redressal of public grievances and monitoring the implementation of reservation policy for Scheduled Castes/Scheduled Tribes, OBCs and physically handicapped persons.

Finance wing

The Finance Wing is mainly responsible for monitoring expenditure on various plan/non-plan schemes, giving advice on financial proposals, preparation of budget, revised estimates, performance budget, work measurement studies and audit objections etc.

The accounting set up headed by the Controller of Accounts comprises the Principal Accounts Office located at New Delhi with seven Pay and Accounts Offices, four located at New Delhi and one each at Faridabad, Pune and Farakka. The Controller of Accounts is assisted by three Deputy Controllers of Accounts, one Assistant Controller of Accounts and seven flay and Accounts Officers. The Controller of Accounts is responsible for compiling the expenditure, preparation of budget and revised estimates, performance budget, reappropriation, allocation of scheme-wise annual plan funds, supplementary grants, vote on account and clearance of projects from the financial angle etc.

Policy and planning wing

All policy matters relating to the development of water resources, preparation of five year plans, annual plans, Twenty Point Programme, administrative matters relating to the Narmada Control Authority, Sardar Sarovar Construction Advisory Committee, matters relating to Sardar Sarovar Project, Central Water and Power Research Station, Central Soil and Materials Research Station and National Institute of Hydrology are being handled in the Policy and Planning Wing. It also looks after the external assistance for multipurpose projects from the international funding agencies.

Project and minor irrigation wing

The Project Wing is responsible for policy matters concerning interstate issues, disputes about waters of interstate rivers except Ravi-Beas and Sutlej Water and Yamuna Water disputes, all administrative and technical matters relating to (i) Farakka Barrage Project, (ii) Public Sector Undertakings under the Ministry i.e. Water and Power Consultancy Services (India) Limited and 'National Projects Construction Corporation Limited and (111) National Water Development Agency, an autonomous body. Matters relating to irrigation and multipurpose projects in various States, including Central Loan Assistance to the States under Accelerated Irrigation Benefits Programme are also looked after by this wing.

The Minor Irrigation Division monitors the progress of development of irrigation created through minor irrigation projects, It implements the centrally sponsored scheme of rationalisation of minor irrigation statistics including census of minor irrigation structures with a view to creating a reliable data base for the purpose. It also assists the State Governments in preparation of schemes for posing to external funding agencies for attracting external assistance for minor irrigation schemes. During the year 1997-98, four such schemes received from Rajasthan, West Bengal, Tamil Nadu and Andhra Pradesh were examined for technical viability.

Eastern river wing

This Wing deals with matters relating to Ganga and Brahmaputra basins and in particular, international aspects of development of water resources and sharing with Bangladesh, Nepal and Bhutan. It also deals with the matters relating to Ganga Flood Control Commission, Patna, and Brahmaputra Board, Guwahati. All matters concerning flood management and sea erosion of the entire country are handled in this Wing.

Indus wing

The Indus Wing is mainly responsible for implementation of the Indus Waters Treaty, 1960 with Pakistan. In addition, matters relating to Ravi-Beas Waters Tribunal, Sutlej-Yamuna Link Canal, sharing of Yamuna waters up to Okhla and Ganga waters up to Haridwar, Upper Yamuna River Board and Upper Yamuna Review Committee, Delhi Water Supply and Flood Control and Drought Management are being handled by this Wing.

Command area development wing

The Command Area Development Wing is concerned with the implementation of the centrally sponsored Command Area Development Programme. The responsibilities of the CAD Wing include monitoring the progress of the works under the Programme, release of central assistance to the States, promoting participatory irrigation management, training of farmers and officials in CAD related activities, action research programmes and adaptive trials etc.

Water management wing

The Water Management Wing is responsible for the implementation of the World Bank assisted Hydrology Project in eight States and five Central agencies. A project Coordination Secretariat for coordinating, monitoring, administering and managing the implementation of the Project has been set up in WM Wing. The Wing is also monitoring the implementation of World Bank assisted Water Resources Consolidation Projects, currently under implementation in Haryana, Tamil Nadu and Orissa. The wing is also dealing with issues relating to National Water Management Project and pricing of water for irrigation.

National water policy

Water as a precious national asset, the National Water Policy embodies the Nation's resolve that planning and development of water resources will be governed by the national perspective. The policy recognises drainage basin as the basic unit of planning for development of water resources and calls for appropriate measures to optimise utilisation of this resource not only for the benefit of the people living in the basin, but also for transfer of surplus water to meet the requirements of areas which have shortage of water. The principal elements of the policy are:-

- Water is a precious national resource and its development should be governed by the national perspectives;
- The available resources, both surface and ground water, should be made utilisable to the maximum extent;
- Planning for water resources to be on the basis of the hydrological unit such as a drainage basin or

sub-basin. Appropriate organisations should be established for the planned development and management of the river basins as a whole;

— Water should be made available to areas where there is a shortage by transfer from other areas including transfers from one river basin to another, after taking into account the requirements of the basins;

— Project planning for development of water resource should, as far as possible, be for multiple benefits based on integrated and multi disciplinary approach having regard to human and ecological aspects and special needs of disadvantaged sections of the society;

— In the allocation of water, ordinarily first priority should be for drinking water, with Irrigation, hydro-power, industrial and other uses following in that order;

— The ground water potential should be periodically reassessed and its exploitation regulated with reference to recharge possibilities and consideration of social equity;

— Due care should be taken tight from the project planning state to promote conjunctive use of surface and groundwater;

— Maintenance, modernisation and safety of structures should be ensured through proper organisational arrangements;

— There should be close integration of water use and land use policies and distribution of water should be with due regard to equity and social justice;

— Efficiency of utilisation should be improved in all the diverse uses of water and conservation consciousness promoted through education, regulation, incentives and disincentives;

— Water rates should be such as to foster the

motivation for economy in water use and should adequately cover the annual maintenance and operational charges and a part of the fixed cost ;

— Farmers should be progressively involved in the management of irrigation system;

— There should be a Master Plan for flood control and management for each flood prone basin. In flood control and management, the strategy should be to reduce the intensity of floods by sound watershed management and provision of adequate flood cushion in water storage projects wherever feasible to facilitate better flood management of each flood prone basin;

— Land erosion by sea or river should be minimised by suitable cost-effective measures. Indiscriminate occupation of, and economic activity in coastal areas and flood plain zones should be regulated;

— Needs of drought-prone areas should be given priority in the planning of projects for development of water resources. These areas should be made less vulnerable through soil-moisture conservation measures, water harvesting practices, the minimisation of evaporation losses, the development of ground water potential and transfer of surface water from surplus areas where feasible and appropriate. Pastures, forestry or other modes of development which are relatively less water demanding should be encouraged;

— A national information system on water resources should be established with a network of data banks and data bases integrating and strengthening the existing Central and State level agencies;

— Training and research efforts should be intensified as an integral part of water resources development programmes.

Follow up action

The Union and State Governments are taking necessary follow-up action for the implementation of the Policy. State Water Policies have been framed by Governments of Kerala, Orissa and Tamil Nadu. The Governments of Arunachal Pradesh, Daman & Diu, Lakshadweep, Maharashtra, Haryana, Bihar, Meghalaya, Rajasthan, Nagaland, Mizoram, Andhra Pradesh, Jammu & Kashmir, Punjab, Himachal Pradesh, Karnataka and Pondicherry have already initiated action to follow policy guidelines. The Government of Madhya Pradesh has drafted the State Water Policy and has taken up the preparation of perspective plan for each river basin.

Updating/revision of national water policy

The National Agenda for Governance provides for adoption of a National Water Policy for effective and prompt settlement of disputes and their time bound implementation. Since the adoption of the National Water Policy in 1987, a number of problems and challenges have emerged in the development and management of the water resources sector. Further, in his address to the Nation on 22nd March, 1998, the Prime Minister had also stated that the Government would unveil a National Water Policy so that no water was wasted and we could clean up our water resources.

The existing National Water Policy needs to be reviewed and updated in the context of existing problems and emerging challenges and also in the light of the experiences of the last ten years of its implementation. Some of the important areas and aspects, which should be considered for their inclusion in the existing National Water Policy, include multi-sectoral perspective and participatory approach towards planning of resources and management, private sector participation and integration of quantity, quality and environmental aspects in the water resources management, mandatory funding of operation and maintenance and related policies for revenue generation and reforms related to legislations, institutions, incentives and disincentives, environment and technology etc. under the water resources sector.

Accordingly, the National Water Board in its meeting on 29.10.1998 reviewed the existing National Water Policy 198 7, considered proposed changes and finalised and updated draft National Water Policy 1998. The updated National Water Policy is being placed before the National Water Resources Council for its consideration and adoption.

National policy guidelines for water allocation among states

Management of country's resources of water should be such as to be able to give people respite from recurrent floods and droughts in the country a possible solution for which involves transfer of water from surplus to deficient areas for which agreements between basin States are required. In view of this fact, the issue becomes very complex.

In most of the cases the interests of upper riparian States are in conflict with lower riparian States as far as sharing of water is concerned, which delays the development and scientific management of water resources.

The National Water Policy was adopted by the National Water Resources Council of India in 1987. At the time of adoption of the policy, the Council had taken note of the necessity for formulating guidelines for allocation of water of inter-State rivers among the States. The National Water Board constituted under the National Water Resources Council has also indicated the need for such guidelines.

The draft of the National Policy Guidelines for Water Allocation among the States were considered in detail in the special meeting of the National Water Board held in June, 1994. In the light of suggestions and discussions in the meeting of the National Water Board, the Ministry of Water Resources has prepared a draft of the National Policy Guidelines for Water Allocation among the States.

The draft of the policy was also discussed in the eighth meeting of the National Water Board held on Sixth November, 1996. As consensus could not be reached, it was decided that a detailed note indicating the points of agreement or otherwise would be prepared and placed before the National Water Resources Council.

As a follow up action on the decision taken in that meeting of the National Water Board, a note indicating the points of agreement or otherwise on guidelines for allocation of waters of interstate rivers among States was prepared and discussed in the subsequent meeting of the National Water Board in November, 1997. It was decided that the draft of the guidelines as finalised by the Board, incorporating necessary modifications based on suggestions received from the Members during the meeting, might be placed before the National Water Resources Council for its consideration and adoption.

The modified Guidelines will now be submitted to the National Water Resources Council together with the draft National Water Policy (1998) for its consideration.

National water resources council

National Water Resources Council (N.W.R.C) was setup by the Government of India in March, 1983 with Prime Minister as the Chairman, Union Minister of Water Resources as Vice-Chairman, and concerned Union Ministers, Chief Ministers of State Governments and

Administrators/ Lt. Governors of the Union Territories as Members. Secretary, Ministry of Water Resources, is the Secretary of the Council. The functions of the Council are as follows:-

— To lay down the National Water Policy and to review it from time to time ;

— To consider and review development plans submitted to it (including alternative plans) by the National Water Development Agency, the River Basin Commissions etc.;

— To recommend acceptance of the plans with Such — modifications as may be considered appropriate and necessary ;

— To give directions for carrying out such further studies as may be necessary for full consideration of the plans or component thereof;

— To advise on the modalities of resolving inter-State differences with regard to specific elements of these plans and such other issues that may arise during planning of implementation of the project;

— To advise on practices and procedures, administrative arrangements and regulations for fair distribution and utilisation of water resources by different beneficiaries keeping in view optimum development and the maximum benefits to the people ; and

— To make such other recommendations as would foster expeditious, environmentally sound and economical development of water resources in various regions.

The Council has held three meetings so far. In the second meeting held in 1987, the National Water Policy was adopted unanimously. The third meeting of the N.W.R.C. was held on Sixth February, 1996, when the following issues/ policy papers were placed before the Council for consideration and adoption.

— Water Information Bill.
— Policy note on setting up of River Basin Organisation.
— National policy for resettlement and rehabilitation of persons affected by reservoir projects.
— Modification of water allocation priorities specified by National Water Policy.
— Overall policy guidelines for water management and pricing of water for industrial purposes.
— An approach to organisational and procedural changes in irrigation sector.
— Irrigation Management Policy.
— Guidelines for planning conjunctive use of surface and ground water in irrigation projects.

The deliberations of the Council on the above item remained inconclusive. The 4th meeting of the National Water Resources Council is being convened to discuss updated draft National Water Policy and Draft National Policy Guidelines for Allocation of waters of Inter-State Rivers amongst States.

National water board

National water board was constituted in September, 1990 with -Secretary, Ministry of Water Resources, as Chairman, Chief Secretaries of all the States/ UTs, Secretaries of concerned Union Ministries and Chairman, CWC as Members in order to review the progress of implementation of the National Water Policy for reporting to the NWRC and also initiate effective measures for systematic development of the country's water resources. Member (Water Policy and Planning), CWC is the Member-Secretary of the Board.

Standing committeefor assessment of water

Under the Government of India (Allocation of Business), (227th Amendment) Rules, 1995, Ministry of Water

Resources is responsible, among other things for planning of water resources from the national perspective and coordinate diverse uses of water for the purpose of holistic planning. With a view to enabling the Ministry to discharge its mandated role mentioned above, a Standing Committee and a Standing Sub-Committee were constituted in the Ministry of Water Resources in 1996. The Standing Committees and the subcommittee have met thrice so far to prepare a document on the "'Assessment of Availability and Requirement of Water for Various Uses in the Country".

The States/UTs have also been requested to set up similar State Level Committees for holistic planning of water resources keeping its diverse uses in view. So far 23 State Governments have set up such Committees.

Private sector participation in irrigation

Financial constraints in the public sector are coming in the way of development of water resources'. It is felt that attracting private sector participation In the sectors of irrigation and hydro-power may give an impetus to the projects, which are under implementation for some time and encourage States to plan new projects.

A High Level Committee under the Chairmanship of the Minister of State for Water Resources was constituted in 1995 to examine the feasibility and scope of private sector participation in irrigation and multipurpose projects. The Committee comprised officials of the Ministry of Water Resources, other related Ministries of the Government of India and representatives of some of the State Governments. The Committee gave its report in December, 1995.

The Committee in its report submitted in December 1995, concluded that private sector participation is feasible in respect of all irrigation (surface and ground water) and multipurpose projects but it would be desirable to introduce this on a pilot basis for projects that did not involve inter-state problems, security issues etc. The recommendations of the Committee have been sent to the States for taking follow up action.

Development of irrigation facilities

Average runoff in the river system of the country has been assessed as 1869 Km^3. Of this, the utilisable portion is estimated as about 690 Km^3. In addition, there is a substantial replenishable ground water potential in the country estimated at 432 Km^3.

Rapid fall in the per-capita availability of water Is, however, becoming evident due to explosive population growth, large scale urbanisation and industrialisation in the country. From a fairly comfortable level of water availability per person in the early stages of development, a significant decline has been noticed in the share of water availability over the years.

The per capita has reduced from about 5277 ml in the year 1955 to the present level in 1970 m^3. The situation may aggravate in future due to the growing water scarcity in the river basins.

Irrigation potential

At the beginning of the era of planning in India in 1951 the irrigation potential was 22 million hectare (m ha). The irrigation potential created up to the end of Seventh Plan was 76.52 m ha against the estimated ultimate potential of 113.5 m ha which has now been reassessed as 13 9.8 9 m ha. On a provisional estimation, it is expected that by the end of the Eighth Plan, it has increased to 89.6 m ha.

Major and medium irrigation

The ultimate irrigation potential of the country from Major and Medium Irrigation projects has been assessed as 58.5 m ha. This includes projects with a culturable command area of more than two thousand hectare. The potential created up to the end of the Sixth Plan (1980-85) was originally reported as 30.01 m ha. This was later on reappraised at 27.70 m ha. The potential created up to the end of Seventh Plan (1985-90) was 29.92 m ha and up to the end of annual Plans 1990-92, it was 30.74 m ha.

A target of 5.09 m ha had been set for creation of additional potential during the Eighth Plan (1992-97) against which, according to a provisional estimate, the potential created is 2.22 m ha. Thus at the end of the Eighth Plan, the cumulative irrigation potential created from major and medium irrigation is anticipated to be 32.96 m ha.

The Plan-wise progress of creation of irrigation potential through major and medium irrigation projects and the expenditure incurred is given in Table 1.

Table 1

Period	*Outlay/ expenditure (Rs. in crore)*	*Potential created (m ha)*	
		During	*umulative*
Pre-Plan Period	–	9.70	9.70
First Plan (1951-56)	376	2.50	12.20
Second Plan (1956-61	380	2.13	14.33
Third Plan (1961-66)	576	2.24	16.57
Annual Plans (1966-69)	430	1.53	18.10
Fourth Plan (1969-74)	1242	2.60	20.70
Fifth Plan (1974-78)	2516	4.02	24.72
Annual Plans (1978-80)	2079	1.89	26.61
Sixth Plan (1980-85)	7369	1.09	27.70
Seventh Plan (1985-90)	11107	2.22	29.92
Annual Plans (1990-92)	5459	0.82	30.74
Eighth Plan (1992-97)	21838	2.22	32.96
Annual Plan (1997-98)	8403 (Approved Outlay)	1.04 (Target)	

Major and medium projects

It is estimated that many major, medium and EPM

projects will spill over in the Ninth Plan from the previous plans. This is given in table 2:

Table 2

	Taken Up	Completed	Spill over into IX Plan
Major	362	200	162
Medium	1081	841	240
ERM	141	67	74

Provisionally, the aggregated present estimated cost of these schemes is Rs. 1,26,3 18.22 crore and the cost of the part spilled over is Rs. 79,3 17.45 crore.

Minor irrigation

All ground water and surface water schemes having culturable command area (CCA) up to 2000 ha individually are classified as minor irrigation schemes. Ground water development is primarily done through individual and cooperative efforts of the farmers with the help of institutional finance and their own savings. Surface water minor irrigation schemes are generally funded from the public sector outlay.

The ultimate irrigation Potential from minor irrigation schemes has been assessed as 81.43 m ha. Up to the end of the Seventh Plan, the potential created through the minor irrigation schemes was 46.60 m ha. During the Eighth Plan, additional irrigation potential of 6.25 (provisional) m ha has been created. Thus, at the end of Eighth Plan, provisionally the cumulative irrigation potential created through minor irrigation schemes is estimated to be 56.60 m ha.

Rationalism of minor irrigation statistics (RMIS)

Minor Irrigation Development in the States/Union Territories is taken up by several agencies and individuals. The Main objective of Central sector scheme of Rationalisation of Minor Irrigation Statistics is to build up a comprehensive and reliable data base in the minor irrigation sector for better planning. Under the scheme, grants are given by the Union Ministry of Water Resources to each State/Union Territory for meeting the cost of a statistical cell. Eighteen States/Union Territories have set up statistical cells under this scheme. These cells are responsible for furnishing quarterly progress reports on minor irrigation development in the State/UT to the Ministry of Water Resources.

The statistical cells also organise surveys, census of minor irrigation projects, collection of statistics of area irrigated under different crops and collection of information on the progress of construction of minor irrigation works.

Census of M.I. works

The second census of minor irrigation works was initiated in September, 1994. Up to January, 1998, 21 States/ UTs had completed the census. The field work has also been completed in four other States/ UTs and computerisation of the data is in progress. The field work in the remaining four States is in progress. Out of a total allocation of Rs. 10. 50 crore, an amount of Rs. 7.26 crore has been released to the different States/UTs/ NIC for conducting the census.

Firming up minor irrigation potential

A Committee headed by the Chairman, Central Water Commission, with representatives from some States and the concerned Departments of the Union Government was set up by the Ministry of Water Resources to firm up the figures of ultimate minor irrigation potential as well as minor irrigation potential created and utilised in the Country. The committee has finalised its report and has made the following recommendations: -

— The present figures of utilisable irrigation potential of 64.05 m ha from ground water and 17.38 m ha from surface water (minor irrigation schemes) may be accepted for the present. These figures need to be reviewed periodically in accordance with the revision in the figures of water availability as well as technical developments taking place in the field of agriculture and irrigation.

— The figures of potential created and utilised during the 8th Five Year Plan has not yet been finalised by the Planning Commission. With the present data base available, firming up of the minor irrigation potential created and utilised up to the end of 8th Five Year Plan is not practicable.

— The Directorate of Economics & Statistics in the Planning Department of the State/ UT should be the nodal department for maintaining the statistics relating to minor irrigation development in the respective States/UTs. All other project implementing agencies Will report their works to the nodal departments.

— There should be uniformity in the type of data — collection.

— In order to assess the potential created/utilised through supplementary irrigation in the command of major and medium schemes, the project authorities should assess the actu al potential utilised in the command. If the figure is more than the actual potential of the project, the excess area under irrigation may be attributed to the supplementary sources of Irrigation.

— As it is difficult to segregate the share of ground water and surface water where the same is being utilised conjunctively in the same command, appropriate weightage should be attributed to the different sources of irrigation in order to recognise the contribution from each source.

Table 3 State-wise number of ongoing major and medium irrigation projects and extension/renovation/modernisation (ERM) schemes spilling over to ninth plan (1997-2002)

Sl. No.	*Name of State*	*No. of ongoing Projects/Schemes spilling over to 9th Plan*		
		Major	*Medium*	*ERM*
1.	Andhra Pradesh	12	20	4
2.	Assam	4	9	3
3.	Bihar	14	29	1
4.	Goa	1	11	1
5.	Gujarat	9	9	9
6.	Haryana	5	–	4
7.	Himachal Pradesh	1	1	1
8.	Jammu & Kashmir	1	9	5
9.	Karnataka	14	15	3
				(Contd...)
10.	Kerala	7	5	2
11.	Madhya Pradesh	23	32	4
12.	Maharashtra	36	66	6
13.	Manipur	2	2	4
14.	Meghalaya	–	1	–
15.	Nagaland	1	–	–
16.	Orissa	1		
17.	Punjab	–	1	8
18.	Rajasthan	6	6	5
19.	Tamil Nadu	–	2	1
20.	Tripura	–	3	–
21.	Uttar Pradesh	18	2	6
22.	West Bengal	3	17	6
	Total	162	240	74

Accelerated irrigation benefit programme

A large number of river valley projects, both multipurpose and irrigation, have spilled over from Plan to Plan, mainly because of financial constraints faced by the State Governments. There are 162 major, 240 medium and 74 ERM projects, which have spilled over from the previous plans to the Ninth Plan and the cost of their completion (at 1998 prices) is estimated to be Rs. 79,317.45 crore.

In order to assist the States to complete the projects in advanced stages, the Government of India launched Accelerated Irrigation Benefit Programme during 199697. It was meant to accelerate the (i) implementation of on-going irrigation/multipurpose projects on which substantial progress had been made and which were beyond the resources of the State Governments and (ii) for other major and medium irrigation projects which were in advanced stages of construction and could yield benefits of irrigation in next four agricultural seasons.

Only those projects are considered under the Programme which have the investment clearance of the Planning Commission. The projects which are already receiving assistance from agencies such as NABARD are not eligible for assistance under this Programme. However, the components of such projects which are not covered under such assistance are considered for inclusion under the Programme. Assistance to large projects is given for their phased completion.

Projects benefiting Tribal/Drought Prone area are given due preference provided they are otherwise eligible. Priority is also given to Inter-State projects and all the party States are eligible for assistance under the Programme individually. Projects with larger irrigated area per unit of additional investment are preferred. Minor irrigation schemes are not eligible for assistance under AIBP because of NABARD's financing for such schemes under Rural Infrastructure Development Fund (RIDF).

The Central Loan Assistance (CLA) to the States is given on a matching basis and is released in two instalments of 50 percent each. The second instalment is released after the States have incurred expenditure equal to twice the CLA already released to them. In the case of North Eastern States and other hilly States, the State Governments are required to contribute only 50 per cent of the CLA released.

The CLA under the programme is in the form of loan at the rate of interest prescribed by the Ministry of Finance from time to time. The loan under the Programme is repayable in 20 equal instalments together with interest on the outstanding balance commencing from the following year. However, 50 per cent of the loan enjoys five years of initial grace period after which repayment of the loans is affected in 15 equal instalments. The loans actually payable will be recovered in 10 equal monthly instalments commencing from June every year.

The projects covered under AIBP are monitored by Central Water Commission. The releases of subsequent instalments are based upon the reports of Central Water Commission.

During 1996-97, Rs. 500.00 crore was released to 52 projects in 18 States. During 1997-98, the Ministry of Finance released an amount of Rs. 9 52.19 crore to 72 projects.

The total irrigation potential likely to be created on completion of these projects receiving AIBP assistance is of the order of 12.63 Million Hectare.

During 1998-99, a budget provision of Rs. 1500 crore exists under AlBP. First instalment of CLA amounting to Rs. 373.205 crore for 33 projects has already been recommended for release to Ministry of Finance in respect of those projects which do not have any shortfall in expenditure. Second proposal amounting to Rs. 182.095 crore for 24 projects is being processed in respect of some new projects and for those projects which have since made up the shortfall in the expenditure. The remaining projects will be recommended only after the concerned States make up the shortfall in expenditure.

Release of second instalment during 1998-99 will depend upon the physical and financial progress of projects which will be reviewed later on during the year.

Command area development programme

High priority was given to the development of irrigation for increasing the agricultural production during the post Independence era. The irrigation potential, which stood at 22.6 m ha till 1950-5 1 had increased to 33.6 m ha by mid sixties. As the potential for irrigation increased, it was realised that utilisation was not keeping pace with it. The Irrigation Commission (1972) analysed this and other concerned problems and recommended systematic development of command areas.

A Committee of Ministers (1973) also looked into the problem of utilisation of irrigation potential and recommended early completion of micro systems for distribution of water and drainage, provision of inputs like seeds, fertilisers, pesticides and other infrastructural facilities and dissemination of technical know-how among farmers and build up a coordinating system to take up all activities related with irrigation water management and irrigated agriculture. As a result, a centrally sponsored Command Area Development (CAD) programme was launched during 1974-75. The Programme's objective was to ensure efficient utilisation of created irrigation potential and to increase the agricultural production from irrigated lands on a sustainable basis through Integration and co-ordination of various activities in irrigated agriculture. To meet this objective a multi-disciplinary team under a Command Area Development Authority/Organisation was created in many States.

Coverage

The Programme began with 60 major and medium irrigation projects coveting 13 States with a Culturable Command Area (CCA) of about 15 m ha. Subsequently, a number of projects were included under the Programme. Presently there are 226 projects under the Programme with a CCA of 21.95 m ha (as on 31.1.1999) spread over 23 States and 2 Union Territories.

Implementation of the programme

The Command Area Development Authorities (CADAs) have been established by many State Governments for one or more projects for the implementation of the CAD Programme. Presently, there are 55 CAD Authorities In the country. Arunachal Pradesh, Himachal Pradesh, Meghalaya, Nagaland, Tamilnadu and Tripura have not constituted CAD Authorities and the Programme is being administered through the concerned Department of the State Governments.

Components

The activities under the Programme are as follows:

(i) On- Farm Development (OFD) Works:

(a) Development of field channels and field drains within the command of each outlet;

(b)Land levelling on an outlet command basis;

(c) Realignment of field boundaries, wherever necessary (where possible, consolidation of holdings should also be combined);

(d) Enforcement of a proper system of "Warabandi" and fair distribution of water to individual fields;

(e) Reclamation of waterlogged areas;

(f) Supply of all inputs and services, including credit; and

(g) Strengthening of extension services.

(ii) Selection and Introduction of suitable cropping pattern.

(iii) Conjunctive use of surface and ground water. Development and maintenance of the main and Intermediate drainage system.

(v) Modernisation, maintenance and efficient operation of the Irrigation system up on the outlet of one cusec capacity.

Financing pattern

The approved financing pattern which has come into force from April, 1996 Is given below.-

Grants

(i) Grants will be admissible on a matching basis to the States for the "establishment', topographical and soil surveys, planning and design of OFD works, supervision of OFD works, construction of field channels, field drains, enforcement of warabandi, adaptive trials, demonstration and training, crop compensation, subsidy to small and marginal farmers on identified items, evaluation studies sponsored by States, reclamation of waterlogged areas and functional grant to Water Users' Associations etc.

(ii) Cent percent grant from the Central Government will be given for orientation training for senior level officers sponsored by Central Government and also for evaluation studies If sponsored by Central Government.

(iii) Subsidy will be admissible for Land Levelling and Shaping, Ground Water Development and Sprinkler and Drip Irrigation to small and marginal farmers for these items of work on the pattern followed under Integrated Rural Development Programme (IRDP).

Loan

(iv) Loan for the purchase of equipment and machinery will be provided to States on matching basis.

Physical performance

The physical progress and targets in respect of core components of On-Farm Development (OFD) works.

Financial performance

An amount of Rs. 1814.59 crore has been released as Central Assistance under the CAD Programme since its inception (1974-75) to March 1998. During the year 1997-98 an amount of Rs. 126.49 crore was spent as against an outlay of Rs. 13 4.00 crore. A revised outlay of Rs. 176.76 crore has been provided under the Central Sector for implementation of the programme during 1998-99.

An important feature of the programme is that Government of Punjab has also decided to implement the Programme and has taken up in Sirhind Feeder canal and Bhaunda Branch canal during 1997-98.

Dissemination of technical know-how among the farmers

This includes activities such as adaptive trials, demonstration of scientific water management, land development, introduction of suitable cropping patterns and varieties and proper dosages and methods of application of fertilisers.

Farmers participation management of irrigation

It is now accepted world-over that stakeholders' participation is necessary for proper management of irrigation. The National Water Policy 1987 has also advocated involvement of farmers in the management of irrigation. The generally accepted term for this is Participatory Irrigation Management (PIM). PIM refers to involvement of irrigation users in all aspects of irrigation management and at all levels.

While the irrigation potential increased nearly four times after 195 1 (22 m ha then to about 89 m ha now), several problems of management of irrigation too arose during this period. These included unreliable and inequitable supply of water especially almost universal tail-end deprivation, poor O&M of the system, poor recovery of water rates, indiscipline in the distribution of water and waterlogging due to seepage and over-irrigation etc. It has now been recognised that participation of beneficiaries is essential for the optimum utilisation of irrigation. The Ministry has taken up several measures to promote this concept which include:

— Creation of awareness and dissemination of information about PIM by organisation of National, State and project level conferences with the participation of officials, NGOs, and farmers ;
— Preparation of manuals for implementation of PIM;-
— Preparation of Guidelines for amendments in the Irrigation Acts of the states to give legal status to water users associations (WUAs);
— Holding of training programmes; and
— Provision of one time functional grant of Rupees Five hundred per hectare to WUAs. This grant is to be shared per hectare at Rs. 225.00 by centre, Rs 225.00 by State and Rs. 50.00 farmers' Association respectively.

These activities have created a good environment in the country for involving the farmers in the management of irrigation. Government of Andhra Pradesh has made a breakthrough by enacting the "Andhra Pradesh Farmers' Management of Irrigation System Act, 1997 (APFMIS Act, 1997) under which elections to more than ten thousand WUAs have already been held. State Government has been providing technical and financial help to these Associations. As a result these Associations have taken up improvement of the irrigation system. This has resulted in increased efficiency of irrigation, increase in irrigated area, agricultural productivity and production in the irrigated commands. Government of Goa has also amended its Command Area Development Act to provide for the establishment of WUAs. Government of Gujarat has taken up thirteen pilot projects to study the modalities of implementation of PIM. Other States are also taking up this concept similarly.

A National Conference on Participatory Irrigation Management was held at Hyderabad from 19th to 23rd January, 1999, in which officers from central and State Governments, NGOs, representatives of the World Bank, Ford Foundation and Economic Development Institute of the World Bank and farmers from different States participated.

The Ministry of Water Resources has facilitated setting up of a Non-Governmental Organisation named Indian Network on Participatory Irrigation Management (IndiaNPIM). The Network has been registered as a society under Societies Registration Act in April, 1998. The objectives of the Society are to promote PIM through dissemination of ideas and information, initiating policy dialogue on PIM, organise training, create data base and a library of literature on the subject and publish literature including a newsletter.

Reclamation of waterlogged areas

The benefits of Irrigation have not been unmitigated. There has been waterlogging and salinisation in certain areas in the commands of Irrigation projects due to seepage in canals, over-Irrigation by farmers, poor drainage and rise of ground water. A new component has been added under the CAD Programme since April, 1996 under which provision of 50 per cent grant as central assistance to State Governments has been made for survey and reclamation of waterlogged areas.

The Ministry has, taken the following steps:

1. An Inter-Ministerial Committee has been constituted under the Chairmanship of Additional Secretary, Ministry of Water Resources, to consider policy issues relating to waterlogging.
2. After scrutiny of proposals received from State Governments by the Core Group of Officers, 18 projects have been approved to be executed by the State Governments.
3. A number of training programmes have been organised in the country on survey and reclamation of waterlogged areas.
4. Water and Power Consultancy Services (India) Limited (WAPCOS) have been engaged to survey the extent of waterlogging and salinity in the commands of Ram Ganga Project (Uttar Pradesh), Chambal Canal Project (Madhya Pradesh), Ukai Kakrapar Canal Command (Gujarat), Gurgaon Canal Command (Haryana) and Nagarjuna Sagar Wight Bank Canal Project (Andhra Pradesh).
5. National Remote Sensing Agency (NRSA) has been engaged, inter-alia, to survey the extent of waterlogging in Sri Rama Sagar Project (SRSP) and Nagarjuna Sagar Project (NSP) in Andhra Pradesh, Jamuna Project and Sukla Project in Assam, Krishna Project, Jayakwadi Stage - I and Majalgaon Project, Girna Project, Upper Tapi Project and Bhima Project in Maharashtra, Chambal Project (Kota) in Rajasthan and DVC Irrigation System, Kangsbati Irrigation System and Mayurakshi Irrigation System in West Bengal.
6. A two days' National Workshop on "Strategy for Prevention and Reclamation of Waterlogged Areas in Irrigated Commands" was held from 20th - 21st August, 1998 at New Delhi with the participation of

officers from Government of India, State Governments and other agencies.

Training

One of the components of the CAD Programme Is the training of functionaries and farmers on various aspects of efficient water management, methods of survey and reclamation of waterlogged areas and participatory irrigation management. The training programmes are meant for officials of the Government as well as the farmers.

During 1998-99, twenty three National Level training programmes and twelve State level training programmes are scheduled to be organised through Water and Power Consultancy Services (India) Ltd., Administrative Staff College of India,. Hyderabad, Water and Land Management Institute, Bhopal and Central Soil and Salinity Research Institute, Karnal on various topics like Participatory Irrigation Management, Command Area Development activities, Waterlogging and On-Farm Development etc.

Impact assessment

With a view to have making an assessment of the impact of the Programme and to identify the constraints in its implementation, seventeen evaluation studies were conducted during the Eighth Five Year Plan for different projects. The studies have been completed and the result of the studies have been communicated to concerned State Governments. A comprehensive study of CAD Programme had also been completed during 1997-98. The work evaluation of thirteen Irrigation projects In Andhra Pradesh, Gujarat, Maharashtra and Rajasthan has been given by the Ministry to the National Remote Sensing Agency.

In order to prepare documentation for PIM, three studies -(i) All India Survey on the Perception and Effects of Participatory Irrigation Management, (ii) Documentation In Participatory Irrigation Management and (iii) Impediments In PIM - Case studies from Maharashtra, were awarded to different researchers. The studies are in progress.

For reviewing the progress of Implementation of CAD Programme In States, a meeting of Secretaries In-charge Of CAD Departments in States, Commissioners and Administrators of CAD Authorities and Chief Engineers was held In New Delhi on 10th- 11th November, 1998.

Conjunctive use of surface and ground water

The Ministry of Water Resources has taken up ten studies on the conjunctive use of ground and surface water through the Central Ground Water Board. Studies of Indira Gandhi Nahar Pariyojana Stage - I, Rajasthan, Mahi Kadana Project, Gujara4 Sarda Sahayak Project, Uttar Pradesh, Hirakud Project, Orissa, Tungabhadra Project, Andhra Pradesh and Ghataprabha Project, Karnataka have been completed and studies of Nagar Junasagar Project, Andhra Pradesh, Indira Gandhi Nahar Pariyojana Stage - II, Rajasthan, Gandak Canal Command, Bihar and Kosl Command Project, Bihar, are continuing. Conjunctive use of ground water and surface water will serve the dual purpose of increasing the area under irrigation on the one hand and reduce waterlogging on the other.

External assistance for development of water resources

The task of development of water resources in various regions of the country requires large financial investments. The Ministry of Water Resources assists the State Governments in obtaining external assistance from different funding agencies to fill up the resource gap for implementation of projects for development of water resources.

The World Bank continues to be the primary source of external assistance in this sector. The other donors are EEC, OECF-Japan, Kfw Germany and Government of Netherlands etc.

Projects completed during the year

World Bank assisted Punjab Irrigation and Drainage Project involving an assistance of US $ 169.208 million has been completed.

UNDP assisted project, Development of capabilities of Hydrological Studies' in National Institute of Hydrology, Roorkee involving an assistance of US$ 3.00 Million has also been completed.

OECF Japan assisted Upper Kolab Irrigation Project of Orissa involving loan assistance of Yen 3 769 million has been completed.

France assisted Pilot Project on Ozone Treatment for Drinking Water of Delhi involving assistance of FF 9.73 million, Pilot Project on Dynamic Regulation of Majalgaon Irrigation Project of Maharashtra involving assistance of FF 7.3 million, Mappint and Control of Water Distribution System of Delhi involving assistance of FF 5. 15 and Hydroplus Fusegates on Four Dams in Gujarat involving assistance of FF 17.8 5 have been completed.

Netherlands assisted Tungabhadra Irrigation Pilot Project, Phase-II involving grant assistance of Dfl 5.00 million and Water Resources Development and Management Project (WARDEMA) involving grant assistance of DfI 6.40 million have been completed.

Projects under consideration

Water Resources Consolidation Projects (WRCP) in Rajasthan and Uttar Pradesh are under consideration for the World Bank assistance. Andhra Pradesh Economic

Reforms (Irrigation Component) Project has already been negotiated and is under implementation with retroactive funding. However, agreement for the same is likely to be signed shortly.

Minor Irrigation Project in Gujarat and Augmenting Surface Water in North Gujarat and North West India Salt Dispoal Studies are under consideration for Netherlands assistance.

Rajasthan Minor Irrigation Project, Phase-II, Maharashtra, Minor Irrigation Project and Himachal Pradesh Minor Irrigation Project are under active consideration for German assistance.

Utilisation of external assistance

In the current financial year up to December, 1998 an amount of Rs. 399.88 crore was received from the World Bank, European Economic Community and other bilateral agencies and utilised by the State Governments and Government of India for implementation of various externally aided projects in the water sector. The total amount of utilisation is likely to exceed Rs. 700 crore by the end of March, 1999.

Hydrology project

The Government of India has launched Hydrology Project with World Bank (IDA) credit assistance of 90. 1 million Special Drawing Rights (US$ 442.0 million). Besides, under the bilateral India-Dutch agreement, the Government of the Netherlands is providing a grant-India assistance of 29.9 million Dutch guilders (US$ 17.4 million) in the form of technical assistance for consulting services and overseas training to all participating States and Central agencies. The Project is being implemented in eight states, Andhra Pradesh, Gujarat, Karnataka, Kerala, Madhya Pradesh, Maharashtra, Orissa and Tamilnadu and five Central agencies, Central Water Commission (CWC), Central Ground Water Board (CGWB), Central Water and Power Research Station, National Institute of Hydrology and India Meteorological Department are involved in its coordination. The duration of the Project is six years.

The implementation of the Project commenced from September, 1995. It will end in September, 200 1. The total cost of the project has been estimated to be Rs. 608.97 crore which comprises Rs. 457.88 crore as baseline costs and the remaining Rs. 15 1.18 crore as physical and price contingencies. The Central and State baseline components under the project are Rs. 168.69 crore and Rs. 2 89.19 crore, respectively. Reckoning the physical and price contingencies, the Central and State components are Rs. 224.35 crore and Rs. 384.62 crore respectively.

Project objectives and scope

The main objective of the Hydrology Project is to improve the institutional and organisational arrangements, technical capabilities and physical facilities available for measurement, validation, collection, analysis, transfer and dissemination of hydrological, hydrometeorological and water quality data within the concerned agencies at Central Government level and in the participating States. The Project will upgrade and expand the physical infrastructure through construction of observation sites and buildings, provision of measuring instruments and equipment and laboratory facilities. The Project will introduce new equipments like Automatic Water Level Recorders, Acoustic Doppler Current Profilers for Surface and Groundwater Observation Systems and Atomic Absorption Spectro-Photometer, gas Chromatograph and UV Spectrometer for Surface and Groundwater quality monitoring.

The project will also help in the development of interactive computerised data banks within the regional offices of CWC and CGWB and the State agencies responsible for collection of hydrological data for surface and ground water. These data banks will be interactive hierarchically and laterally with NICNET system of National Informatic Centre serving as communication link. Separate National Data Centers will he established at CWC and CGWB headquarters for surface water and groundwater respectively, with VSAT facilities. The State Data Centers as well as CWC and CGWB regional data banks will transfer their data bases to the National Data Centre-The above arrangement will help to develop comprehensive, easily accessed and user friendly data base covering all aspects of the hydrological cycle, including surface water and ground water in terms of quality and climatic measurements. The State-of-the-art computer hardware and software and communication systems will be provided under the project forth is purpose.

The project will introduce standard procedures for data collection, processing, validation and management including the use of software for routine quality control and other analyses. It is necessary to train the staff for these activities. The training contemplated to be given under the project will ensure that these standardised procedures are followed uniformly throughout the area of the project and the capabilities of the staff developed during this period by continuous internal training within the agencies are sustainable without further external support.

Arrangement for coordination and monitoring

Considering the number of agencies involved in the implementation of the project, extensive coordination and monitoring arrangements have been put in place both at the Central and the State level. At the Central level, a National Level Steering Committee (NLSC) has been set up under the Chairmanship of Secretary Water Resources) in which Secretaries of the concerned departments of the State Governments and the heads of central agencies are represented. Under NLSC, a National Coordination Committee (NCC) has been set up, which is chaired by Member (RM) of Central Water Commission. The NCC coordinates different aspects of the Project and also renders advice to the project coordinating groups in the States. In addition, a Project Coordination Secretariat (PCS) has been set up in the WM Wing of Ministry of Water Resources to provide secretarial assistance to NLSC and NCC. The World Bank also monitors the implementation of the Project through supervision missions at regular intervals. The Project consultants are also assisting in the implementation. The arrangements for coordination and monitoring set-up in the States mirror those at Central level.

Benefits of the project

The project is expected to generate substantial benefits by improving the data base of the participating agencies concerning water resources and climate. This will also make the availability of data from computerised data banks easy for the users. The reliable water data, with adequate coverage in time and space are, the foundations on which planning, development and management of water resources are based. The improved hydrological and hydrometeorological information will help in making reliable and economic, a) investment decisions in which the availability of water resources is a dominant determinate (i.e. irrigated agriculture, water supply and sanitation, industrial water use, etc. and b) operational decisions in existing enterprises in which water is an essential input to achieve predicted impact.

Progress of implementation of the project

The duration of the project is six years. It is designed in a manner to complete all infrastructural facilities for observation stations, laboratories and data centres Annual Report 1998-99 during the first three years of the project and to improve data collection, storage, transfer, and usage facilities during the second phase. The progress so far is behind the SAP, targets. An Expenditure of about Rs. 20.6 3 crore was incurred by all the agencies up to September, 1998 during the year 1998-99 raising the total cumulative expenditure incurred under the project up to September, 1998 to Rs. 87.7 crore or 19.2 per cent of the project's baseline cost. The major reasons that held up the project in the initial years are:-

— Delay in the commencement of the Project. The implementation of the project commenced from April, 1996 instead of September, 4995 because of delay in administrative clearances;
— The implementing agencies took time to get accustomed to the World Bank Procurement procedures;
— Certain policies of the State/Central Governments such as ban on creation of new posts and procurement of new vehicles hampered the progress;
— Lack of experience in the country in the use of hi-tech equipments, procured for use under the project; and
— Delay in transfer of Government land for buildings.

Water resources consolidation projects

Under the Water Resources Consolidation Project, the World Bank has extended credit assistance for a period of six years individually to Haryana, Orissa and Tamil Nadu. The main objectives of WRCP are improving institutional and technical capabilities for managing the States' water resources, planning of water resources by river basin across all uses of water, improving agricultural productivity through rehabilitation and completion of irrigation schemes and farmers' participation, assuring sustainability of infrastructure and environment. In WRCPs, the major thrust is on improving the productivity of systems of irrigation through renovation and modernisation of existing irrigation and drainage schemes and associated agricultural improvements linked with farmers' participation. Priority is given to the schemes where water users organisations (WUAs) are established where water services are unreliable and inequitable, resulting in agricultural productivity substantially below potential. An improved package of agricultural practices is required to be provided for Intensive agriculture. Due stress is given to the formation of WUAs along with funding for deferred maintenance to improve the performance of the irrigation system, to improve the recovery of water rates to ensure adequate and sustainable levels of services. The Project also involves an institutional reorganisation to build up the capabilities of irrigation departments and farmer organisations.

Haryana water resources consolidation project

The Haryana Water Resources Consolidation Project has been structured as a six year operation commencing from 1994-95 and targeted to be completed by December, 2000. The project is estimated to cost Rs. 18 58.2 5 crore (equivalent of U S $ 48 3.4 Million) and will finance the works under Bhakra and Yamuna canal systems including Gurgaon canal system of the State. The Bank assistance for the project is US $ 258 million. An expenditure of Rs. 503 crore had been incurred up to September, 1998 under this project. For the current financial year up to June, 15, 1998, further expenditure of Rs. 50 crore has been incurred. The proposed budget provision for the project for 1998-99 is Rs. 411 crore.

Tamil Nadu water resources consolidation project

The Tamilnadu Water Resources Consolidation Project was negotiated in April 199 5 for an assistance of US $

282.9 million (approximately Rs. 887.5 crore). The project is estimated to cost Rs. 726 crore with an implementation schedule of six years. On completion of the project, an area of 0.53 million hectare is likely to be benefited. The cumulative expenditure up to June 30, 1998 is reported to be Rs. 8 1.98 crore. Although the progress of expenditure has not been satisfactory, it is reported that the State Government has been making intensive efforts for better implementation of the project. As per the report of the last Supervision Mission of the World Bank during June 1998, the progress of the project has been rated as satisfactory.

Orissa water resources consolidation project

The Orissa Water Resources Consolidation Project was negotiated during 1996. The project is to be implemented in a period of six years with the World Bank assistance of US $ 2 90 million (approximately Rs. 977 crore). The latest estimated cost of the project is Rs. 912.5 crore as against which a cumulative expenditure of Rs. 449.4 crore has been incurred up to June 30, 1998. The overall progress of the project has been reported to be satisfactory.

National water management project

National Water Management Project (NWMP) was designed to supplement the resources of the states to promote the process of improved water management through upgradation of the main systems of the selected irrigation schemes. The basic objective of the project was to improve irrigation coverage and agricultural productivity and thereby increase incomes of farmers in the command through a more reliable, predictable and equitable irrigation service. The first phase of the programme lasted from June, 1987 to March, 1995. The Project has given encouraging results.

In view of the Importance and usefulness of NWMP in Improving the performance of Irrigation schemes,

Ministry of Water Resources (MOWR) had Initiated action on its follow-up phase. The objectives, approach and strategy under the proposed NWMP-II were firmed up in the light of NWMP-I experience. Detailed consultations with the willing participating states had been held and comprehensive proposals for NWMP-II were formulated by the MOWR and forwarded through the Department of Economic Affairs, Ministry of Finance, to the World Bank for financial assistance. The Project will be taken up for Implementation, only after the clearance from the World Bank has been obtained.

2

Energy and Environment Sectors

Energy, an essential input for economic development, is consumed in a variety of forms in India. Fuelwood, animal waste and agricultural residues are traditional sources of energy that continue to meet the bulk of the energy requirement in the rural areas.

The Government has formulated an energy policy with the objectives of ensuring adequate energy supply at a minimum cost, achieving self-sufficiency in energy supplies and protecting environment form adverse impact of utilising energy resources in an unjudicial manner. The development and promotion of non-conventional/alternate/new and renewable sources of energy such as solar, wind and bio-energy, etc., are also getting sustained attention from the Department of Non-Conventional Energy Sources, created in september 1982. Nuclear energy to * contribute significantly to the overall energy avalalbility in the country.

Electricity is the most convenient and versatile form of energy. Demand for it, therefore, has been growing at the rate faster than other forms of energy. Power industry too has recorded a phenomenal rate of growth both in terms of its volume and technological sophistication over the last few decades. Electricity plays a crucial role in both industrial and agricultural sectors and, therefore, consumption of electricity in the country is an indicator of productivity and growth. In view of this, power development has been given high priority in development programme.

Studies have shown that while the demand for electricity in the entire economy has riisen at the rate of 9.73 per cent during 1986-87, the demand in the residential and agricultural sectors has been increasing at an alarming rate of 14.03 per cent and 14.58 per cent respectively per year. Installed power generation capacity in the country has increased from a meagre 1,400 mw in 1947 to 81,164.41 mw at the end of 1994-95 comprising 20,829.04 mw hydro (25.66 per cent) and 58,110.37 mw thermal including gas, diesl and wind (71.60 per cent) and 2,225.0 mw nuclear (2.74 per cent).

Various measures being taken to improve power generation in the country include commission of new generation capacity, renovation and modernisation of old units, assistance to Electricity Boards in undertaking plant betterment programme, supply of requisite quantity and quality of coal, training of operation and maintenence personnel and strengthening of transmission and distribution system and implementation of short gestation projects, reduction in T & D losses, implementation of demand management and energy conservation measures. The target of power generation during 1995-96 has been 377.15 billion units out of which 297 billion units are programmed for generation by thermal stations 72.3 billion units by hydro stations and 7.85 billion units by the nuclear stations. Thus an increase of about 7.4 per cent over the generation achieved during 1994-95 is envisaged.

The Plant Load Factor (PLF) has shown a steady improvement over the years. It has improved from 53.8 per cent in 1990-91 to 60 per cent in 1994-95. The following table highlights the achievement of the power sector in major areas during 1994-95.

Energy and power

Electricity is a concurrent subject at Entry 34 in the List III of Seventh Schedule of the Constitution of India. The responsibility of its development lies both with the Central and state governments. At the Centre, the Ministry of Power is responsible for the administration of the Electricity (Supply) Act, 1948 and the Indian Electricity Act, 1910. The Ministry is also concerned with perspective planning, policy formulation, processing of projects for investment decision, monitoring of the implementation of power projects and training and manpower development.

The Central Electricity Authority (CEA), constituted under the Electricity (Supply) Act, 1948, advises the Ministry of Power on technical and economic matters. The construction and operation of generation and transmission projects in the Central Sector are entrusted to Central sector power corporations, namely, the National Thermal Corporation (NTPC), the National Hydroelectric Power Corporation (NHPC), the North Eastern Electric Power Corporation (NEEPCO) and the Power Grid Corporation of India Limited (POWERGRID). POWERGRID, which was incorporated on the 23 October 1989, is responsible for all the existing and future transmission projects in the Central sector and also for the formation of the National Power Grid. There are two joint ventures power corporations under the administrative control of the Ministry of Power, namely, Nathpa Jhakri Power Project and projects of the Tehri Hydro Power Complex. The Damodar Valley Corporation (DVC), constituted under the DVC Act, 1948, the Bhakra Beas Management Board (BBMB) constituted under the Punjab Act, 1966, and three autonomous bodies, namely,

Central Power Research Institute (CPRI), the National Power Training Institute (NPTI) and the Energy Management Centre (EMC) are also under the administrative control ofthe Ministry. Programmes of rural electrification are within the purview of the Rural Electrification Corporation (REC). The Power Finance Corporation (PFC) provides term-finance to projects in the power sector. There is one subordinate office Badarpur Management Control Cell (BMCC), directly under this Ministry and 16 subordinate offices under the Central Electricity Authority.

Significant progress has been made in expansion of transmission and distribution facilities in the country. Total length of transmission lines of 66 kv and above voltage level increased form 10,000 ckt km in December 1950 to about 2.36 lakh ckt in March 1994. Highest transmission voltage at present is 400 kv and about 30,240 ckt km of 400 kv lines had been constructed upto March 1994. In addition, the first +500 kv HVDC bipole Rihand-Dadri transmission line of about 820 km length is also in operation. An inter-regional link (vindhyachal 2 × 250 mw HVDC back-to-back) connecting western and northern regions is also in operation.

Five regional grid systems, namely, northern, western, southern, eastern and north-eastern covering all the states of the country are already existing. All the regions except north-eastern have fairly well inter-connected systems of 220 kv voltage level with progressive overlay of 400 kv transmision systems. The Union Cabinet in 1981 approved in principle the establishment of a Centrally owned and operated National Power Grid. The National Power Grid would eventually comprise strong regional networks with suitable synchronous HVDC links between the regions. Power Grid Corporation of India Limited (*POWERGRID*), created in October 1989, has been vested with the responsibility of developing a National Power Grid. The development of National Power Grid is an evolutionary process and would be achieved over a period of time through development of the regional grid systems and further inter-connections between the regions. National Power Grid will promote integrated operation and transfer of power from one system to another with ultimate objective of ensuring optimum utilisation of available resources in the country.

In order to promote integrated operation of power systems, the country has been demarcated into five regions, namely, north, west, south, east and north-east. Regional electricity boards were set up in 1964 in each of these regions. Northern region covers Haryana, Himachal Pradesh, Jammu and Kashmir, Punjab, Rajasthan, Uttar Pradesh, Chandigarh and Delhi, western region covers Gujarat, Maharashtra, Madhya Pradesh, Goa, Daman and Diu and Dadra and Nagar Haveli; southern region covers Andhra Pradesh, Karnataka, Tamil Nadu, Kerala and Pondicherry; eastern region covers Bihar, Orissa, West Bengal and Sikkim and north-eastern region covers Assam, Manipur, Meghalaya, Nagaland, Tripura, Arunachal Pradesh and Mizoram.

To coordinate operation of the grids of the constituent power systems and to optimise utilisation of the existing generation capacity, regional load despatch centres (RLDCs) have been set up in each region. RLDCs, hitherto functioning under the Central Electricity Authority/regional electricity boards, are being transferred to *Powergrid* in phased manner. In the northern, western and eastern regions, permanent RLDCs equipped with computer based telemetry and the data acquisition system were establilshed around mid 1980s. In the southern region, RLDC equipped with analog telemetry equipment, mimic board, transducers, speech communication, telex and teleprinters facilities is working. In the north-eastern region, an interim regional load despatch centre is operating. Unfied schemes covering the long-term requirements of RLDC and constituents systems in respect of all the five regions are in different stages of formulation. The schemes in respect of southern, northern, and north-eastern regions have got technoeconomic clearance of Central Electricity Authority while the scheme pertaining tothe eastern and western regions are still under finalisation.

Efficient operation of integrated power systems through moderanised computer-based load despatch centres is vitally dependent on efficient data transfer over distance. Thus there is a need for developing a highly reliable communication network. Subsequent to an in-depth analysis of requirements carried out by the Planning Commission, the Central Electricity Authority (CEA)) has developed a Master Telecom Plan for the power sector. Concrete schemes have been framed based on modern communication system. Several such schemes have been techno-economically approved by CEA and most ofthese have also cleared by DOT.

With a number of inter-regional links commissioned during the Eighth Plan period and subsequent years in form of National Grid and the five regional load despatch centres already in operation, National Electric Power System Information Centre (NEPSIC) has been set up which is equipped with PC-based data acquisition system linking all the RLDCs in the country. The data acquired from RLDC is also available at CEA headquarters for getting an overview of current power system status. Teleconferencing and FAX facilities are also provided. The system is fully functional since June 1993.

State electricity boards have been established in 18 out of 25 states. These are mainly responsible for generation and distribution of electricity in their respective states. Arunachal Pradesh, Goa, Manipur, Mizoram, Nagland, Sikkim and Tripura are yet to establish their electricity boards.

The first major step in this direction had been the setting up of 336 mw Chukha Hydroelectric Project in Bhutan at a cost of Rs. 243.71 crore with Indian technical and financial assistance under an agreement signed in March 1974. The first unit of the project was commissioned in September 1986 and all the four units of 84 mw August 1988. Since then the project has been generating power, the bulk of which has been exported to India. Bhutan has earned the entire cost of the project in about five years time by export of power to India alone besides their internal consumption.

Gratified with the success of Chukha Project the Royal Government of Bhutan are keen on development of their Hydro Resources for the mutual benefit of the two countries. To this end, India and Bhutan have signed an agreement in February 1994 for implementation of Kurichu Hydroelectric Project (3×15 mw) in western Bhutan at a cost of about Rs. 310 crore on a turn-key basis through NHPC within a period of five years. India and Bhutan have agreed to execute Tala HE Project downstream of existing Chukha Project with an installed capacity of 1,020 mw. Discussions have been held between the two countries and modalities for implementation of this mega project are being worked out.

India had constructed a number of mini/micro hydel schemes at Thimpu (360 kw), Gidakom (1000 kw), Wangdi (3000 kw), Gyesta (1500 kw), Khaling (600 kw), Chenarry (750 kw), Lhuntshi (20 kw) during 1960-80. These projects have been identified for rehabilitation in a phased manner by the Government of India. Proposals for taking up impementation of new mini/micro hydro schemes at Ungrichu, Yonglachy, Dongdichu and Chhalori are under consideration.

Energy Conservation has been identified as one of the major thrust areas in the Eighth Plan, as a part of the National Energy Efficiency Programme, with an objective of saving 5,000 mw of installed capacity by the terminal year of Eighth Plan. Apart from the awareness campaign and launching of demonstration projects in agricultural and industrial sectors for promoting energy efficiency technologies, other main activities relate to organising training programmes and studies in the field of energy conservation. A number of internationally supported projects for cooperation on energy conservation in Indian industries and other areas have also been undertaken.

Concerned with the deterioration in the performance of the thermal power stations in the country, Government of India launched a Centrallysponsored programme for renovation and modernisation (R and M) of thermal power stations to improve their performance. Likewise, a programme for renovation, modernisation and uprating (RM and U) of hydro-electric power stations was formulated by the Central Electricity Authority in 1987. R and M schemes are relevant also in the context of energy conservation and optimum energy usage.

At present, 3,544.58 mw (around 4.4 per cent of India's installed capacity) is in the private sector. The Government of India announced in September 1991 the policy to encourage private enterprises participation in the electricity sector. In pursuance of the policy announcement, the legislation governing the electricity sector was amended in October 1991 and the two part tariff notification was issued on 30 March 1992. The primary objective of the policy was to bring a additionality of resources, increase efficiency in operation and encourge commercial operations in this sector. The response has been encouraging. As on date, interest has been expressed in putting up 196 power projects for a total capacity of 77,720 mw involving an investment of Rs. 2,88,252 crore.

Coal is the main source of energy in the country and it accounts for about 60 per cent of the country's commercial energy requirement. Coal is also an essential input in steel and carbo-chemical industries.

An on 1 January 1995, the coal resources of India (upto a depth of 1,200 metre) have been estimated by the Geological Survey of India at 1,96,891.87 million tonnes.

Coal production which was around 78.71 million tonnes atthe time of nationalisation of the coal industry in 1973-74, rose to a level of 253.80 million tonnes in 1994-95. India is now the third largest coal producing country in the world. The coal production is slated to reach 300 million tonnes by 1996-97. Strategies adopted to achieve higher rate of production are: re-organising existing mines and opening up on new projects, both underground as well as opencast.

Distribution of coal is controlled statutorily under the Colliery Control Order., 1945. The distribution is to be done by the Coal Controller. However, if for any reason Coal Controller is not able to do so, coal companies have been allowed to distribute coal on the basis of linkages/ sponsorships. Short term linkages for important sectors of economy, like power and cement are decided by Standing Linkage Committee set up under the mInistry of Coal. Linkages to other consumers execpt steel are within the purview of coal companies, which allot coal to actual users as per advice receeived by them from the various sponsoring authorities. New allotments by coal companies to industries are of the order of 5,000 tonnes per month. Off-take of raw coal during 1993-94 and 1994-95 to major sectors of economy is given in table 21.

Under the present delegation of powers, coal projects costing upto Rs. 50 crore are sanctioned by the Board of Directors of the Coal India Limited. The subsidiary companies of Coal India Limited have powers to sanction projects upto Rs. 20 crore. Singareni Collieries Company Limited Board can also sanction coal projects upto Rs. 50 crore. Projects costing more than Rs. 50 crore are sanctioned by the Government. After the nationalisation of the coal industry in 1973 and till December 1994, the number of projects sanctioned (each costing Rs. two crore and above) was 633. A total investment of Rs. 20,718.97 crore has been sanctioned in these projects. Og these, 419 are mining projects and remaining 214 are non-mining projects like washeries, fire control schemes, captive power plants, water supply schemes etc. Out of 633, 340 projects have been completed and 293 are at different stages of implementation. Mining projects on completion will have a capacity of 338.08 million tonnes of coal per annum.

Even though history of Indian coal mining dates back more than two centuries, real sprut in coal production took place only after the nationalisation of the coal industry. Coal production in the country is now allmost completely in the public sector companies e.g. Coal India limited (CIL) and Singareni Collieries Company Limited (SCCL) except few captive mines of TISCO, IISCO and DVC. Coal India Limited producing over 90 per cent of the country's total coal production, has seven coal producing subsidiaries, namely, eastern Coalfields Limited (ECL), Bharat Coking Coal Limited (BCCL), Central Coalfields Limited (CCL), Northern Coalfields Limited (NCL), South Eastern Coalfields (SECL), Mahandi Coalfields Limited (MCL) and Western Coalfields Limited (WCL). The eight subsidiary Central Mines Planning and Design Institute Limited (CMPDIL) is the planning and design institute. SCCL is a joint venture of the Centre and Government of Andhra Pradesh. About 72 per cent of the coal production is obtained through opencast mmines which are almost completely mechanised deploying dragllines, shovels, dumpers, drills, dozers, etc. Mechanisation of underground mines has also been taken up in a big way. Most of the equipment used in coal mines ae indigenously available. At present there are 19 coking coal washeries with an annual capacity of 32.56 million tonnes.

Conservation of coal is an integrated part of mine planning and operation. This is ensured by maximum recovery of *in situ* reserves of coal. Since coal deposits in India are mostly in thick seams and occur at shallow depths, special techniques for maximising recovery are being developed.

Difficult geo-mining conditions prevailing in coal bearing areas like steep and irregular coal seam deposits, gassy seams contifuous and multisection seams necessitate the introduction of some suitable technology for exploitation of such deposits from coal conservation and also safety point in view. Some of the newly introduced methods of mining are: (a) to exploit seams developed in multi-sections and seams with thickness of 6 to 8 m and standing pillars, methods such as blasting gallery and sub-level caving have been adopted in Katras Project, BCCL. Blasting gallery method with sub-pannelings has been planned in Chora Colliery of ECL and GDK-10 and CDK-8 of SCCL Colliery; (b) keeping in view the limitations of conventional underground methods in terms of quantum of output as well as conservation, both Coal India Limited and Singareni Collieries Company Limited have introduced mechanised longwall technology that ensures higher extractability; (c) diversion of rivers, shifting of colonies and townships have been taken up to release sterlised coal underground;

(d) adequate measures have been asopted to deal with coalfijeld fires particularly in Jhria Coalfield and latest technology like remote sensing is being applied for fire management; (e) in steep and thick seams of Margheritta Area (Assam), the system of Shield Mining has been introduced. The extraction percentage of coal by traditional system which was 25 per cent to 35 per cent has now improved to nearly 70 per cent or even more in the system of shield mining. The flexible roofing method of mining in the thick seams of North Eastern coalfield has also been applied where the thickness of the seam exceeds 4.5 meter. The system has, however, a limited application ; and (f) since opencast working ensures better conversation, application of opencast working is now followed with much higher cut-off ratios utilising high capacity machineries. Singareni Collieries Company Limited has also made a breakthrough in a small way for extraction of Developed pillars by opencast methods. The company has of late been making efforts to convert existing underground mines into high capacity mechanised Opencast projects at Ramagundam and Kothagudem areas.

The Coal mines Conservation and Development Act, 1974 provides for imposition of excise duty on coal despatches for meeting activities like conservation of coal, development/introduction of new technology in coal mines, safety in Mines and assistance in mining operation. A number of research and development activities in coal sector are carried out under overall guidance and supervision of Standing Scientific and Research Commmittee and its four sub-committees. The applied research is carried out in the fields of production, productivity, safety coal preparation, coal utilisation, environment and ecology.

Special efforts to improve lthe standard of safety in the coal industry have brought down the rate of fatalities per million tonne of output in Coal India Limited to 0.40 and in Singareni Collieries Companies Limited to 2.04 in the year 1994. A Standing Committee on Safety regularly review safety standards in coal mines.

Coal industry employs over seven lakh workers. Since nationalisation of coal mines, welfare of coal miners by way of providing facilities like housing, water supply, medical care, education, etc., is bieng given greater attention.

Lignite reserves in the country have been estimated at around 26,200 million tonnes. Out of the above, 3,300 million tonnes spread over 480 sq km is in the Neyveli Lignite fields in South Acrot Vallalar district and about 2,000 mt has been identified as minerable under the presently adopted mining parameters. Geological reserves of about 1150 mt of lignite have been identified in Jayamkondacholapuram of Trichy district of Tamil Nadu. In Mannargudi and east of Veeranam, geological reserves of around 18,200 mt and 1,340 mt of lignite respectively have been estimated. Smaller deposits exist in Rajasthan, Gujarat and J&K. Lignite reserves at Neyveli are exploited by Neyveli Lignite Corporation (NLC) Ltd. It was incorporated as a private limited company in 1956 wholly owned by Government of India. The Corporation was converted into public company w.e.f. 7 March 1986.

The main constituents of the company are lignite mines, thermal power stations, fertilizer plant and briquetting and carbonisation plant. Mine-I (6.5 million tonnes of Lignite per annum) feeds thermal Power Station-I (600 mw), Briquetting and Carbonisation Plant (2,62,000 tonnes of coke-achievable capacity) and the Process Steam Plant. Mine-II (10.5 million tonnes of lignite per annum) feeds it captive Thermal Power Station-II (7×210 mw). The Fertilizer Plant (achievable capacity 1,29,200 tonnes of urea per annum) which initially used raw lignite as feed stock changed over to oil gasification in July 1979 on operational and technological consideration. The power generated from Thermal Power Station-I after meeting the NLC's requirements is fed into Tamil Nadu Electricity Board grid which is the sole beneficiary. Power generated from Thermal Power Station-II after meeting the needs of Second Mine is shared by southern states *viz.*, Tamil Nadu, Kerala, Karnataka, Andhra Pradesh and Union Territory of Pondicherry. NLC produced 154.10 lakh tonnes of lignite and generated 10,890.29 million units of power during 1994-95, registered an increase of about 23 per cent and 36 per cent respectively over 1991-92.

Raw lignite sales (12,34,001 tonnes) and power export (8916.36 million units) had registered an increase of about 61 per cent and 40 per cent respectively in 1994-95 over 1991-92. The company has been making profits since 1976-77 and its profit of Rs 171 crore (provisional) for 1994-95 is the highest profit achieved for any year since inception. In 1994-95, the sales turnover has recorded a growth of 33.23 per cent and net profit of 50 per cent over 1993-94.

India is richly endowed with minerals. Under the Constitution, minerals rights and the administration of mining laws are vested in the state governments. The Centre, however, regulates the development of minerals under the Mines and Minerals (Regulation and Development) Act, 1957 and the rules and regulations framed under it. This Statute empowers the Centre to formulate rules for: (i) the grant of prospecting licences and mining leases for schedule minerals, (ii) the conservation and development of minerals., and (iii) the modification of old leases. The Act, came into force on 1 June 1958. Amendments to this Act were made in 1972, 1986, and 1994.

Principal mineral found in the country along with their estimated reserves are given below.

Coal is India's largest mineral resource and presently India is the fifth largest producer of coal in the world. Vast deposits of coal of Gondwana formations occur in West Bengal, Orissa, Bihar, Madhya Pradesh, Andhra Pradesh, Uttar Pradesh and Maharashtra. It also occurs in tertiary formation in Assam, Arunachal Pradesh, Meghalaya and Nagaland. Total known reserves of all types of coals in Gondwana and tertiary coalfields estimated stands at 192 billion tonnes. Out of these, reserves of prime-coking coal have been estimated at 5.3 billion tonnes. Total reserves of lignite stands at 6.5 billion tonnes, located in Tamil Nadu, Gujarat, Rajasthan, Kerala, Pondichery and Jammu and Kashmir.

The total recoverable reserves of bauxite in the country are placed at 2,525 million tonnes while the total *in situ* reserves are 3,037 million tonnes. The conditional resources of bauxite are about five lakh tonnes. In addition, prospective resources are placed at 90 million tonnes. Orissa, Andhra Pradesh, Madhya Pradesh, Gujarat, Maharashtra and Bihar are the principal states where bauxite deposits are located. Major reserves are concentrated in the East Coast Bauxite deposits of Orissa and Andhra Pradesh.

Total recoverable reserves of chromite are estimated at 8.8 million tonnes. Deposits of economic significance occur in Andhra Pradesh, Bihar, Karnataka, Maharashtra, Manipur, Orissa and Tamil Nadu. However, refractory grade reserves of chromite are very meagre.

The total recoverable reserves of copper ore in the country are 415.86 million tonnes equivalent to 4.14 million tonnes of metal content. The all-India conditional resources of copper are 695.29 million tonnes (1.99 million tonnes of copper metal) and prospective resources are 769.9 million tonnes of copper ore. Major and important copper ore deposits are located in Singhbhum district (Bihar), Balaghat (Madhya Pradesh) and Jhunjhunu and Alwar (Rajasthan). In addition, small copper ore deposits are in Andhra Pradesh, Gujarat, Karnataka, Sikkim, Orissa, Uttar Pradesh and West Bengal.

There are three important gold fields in the country, namely, Kolar Gold Field, Kolar disrict, Hutti Gold Fields in Raichur district (both in Karnataka) and Ramgiri Gold field in Anantpur district (Andhra Pradesh). Total gold metal ore reserves are estimated at 176.9 lakh tonnes.

The total recoverable reserves of iron ore in the country are about 9,606 million tonnes of haematite and 3,143 million tonnes of magnetite. Haematite resources are located in Andhra Prades, Bihar, Goa, Karnataka, Madhya Pradesh, Maharashtra, Orissa and Rajasthan. Magnetite resources are located in Andhra Pradesh, Bihar, Goa, Karnataka and Kerala.

Lead-zinc resources are located in Rajasthan, Gujarat, West Bengal, Andhra Pradesh, Meghalaya, Orissa, Sikkim, Tamil Nadu and Uttar Pradesh. Total recoverable reserves (all grades) of lead and zinc ores are 198.5 million tonnes comprising of metal content of 2,390 thousand tonnes of lead and 9,866 thousand tonnes of zinc metal. The conditonal resources of lead-zinc are 200.29 million tonnes in the country.

The total recoverable reserves of manganese ore are 233.33 million tonnes out of which 41.05 million tonnes are proved , 142.03 million tonnes probable and 50.25 million tonnes of possible category. Main reserves are in Karnataka followed by Orissa, Madhya Pradesh, Maharashtra and Goa. Minor occurences of manganese are in Andhra Pradesh, Bihar, Gujarat, Rajasthan and West Bengal.

The total estimated conditional resource of nickel ore is 294 million tonnes located in Orissa (285 million tonnes) and Bihar (9 million tonnes). Minor occurrence of nickel in Tamil Nadu, Maharashtra and Goa are indicated. The recoverable reserves of tungsten ore have been estimated at 25.89 million tonnes or 77.32 thousand tonnes of WO_3 content. The main reserves are at Degana, Rajasthan. It also occurs in Maharashtra, Karnataka, West Bengal and Uttar Pradesh.

The recoverable reserves of barytes are 70.15 million tonnes. The Mangampet deposit occuring in Cuddapah djistrict (Andhra Pradesh) is the single largest deposit in the world containing 67 million tonnes of recoverable reserves. Minor occurences of barytes are located in Rajasthan, Madhya Pradesh, Maharashtra, Himachal Pradesh, Tamil Nadu, Uttar Pradesh and Bihar.

Diamond deposits occur in three types of geological settings such as kimberlite pipes, conglomerate beds and alluvial gravels. The main diamond bearing areas in India are Panna belt in Madhya Pradesh, Munimadugu-Banganapalle conglomerate in Kurnool district, Wajrakarur kimberlite pipe in Anantpur district and the gravels of Krishna river basin in Andhra Pradesh. Reserves * of about a million carats, there are conditional submarginal of 265 thousand carats.

Dolomite occurrences are widespread in almost all part of the country. The total recoverable reserves of all grades of dolomite are 4,967 million tonnes. Of the total all India recoverable reserves, major share of about 92 per cent reserves is distributed in seven states– Madhya Pradesh, Orissa, Gujarat, Karnataka, West Bengal, Uttar Pradesh and Maharashtra.

Fireclay occurs as a bedded deposit, mostly associated with measures of Gondwana and Tertiary periods. Important deposits are associated with Jharia and Raniganj coalfields in Bihar and West Bengal, Korba coalfields in Madhya Pradesh and Neyveli Lignite field in Tamil Nadu. Notable occurrences of fireclay not associated with coal measures are known in Gujarat, Jabalpur region of Madhya Pradesh and Belpahar-Sundergarh areas of Orissa. The recoverable reserves of fireclay are about 697 million tonnes.

Total recoverable reserves of fluorspar in India are 2.15 million tonnes. Rajasthan and Gujarat are the only producing states in India. Fluorspar occurs in Gujarat, Madhya Pradesh, Maharashtra and Rajasthan.

The recoverable reserves of gypsum are estimated at 239 million tonnes. Out of the above, 70,000 tonnes surgical plaster grade, 39 million tonnes of fertilizer/pottery grade, 38.6 million tonnes of cement/paint grade, four million tonnes of soil reclamation grade and the rest is unclassified. The production of gypsum is confined to Rajasthan, Tamil Nadu, Jammu and Kashmir, Uttar Pradesh, Himachal Pradesh and Gujarat. Rajasthan is the main producer of gypsum followed by Tamil Nadu.

The recoverable reserves of graphite are 3.11 million tonnes. Orissa is the major producers of graphite. Almost the entire reserves under proved category are in Ramanathapuram district, Tamil Nadu. Resources of graphite are in Andhra Pradesh, Orissa, Tamil Nadu, Kerala, Bihar, Gujarat, Rajasthan, Madhya Pradesh and Maharashtra.

The recoverable reserves of ilmenite are 86.75 million tonnes. Ilmenite occurs mainly in beach sand deposits right from Ratnagiri coast in the west to Orissa coast in the east. These minerals are found in Kerala, Tamil Nadu and Orissa.

The all India recoverable reserves of kaolin, including white clay of all categories are about 986 million tonnes. Principal producing states are Bihar, Gujarat, Rajasthan and West Bengal. Kerala, Haryana, Orissa and Madhya Pradesh also produce significant quantities and ball clay is mainly produced in Rajasthan, Andhra Pradesh and Gujarat.

The total recoverable reserves of limestone of all categories and grades are placed at 76,446 million tonnes. The conditional reserves have been estimated at 360 million tonnes. Major producing states are Madhya Pradesh, tamil Nadu, Andhra Pradesh, Gujarat, Bihar, Orissa, Rajasthan and Karnataka.

India is the world's leading producer of sheet mica and accounts for about 60 per cent of global mica trade. Economic deposits of mica occur in three important belts in Bihar, Andhra Pradesh and Rajasthan.

The total recoverable reserves of magnesite are about 233 million tonnes of which 41 million tonnes are in theproved category. Magnesite is found in Uttar Pradesh, Tamil Nadu and Rajasthan while minor occurrences are in Karnataka, Jammu and Kashmir and Himachal Pradesh.

The total recoverable reserves of kyanite and sillimanite in the country are 2.7 million tonnes respectively. Besides, conditional resources of 175.84 million tonnes of kyanite are also estimated. For sillimanite conditional resources of 5.9 million tonnes and prospective resources of 0.8 million tonnes have been estimated.

Kyanite deposits are located in Andhra Pradesh, Bihar, Karnataka and Maharashtra. Sillimanite resources are in Kerala, Orissa, Madhya Pradesh, tamil Nadu and minor occurrences in Andhra Pradesh, Assam, Bihar, Karnataka, Maharashtra, Meghalaya, Rajasthan and West Bengal.

Deposits of phosphorites are located in Madhya Pradesh, Rajasthan and Uttar Pradesh. Besides, apatite deposits of commercial importance are reported from Bihar, Andhra Pradesh, Rajasthan, West Bengal and Tamil Nadu. Recoverable reserves of rock-phosphate are estimated at 146.95 million tonnes of all grades and of apatite at 13 million tonnes.

Other minerals occuring in significant quantities in India are bentonite (Gujarat, Rajasthan, Bihar, Jammu and Kashmir and Tamil Nadu), corundum (Maharashtra, Madhya Pradesh, Andhra Pradesh * and Gujarat), fullers earth (Rajasthan, Karnataka and Andhra Pradesh), garnet (Tamil Nadu, Rajasthan and Andhra Pradesh Pradesh), pyrites (Bihar and Rajasthan), steatite (Rajasthan, Uttar Pradesh, Andhra Pradesh, Tamil Nadu and Bihar), wollastonite (Rajasthan and Gujarat), zircon (beach sand of Tamil Nadu, Kerala and Orissa) and quartz and silica minerals are wide spread and occur in about all states. Besides, the country has vast resources of building dimension and ornamental stones such as granite, marble and slate. Granite is mainly mined in Tamil Nadu, Karnataka, Andhra Pradesh and Rajasthan, marble in Rajasthan, Uttar Pradesh and Gujarat and slate in Madhya Pradesh, Andhra Pradesh and Haryana.

The petrochemical industry, which forms a part of the chemical industry, is one of the fastest growing sectors in the Indian economy. The annual growth rate of the industry has been around 12-15 per cent compared to about 10 per cent in the chemical industry and 8 per cent of industrial sector as a whole. Petrochemicals, particularly plastics and fibres, make a substantial contribution to the national exchequer directly by way of excise and customs duty and other taxes. The plastic processing industry offers direct employment to over two lakh persons with the potential of over three lakh persons by 2000 AD. Starting from the stage of raw material production to the conversion of finished products, employment gets generated in a cascading manner.

In the initial years, since indigenous capacity was small, the growth was mainly import driven. Consequent to the strong leadership provided by the Indian Petrochemicals Corporation Limited (PCL), a public sector company, and perceiving the greater growth and scope for returns on investments, several private sector companies entered this field. Consumption of all major petrochemicals increased from 7.5 lakh mt in 1979-80 to 29.73 lakh mt in 1990-91 and 34 lakh mt in 1993-94, and is expected to reach the level of over 70 lakh mt by 2000 AD. To meet the growing demand of petrochemicals, Government have sanctioned several mega petrochemical complexes involving a total investment of about Rs. 35,000 crore. This would make India largely self-sufficient in petrochemicals. Petrochemicals have emerged as cost effective energy saving versatile materials serving the needs of the common people.

Exports in petrochemicals have been growing reasonably well. The country has been able to make some exports of polyester staple fibre and LAB. In addition, export of plastic processed goods has increased from Rs. 415 crore in 1992-93 to Rs. 815 crore in 1993-94. The export of man made/synthetic fibres/yarns (including blended spun yarns) was for Rs. 712 crore in 1992-93 and Rs. 514 crore in 1993-94.

There are three public sector organisations in the petrochemical sector under the administrative control of the Department of Chemicals and Petrochemicals. Indian Petrochemicals Corporation Limited (IPCL) is a public sector undertaking incorporated in March 1969. The company has been entrusted with the responsibility of manufacturing and distribution of various petrochemicals like polymers, synthetic organic chemicals, fibres and fibre intermediates. IPCL's mega petrochemicals complex at Vadodara was commissioned in 1993 and the Olefin Complex was commissioned in 1978. The company has set up another Olefin complex in Nagothane in Maharashtra. It has been commissioned and production is stabilising. The third such complex has been approved by the Government in Gandhar in Gujarat. IPCL is a profit making company which earned a net profit of Rs. 562.32 crore during 1994-95.

Petrofils Cooperative Limited (PCL) is a joint venture company of the Government of India and weavers' cooperative societies. It produces polyester filament yarn and nylon filament yarn at its three plants located at Vadodara and Naldhari in Gujarat. The Society has set up spandex plant at Naldhari, which will manufacture spandex yarn for the first time in the country. The spandex yarn having elastic properties is used in swimming suits, underwear garments etc. The company has a turnover of Rs. 322 crore during 1993-94. It has made a net profit of about Rs. 5.40 crore during 1993-94 as against a net loss of Rs. 15.83 crore in 1992-93.

The Central Insititute of Plastics Engineering and Technology (CIPET) is a training institute set up at Madras by the Government as a registered society with the primary objective to develop skilled manpower and provide technical services to the plastic industry. Besides training, the Institute also provides testing, standardisation and quality control, advisory and consultancy services to the plastic industry. To meet the increasing demand of trained personnel in the field of plastics, CIPET has set up nine extension centres at Ahmadabad, Amritsar, Bhopal, Bhubaneswar, Hyderabad, Imphal, Lucknow and Mysore including the headquarter centre at Madras. A service centre and a training centre of CIPET have also been opened at Goa and Patna respectively to cater to the demands of plastic industry in and around these places.

The production of crude oil which reached a peak of 34.09 million tonnes in 1989-90 declined to the level of 26.95 million tonnes in 1992-93. Therefore, to increase the production, a number of short-term and medium-term measures such as early production from satellite fields, use of state-of-the-art technology i.e. horizontal drilling, drainhole drilling etc., were initiated in 1993. As a result of these measures, the decline in crude oil production was arrested in 1993-94 with the production level of 27.02 million tonnes which has further increased to 32.24 million tonnes in 1994-95. The substantial increase in the production in 1994-95 has been due to commissioning of major development schemes such as the additional development of L-II, L-III, Neelam field and South Heera field in the Western Offshore. The crude oil production during 1995-96 is expected to be 37.24 million tonnes. This increase over 1994-95 of around five million tonnes will come mostly from increased production in the Western Offshore fields. The production of crude oil is likely to reach the level of 38.57 million tonnes in 1996-97. Government have also initiated action for increasing indigenous crude oil by offering small and medium sized fields for development through private/joint venture participation. Some small sized fields have been offered for development through private participation.

India is importing a substial part of its oil needs. During 1992-93, the gross import of crude oil and petroleum products was 40.5 million tonnes costing Rs. 17,046 crore in foreign exchange. During 1993-94, the import of crude oil and POL was at 42.9 million tonnes valued at Rs. 17,730 crore. The gross import of crude oil and POl products during 1994-95 was 41.3 million tonnes valued at Rs. 17,838 crore.

Research and development activities by Oil and Naturtal Gas Commission (ONGC) and Oil India LImited (OIL) and Gas Authority of India Limited (GAIL) in the field of crude oil and natural gas exploration and production, processing and marketing sectors are carried out at their respective R and D centers. ONGC has established eight institutes, viz., Kishav Dev Malviya Institute of Petroleum Exploration (KDMIPE), Dehra Dun; Institute of Reservoir Studies (IRS), Ahmadabad; Institute of Engineering and Ocean Technology (IEOT), Bombay; Institute of Oil Gas Production Technology (IOGPT), Bombay; Geophysical Data Processing and Interpretation Centre (GEOPIG), Dehradun; Institute of Petroleum Safety and Environment Management (IPSEM), Goa; Institute of Biotechnology and Geotectonics (INBIGS), Jrhat; and Institute of Drilling Technology (IDT), Dehra Dun.

The main objective of the KDMIPE is to provide back-up services to exploration efforts of ONGC. IRS provides R and D back-up for preparation of development plans of ONGC"s oil and gas fields and application of enhanced oil recovery methods with a view to improve their oil and gas recovery. IDT attends to the development of techniques for drilling difficult wells in high pressure/high temperature regime as well as super deep wells in technically complex areas. IEOT carries out design review for all offshore platforms, deep water production systems. * IOGPT had been set up to provide continuous back-up to situation specific production problems and long term application of appropriate techniques and technologies. GEOPIC is ONGC's premier seismic, gravity, magnetic, logging and geochemical data processing and interpretation center. IPSEM aims at creating awareness for improved safety and environment management and minimize the pollution accidents and loss of life caused by petroleum exploration and production operations. INBIGS, when fully operational, will be able to provide genetic probes for direct detection of hydrocarbons. Additionally, ONGC has set up a joint ONGC-Schlumverger Wireline Research Center at Delhi to meet the long term need of high technology requirement for wireline logging and related fields. OIL has its R&D center at Duliajan, mainly dealing with exploration, oil field chemicals, EOR and production engineering related matters. GAIL is also developing in-house R&D facilities mainly in the area of gas processing storage, distribution and utilisation.

Production of natural gas in 1994-95 was 19.38 BCM as compared to 18.33 BCM in the year 1993-94. The utilisation in 1994-95 was 17.35 BCM as compared to 16.41 BCM in 1993-94. The balance recoverable reserves as on 1 April 1994 were around 700 BCM.

Gas Authority of India Limited (GAIL) was incorporated i 1984 for the transportation, processing and marketing of natural gas and was assigned the priority task of setting up the cross country HBJ pipeline. Presently GAIL is the largest company in India for marketing natural gas. It operates over 3,000 km of pipelines in the country and supplies gas to power plants for the generation of 6,000 mw of power to the fertilizer sector for the production of 10 MTPA of urea and to about 150 industrial units.

GAIL is operating on the plants LPG at Bijaipur (Madhya Pradesh) and Vaghodia (Gujarat). It is putting up two more LPG plants at Lakwa (Assam) and Usar (Maharashtra), a petro-chemical complex at Auraiya (Uttar Pradesh) and proposes to put up a gas processing complex at Gandhar. GAIL has formed a joint venture company with British Gas to implement the Bombay City Gas Distribution Project. It is also upgrading the HBJ pipeline capacity from 18.2 MMSCMD to 33.4 MMSCMD.

The Government of India has been inviting offers from Indian and foreign companies for development of discovered oil fields as well as for exploration of oil and gas in various blocks in India. Against the offer of discovered oil field made in August 1992, contracts for development of five medium sized fields and 12 small sized fields have been signed. The medium sized fields * are MId and South Tapti, Mukta and Panna (Bombay offshore); Ravva (Krishna-Godavari offshore) and Kharsang (Arunachal Pradesh). The small fields are Hazira, Cambay, Bhandut, Matar, Sabarmati, Indora, Bakrol, Lohar, Dholka, Wavel, Baola and Asjol in Gujarat.

The medium-sized fields would be developed through joint ventures between Oil and Natural Gas Commission (ONGC) Oil India Ltd. (OIL) on the one hand and private companies on the other. These joint ventures could be either incorporated or unincorporated ventures. Where they are incorporated, ONGC/OIL would have a 49 per cent share in the equity of the venture. In unincorporated ventures, ONGC/OIL would take a 40 per cent share in the venture.

The small-sized fields would be developed by commmpanies on their own, with no participation by ONGC/OIL, under production sharing contracts to be signed by the companies with the Government of India. In both cases, companies would also be required to bear their share of statutory levies like royalty, cess, etc. Foreign companies would be levied income-tax at a fixed rate of 50 per cent, while Indian companies would be governed by the relevant provisions of the Income Tax. The Government has the first right of refusal in respect of the contractor's share of oil, with international price being payable. Companies have also been exempted from payment of customs duty on goods imported for use in petroleum operations.

In addition to the above, the Government has signed production sharing contracts for exploration of oil and gas in four blocks under the fourth round of bidding. These blocks are: (i) in Pranhita-Godavari (Gondwana) onshore basin; (ii) Krishna-Godavari offshore basin; (iii) Rajasthan basin and (iv) Cauvery offshore basin.

Government is actively encouraging the acquisition of acreages overseas to enhance the flow of equity oil into the country. As part of this policy, ONGC Videsh Ltd. (OVL) has been aggressively pursuing opportunities overseas to acquire exploration and producing acreages.

OVL entered into a production sharing contract in 1988 with Petro-Vietnam for exploratiion for hydrocarbons in blocks 6,12E and 19 in offshore Vietnam. Subsequently, in 1992. OVL assigned 45 per cent of its interest in the blocks to the alliance of British Petroleum (BP), UK and Statoil, Norway.

The OVL-BP-Statoil consortium carried out further survey and drilling work during the second phase of exploration between May 1992 and November 1994, leading to a discovery of about two trillion cubic feet (TCF) of gas in the Lan Tay and Lan Do structures in block 6. Techno-economic appraisal of the gas discovery with a view to its development is currently in progress. OVL has so far spent about US dollar 30 million on this venture.

OVL signed an agreement with British Gas, UK, in June 1995 for taking a 50 per cent participating interest in the North Zaafarana concession in Egypt. Under this agreement, OVL is scheduled to drill an exploratory well with and expenditure of about US dollar 7 million. It has also signed an agreement with Command Petroleum, Australia in July 1995 for taking a 40 per cent participating interest in the Fejaj permit in Tunisia. Drilling of an exploratory well is currently in progress.

In addition to the above, OVL is also engaged in negotiations with British Gas for taking a participating interest in offshore block in Yemen. It is also actively evaluating exploration and production opportunities in a number of other countries in order to enhance its reserves in overseas acreages so that a significant contribution to the equity oil accruing to the country from overseas ventures can be made.

The total refining capacity in the country as on 1 April 1994 was 53.40 MMTPA spread over 13 refineries. The actual crude processed was 54.30 MMTPA year 1993-94 representing a capacity utilisation of 101.7 per cent. The cumulative refinery production from April-August 1995 was 24.12 thousand tonnes as against the *pro-rata* installed capacity * . While making projections for the Eighth Five Year Plan, it has been estimated that the demand of petroleum products will be around 79 MMTPA in the terminal year of Eighth Plan and around 102 MMTPA by the end of Nineth Plan *i.e.* in the year 2001-20002. To meet the consumption levels, Government approved proposals to set up the following new refineries in addition to implementation/expansion/ debottlenecking of existing refineries: (i) Mangalore Refinery (JV)-Three MMTPA; (ii) Numaligarh Refinery-Three MMTPA and (iii) Panipat Refinery-Six MMTPA. With the modernisation of Digboi Refinery, its capacity would be increased from 0.5 to 0.65 MMTPA. Further expansion of Bongaigaon Refinery and Petrochemicals Limited (BRPL) from 1.35 MMTPA to 2.35 MMTPA has already been implemented. Haldia and Vizak refineries plans have been also approved for expansion by one and three MMTPA respectively. Besides, the Government had decided in July 1992 for setting up of three new grass-root refineries during the Eighth/Ninth Plan, each with a capacity of six MMTPA as joint ventures with suitable private parties from India or abroad.

The Government of India has welcomed proposals for private investment including foreign investment in the refining sector following liberalisation of industrial policy. In pursuance of this policy, Letters of Intent have been granted to 11 companies for setting up refineries in the private sector including EOU refineries to the extent ofabout 60 MMTPA. In case all the approved refineries are implemented by the end of century, India will be mot self-sufficient in the refining capacity but also export some products.

Lubrizol India Limited (LIL), a public sector undertaking was incorporated in 1966 in collaboration with the lubrizol Corporation, USA under the Companies Act. The authorised and paid-up share capital of the company is Rs. 19.20 crore. The Government of India holds 60 per cent of the subscribed equity capital of the company and the Lubrizol Corporation, USA 40 per cent thereof. LIL develops, manufactures and markets additive systems for autommotive and industrial lubricants and also develops other speciality chemicals for catering to the needs of the petroleum industry. The company has one manufacturing unit and the second unit for manufacturing of extreme pressure additives at Taloja, district Raigad, was commissioned on 30 March 1995.

The Engineers India Limited (EIL) was established in 1965 in collaboration with the Bechtel Corporation, USA mainly to indigenise engineering and project management capabilities in the petroleum sector. In 1967, the shareholding of Bechtel was taken over the Government of India and since then the company has been a fully-owned public sector undertaking. The authorised and paid up capital of EIL is Rs. two crore as on 31 March 1994. The reserves and surplus of the company have grown to Rs. 197.90 crore as on 31 MArch 1994 and its net worth on that date was Rs. 199.90 crore.

EIL today provides a complete range of project services in the fields of petroleum refining, petrochemicals, oil and gas processing pipelines, ocean engineering, ports and harbours, fertilizer and non-ferrous metallurgy, cement, paper, etc., and has emerged as South Asia's leading design and engineering company. In order to increase its global competitiveness, EIL has adopted a three-pronged strategy, *i.e.* setting up of joit ventures, formation of strategic alliances and stand alone ventures. The company has formed a joint venture company in the name of AMEC Engineers India Limited (AEIL) in 50:50 partnership with M/s AMEC Process and Energy International, in UK.

The EIL has also formed a wholly-owned subsidiary in India under the name Certification Engineers International Limited (CEIL) in order to provide certification, recertification and third party inspection services to the Indian as well as overseas clients. The company is also in process of establishing a wholly-owned subsidiary company in Malaysia under the name EIL, ASIA PACIFIC SDN BHD. It has diverse consultancy assignments in Iran, Algeria, Qatar, Abu Dhabi and Malaysia.

The growing demand for petroleum products has been casting a heavy burden on the economy. Hence a very high priority is being attached to the conservation of petroleum products. A variety of measures taken by the Petroleum Conservation Research Association * (PCRA), a registered society under the Ministry of Petroleum and Natural Gas, to promote conservation of petroleum products cover transport, industrial, agricultural, household and oil sectors which account for the PCRA are creation of mass awareness on the need for the conservation of petroleum prosucts, promotion of measures to curb wasteful practices, and improve the oil use efficiency of equipment, devices and vehicles and research and development for improving oil use efficiency in various end uses. As a result of these efforts it has been possible to achieve quantifiable savings of about Rs. 491 crore during 1994-95 including recurring saving of Rs. 417 crore achieved as a result of efforts made by and through the PCRA.

In addition, new areas or the inadequately covered areas are also being taken up including promotion of inter-seul subsititution. As part of a programme for inter-fuel substitution, CNG was introduced as an alternate fuel in the road transport sector. In all 1,677 petrol driven vehicles have been converted for CNG operation.

Marketing and distribution network of the Indian pteroleum industry is widespread and, by and large, under the control of the public sector oil companies. Apart from over 2,736 km of product pipeline, the industry has a network of about 16,023 MS/HSD retail outlets, 6156-light diesel oil/kerosene dealers and over 4,673 LPG distributors up to April 1995. Fair distribution of products all over the country at stipulated prices is generally ensured.

A major landmark development in the petroleum marketing has been the decanalisation of kerosene, LPG and LSHS and the introduction of parallel marketing of these products to augment their domestic availability. As a result of this liberalisation, the private entrepreneurs can now undertake import of these commodities and sell them at market determined prices. As on 31 July 1995, about 73.5 TMT of LPG and 817.3 TMT of kerosene has been imported. The private sector has also been allowed to invest in the development of infrastructure for petroleum marketing. Private investment has been invited for setting up and operation of depots, tank farms, import facilities, product and crude pipeline and manufacture of railway tank wagons for use by the oil industry. Several products like naptha, hexane, toluene, petroleum coke, carbon black feed stock, lube oil base stock, etc., have been decanalised for better availability of these products.

In order to inform and educate the public about the credentials and credibility of parallel marketers, a system of rating has been introduced in June 1995, by which every parallel marketer is required to obtain a rating certificate from one of the approved rating agencies.

Several joint ventures have been set up in the petroleum sector by both the public and private enterprises. Six joint ventures have been set up by the public sector oil marketing companies with reputed international companies for manufacture and marketing of lubricants, bitumen emulsions, and insfractructure for LPG. Several private sector companies have also entered into joint venture agreements with transnational companies. These are expected to bring in foreign investment as well as help in upgrading the indigenous technologies.

Indian Oil Corporation (IOC) was set up in September 1964, by amalgamating Indian Refineries Limited with Indian Oil Company Limited. The Corporation has three division, namely, (i) Marketing Division with headquarters at Bombay. (ii) Refineries and Pipelines Division with headquarters at Delhi; and (iii) Assam Oil Division with headquarters at Digboi. IOC has a Research and Development Centre at Faridabad in Haryana. The Centre provides technical service to customers and is engaged in development of sophisticated lubrication oils. It is actively working on possibilities of production and utilisation of viable substitute fuels. IOC is also having a wholly-owned subsidiary called Indian Oil Blending Limited (IOBL) which is engaged in blending lubricants.

The market share of the Corporation was 55.76 per cent of the total oil industry's sales in April 1995. The Corporation had in existence 2,295 cooking gas (LPG) distributorships, 6,277 retail outlet (petrol/diesel) dealerships and 3,283 kerosene/light diesel oil dealerships in the country.

Following government's acquisition of two Burmah-Shell companies in January 1976, name of Burmah-Shell Refineries Limited was changed to Bharat Refineries Limited from 12 February 1976. Being an integrated refining and marketing company, name of the company was changed to Bharat Petroleum Corporation Limited (BPCL) from 1 August 1977.

The company is engaged in processing of crude oil in its refinery at Bombay and storage, distribution and marketing of petroleum products in country. In addition, it is in the process of diversifying into ptero-chemicals using certain refinery streams as feed stock. Market share of BPCL in 1994-95 was 20.01 per cent of total oil industry's sales. As on 1 April 1995, the company had a total of 948 cooking gas (LPG) distributorships, 4,204 petrol/diesel retail outlets and 937 kerosene oil/light diesel oil dealership.

Hindustan Petroleum Corporation Limited (HPCL) was set up on 15 July 1974 by acquiring assets in India of ESSO Eastern Inc. USA and became a wholly government-owned company. On 21 December 1976, Government acquired Caltex Oil Refining (India) and merged it with HPCL. The main activities of HPCL are refining of crude oil, manufacturing lubricating base oil, manufacturing and blending of lubricants, grease and petroleum products and related automative accessories all over the country and marketing of petroleum products including LPG. Market share of HPCL in 1994-95 was 19.54 per cent of total oil industry's sales. As on 1 April

1995, the company had a total of 1307 cooking gas (LPG) distributorships, 4154 retail outlets (petrol/diesel) and 1,580 kerosene/light diesel oil dealerships.

IBP Company Limited has three divisions, namely, oil, chemicals and engineering. Oil division has a country-wide retail network marketing petroleum products which it obtains from other oil companies in the absence of its own refining facility at present. The Company had in existence 1388 retail outlets (petrol/diesel) dealerships and 356 kerosene/light diesel oil dealership in the country.

As India is one of the lowest cost refiners in the world, experts believe that it might become a net exporter of petroleum products in the coming century and a "swing producer" to stabilise global product markets. Though the first oil well in India was completed late in the last century—drilling for the oil well at Digboi in Assam was begun in September 1889 and completed in November 1890—the search for oil in a big way started only after the country gained Independence. The first well at Digboi was drilled by the Assam Railway and Trading Company. Later the Assam Oil Company (AOC) came into existence, which sold its rights to the Burmah Oil Company.

These were the beginnings of Oil India Limited, which became a fully-owned Government company in the early eighties. Thus at the time of Independence, indigenous production of crude oil was confined to Assam. Since this was hardly enough to meet the country's needs for petroleum products, the Government of India took a conscious decision to develop the country's oil resources, both onshore and offshore.

Creating a Petroleum Division within the Geological Survey of India in October 1955, exclusively for country-wide oil exploration, was the first step. It did not take much time for GSI's Petroleum Division to grow into the Directorate of Oil and Natural Gas, and subsequently into an autonomous Oil & Natural Gas Commisssion through an act of Parliament in October 1959. Now, of course, the Commission is known as Oil & Natural Gas Corporation Limited.

The real fillip to the development of the indigenous petroleum industry was given by the late Keshav Deo Malaviya, who gave ONGC the necessary push and was also responsible for the creation of Indian Oil Corporation, India's first national refining and marketing corporation.

Later, of course, the refineries and marketing companies owned by Burmah-Shell, Esso and Caltex (not to talk of the small Digboirefinery owned by Burmah Oil Company) were nationalised giving birth to two more national oil companies, i.e. Bharat Petroleum and Hindustan Petroleum. Today there are 14 refineries (including the two mentioned above)—13 in the public sector and one in the joint sector. The Gas Authority of India Limited (GALL) was set up in 1984 for planned utilisation of gas reserves and was given the responsibility to set up the HBJ pipeline.

These are briefly the main operators in the oil and natural gas sector, which is basically a public sector monopoly now. While Oil India's operations, in the initial stages, were confined to the north-eastern region, ONGC's initial successes came in the western region. The first discovery of oil and gas made by ONGC was in 1958 in the Cambay onshore basin in Gujarat. Also in Gujarat, the first giant oilfield was discovered at Ankleshwar in 1960.

In what was termed as "Samudra Manthan" in the early sixties, ONGC decided to step up its offshore exploration activity in earnest. Seismic surveys helped in the discovery of the Aliabet structure at the mouth of the Narmada and later in "Bombay High". A big debate raged in the late sixties whether we should develop "Bombay High" on our own or entrust the job to foreign compaines. The first option was chosen and ONGC acquired its first jack-up type rig "Sagar Samrat" (built for the Commission in Japan) in 1973. "Sagar Samrat" started drilling in "Bombay High" in January 1974 and about a month later oil was discovered at the very first well it drilled in this oilfield, which has met part of the country's crude needs for the past 15 years or so.

This writer was fortunate enough to be among the group of reporters who were on board the "Sagar Samrat" in early 1974 to witness the drilling for the first well. By the time we returned to shore and about to report this first experiment in offshore drilling, news arrived that oil has been found. February 1974 will thus be a landmark in the development of offshore oil production in India.

ONGC has travelled quite far in the 22 years since oil was established in "Bombay High". Crude oil production from offshore areas (which is solely from ONGC) has risen from five million tonnes in 1980-81 to a high of 21.2 million tonnes in 1990-91. It was around 20.2 million tonnes 1994-95. Total crude production both from onshore and offshore areas (i.e. the total output of OIL and ONGC) was around 35.2 million tonnes in 1995-96.

But the country's requirements of petroleum products have grown at a rapid rate, from 30 million tonnes in 1980-81 to almost 75 million tonnes in 1995-96. Current estimates indicate that it would reach a level of about 113 million tonnes by 2001-02.

Looked at from a different perspective. India's domestic oil production vis-a-vis petroleum product consumption indicate that the percentage of slefsufficiency has declined from 55.6 per cent in 1990-91 to 43.7 per cent in 1995-96 and is estimated to decline further to 23.5 per cent by 2006-7. In other words, the percentage of self-sufficiency in another 10 years (which is not far away) will be half of what it was in 1990-91.

While of course it is true that it is the Centre's responsibility to find adequate funds to develop the oil and gas industry, the above figures only highlight the need to let the oil and gas industry generate more internal resources to finance its future development. It is an open secret that the Government of India's finances are none too rosy and there are too many competing claims on the limited kitty available with the Centre.

All the more reason for immediate reforms in the hydrocarbons sector. Though it is difficult to quantify in monetary terms the benefits of reforms, the R Group has estimated that the net present value of the reforms it has suggested would amount to around Rs. 100,000 crore. And that is a lot of money.

The controversy that is raging at the moment over raising the prices of some of the heavily subsidised petroleum products only serve to highlight the problems that arise in opening up the oil and gas sector in line with the changes that are taking place in other sectors of the economy.

For instance, it is widely admitted (even in official publicity material) that a level playing field should be given to national oil companies "particularly by paying them international market price of oil". This will help them to raise more revenue, but this good intention still remains on paper only.

"If discovered fields are offered in future for improving economic viabiloity, the national oil companies, who have discovered the fields, should be reimbursed the past costs incurred by them", says an official note explaining the short-term measures to be taken for development of the oil sector. This is another contentious issue on which there is more noise than action.

The Government has allowed entry of private sector in a major way into the oil refining sector (proposals, including export-oriented refineries, adding up to 70 million tonnes per annum have been cleared so far). Similarly, parallel marketing in gas has been allowed (though this has yet to pick up) and with the approval in principle for the Southern Gas Grid, several policy decisions with regard to the natural gas sector have also to be taken. For instance, natural gas is underpriced and there is a recommendation that it should be raised.

Development of the natural gas sector (which will, as per present indications, will be largely based on imported gas) means heavy investment in pipelines, port and storage facililties, etc. It takes years to set up these. Here again, to facilitate and encourage investment, a rational pricing policy must be in place, the sooner the better.

Since the country has mastered the art and science of setting up refineries as well as running them, experts believe that india might become a net exporter of petroleum products in the coming century and a "swing producer" to stabilise global product markets. This expectation is based on the fact that India is one of the lowest cost refiners in the world.

But, to quote Dr. Kelkar again, "our present administered prices regime is non-transparent and certainly not efficency compatible. Further, our current tariffs provide negative rate of protection for the refining sector and as such it discourages provate investors to bring in new investments". Hence, what is required is comprehensive reforms of pricing and tariff policy as that alone can promote adequate infusion of capital and efficient use of these resources, he argues.

Now, that prescription applies not only to the refining sector, but to the entire oil and natural gas sector. This is not the place to go into specific details, but a visionary approach is needed similar tot he one shown by many of those who have helped paying the foundation for the oil and gas industry.

The great institutional base built up within the country over the past several decades in exploration, production and refining should be strengthened further, along with the entry of a range of new actors. Major investments are taking place in sectors like automobiles, but these can become infructuous if the main engine of growth (here one means both industrial and agricultural growth) i.e. the oil and gas sector, is not properly taken care of. It is time we put this sector on a faster track.

Both at the central and state level, the Government has initiated and supports many efforts towards capacity-building. The major thrust of development is on the implementation of sectoral programmes, particularly those related to agriculture and allied sectors. Programmes such as the National Rural Employment Programmes (NREP), Rural Landless Employment Guarantee Programme * (IRDP) aim to alleviate rural poverty. Programmes such as Hill Area Development are designed to tackle hostile environmental factors which affect development of certain areas. In the Drought-Prone Areas Programme (DPAP) and Desert Development Programme (DDP), the emphasis is on water and moisture conservation.

India has sovereign rights and jurisdiction in the economic zone extending 200 nautical miles from the coastline. The Government has established a wide-ranging network of legislative and institutional frameworks for protecting and preserving the marine environment.

The programme of the Department of Ocean Development and associated organizations include Development of Coastal Zones and Islands, Monitoring and modelling of the Marine Environment, Control of Marine Pollution, Wave Power Generation, Ocean Modelling, Sea Level Monitoring and Modelling, and Coastal Mapping.

Marine Satellite Information Secvice centres and a multi-institutional Marine Pollution Coastal Ocean Monitoring and Predictive System have been established.

The National Environmental Awareness Campaign (NEAC), which began in 1986, is a major programme of the Ministry of Environment and forests. The programme seeks to increase environmental awareness through the involvement of governmental and non-governmental organizations. Activities under the NEAC include seminars, workshops, rallies, teacher training, eco-clubs, environmental campus etc.

The Ministry of Environment and Forests set up the Environmental Information System (ENVIS) in 1982 as a decentralized system using a network of databases to ensure integration of national efforts in collecting information related to environment.

ENVIS has ten centres working in diverse areas such as pollution control, coastal ecology, environmentally sound and appropriate technology etc. It has a documentation service and processes queries from national and international useres. A quarterly abstracting journal Paryavaran Abstracts is published after scanning nearly five hundred scientific journals. ENVIS maintians a close liaison with other national information systems like National Information System on Science and Technology (NISSAT) and Biotechnology Information System (BTIS).

The Central Arid Zone Research Institute (CAZRI) was set up at Jodhpur in Rajasthan by the Government of India to undertake studies on land, soil water and vegetation resources of arid and semi-arid areas. The Institute carries out studies on precipitation, the regional dynamics of the landscape and the impact of climatic conditions and man-animal activities on it in order to determind the optimal natural plant community of major environments, and to optimize the use of water and land. CAZRI is also involved in transfer of technology, publicity and extension work to create awareness about the desertification process, and to achieve public participation in the development programmes of arid and semi-arid regions.

In the area of formal education, the National Policy on Education (1986) stresses the paramount need to create consciousness about the environment. This must permeate all ages and sections of the society, beginning with the child. The Policy gives unqualified priority to universalization of elementary eduction and substantial improvement in the quality of education. Detailed school mapping exercises have been planned under a master plan for universal provision of facilities for environment education. The National Council of Educational Research and Training (NCERT) has been assigned the responsibility of developing model syllabi and instructional packages in ten core cureicular ares, of which protection of environment is one.

The Ministry of Human Resource Development (MHRD) has taken a major initiative in the field of environment education through the launching of the Environment Orientation to School Education scheme.

Under this scheme special cells have been created in the state departments of education. Support is also extended to NGOs to facilitate the development of locale-specific programmes and materials.

The Ministry of Environment and Forests supports two centres of excellence in the area of environmental educationl. These are the Centre for Environment Education, Ahmedabad, and the CPR Environmental Education Centre, Madras. The Centre for Environment Education, Ahmedabad, is involved in developing innovative programmes and materials to increase awareness about the environment.

The National Museum of Natural History (NMNH), New Delhi, is a unique facility which provides people an opportunity to acquire a direct understanding of the world of nature, the inter relationships among plants, animals, and the environment, and the need to develop a new approach and ethic towards the natural environment. NMNH also has centres at Mysore, Bhubaneshwar and Bhopal.

The Government of India supports research projects for the study of ecosystems and the causes of their degradation. In this regard, two committees—the Environmental Research Committee (ERC) and Man and the Biosphere (MAB) Research Committee function as advisory bodies under the Ministry of Environment and Forests. The research is followed up by formulation of action plans for optimal utilistion of resources leading to sustainable development.

Man and the Biosphere programme is an inter-disciplinary programme of research and training which emphasized and ecological approach to the study of inter-relationships between humans and their environment. The programme aims to provide scientific basis to solve practical problems of resource management through understanding the environmental problems in the ecosystem context.

The Environmental Research Committee addresses problems of chemical, engineering and technological aspects of environmental management, and promotes research in all subjexts concerned with the human environment that are not covered by the MAB programme. ERCs thrust areas include environmental aspects of rural and urban settlemens, resource management, environmental degradation, planning, training and education. It promotes integrated action-oriented programmes which deal not only with research but also its demonstration and extension. Such action-oriented research has been taken up in the Himalayan region, and in the Western and Eastern Ghats, besides multinational project of integrated studies on the Kaveri river.

The Ministry of Environment and Forests has so far supported about 500 environmental research projects in different parts of the country. Of these, about 300 had been completed by March 1990. The findings of the research projects are published in a departmental publication and also in scientific journals and the popular press. Some of the findings have direct applicability while others contribute to the data base for environmental planning and management.

Various other research organizations set up by the Government and other agencies are concerned with different aspects of evnironment. The physical Research Laboratory (PRL) Ahmedabad, is a premier national centre for research in space and allied sciences; the Indian Institute of Remote Sensing (IIRS), Hyderabad, imparts training in remote sensing techniques and promotes research in areas like thematic mapping of land.

The functions of the Council of Scientific and Industrial Research (CSIR) include institutional financing, awarding fellowships, collecting and disseminating information on research and industrial matters. It has a chain of 39 laboratories and about 80 field centres. From aeronautical products to oceanography, and from drugs to salt and marine chemicals research, CSIR is involved in helping the country enter frontier areas of research.

Its centres include the Central Drug Research Institute, Lucknow; National Environmental Engineering Research Institute, Nagpur; Indian National Scientific Documentation Centre, New Delhi; National Chemical laboratory, Pune; Central Institute of Medicinal and Aromatic Plants, Lucknow; Industrial Toxicology Research Centre, Lucknow; Indian Institute of Chemical Technology, Hyderabad; and Central Food Technology Research Institute, Mysore.

Council for Advencement of People's Action and Rural Technology (CAPART), set up in 1986 is the central agency for funding rural development projects of voluntary agencies. It assists voluntary efforts which aim to implement locale-specific rural development projects. Funding for projects coming under several government programmes like the Drought Prone Area programme, Integrated Rural Development Programme etc., are disbursed through CAPART.

CAPART gives financial assistance to registered voluntary organization. Up to 80 per cent of the project expenditure is made available and the remaining has to be raised by the organization for other sources.

The Department of Science and Technology, Government of India, is involved in research and development related to several environmental issues throuhg its institutions.

The Indian Institute of Tropical Meteorology, Pune, is involved in studies of atmospheric ozone, effect of aerosols on climate change, effect of stratospheric changes and anthropogenic activities on climate change, carbon dioxide studies etc.

The Birbal Sahni Institute of Paleobotany, Lucknow, is engaged in paleobotanical research which aims to build up an evlutionary sequence charting the history of modern vegetation. It is also involved in investigating past climates.

The Wadia Institute of Himalayan Geology, Dehra Dun, has been studying various aspects of the chemistry of Himalayan glaciers. It has also conducted studies on the impact of growing human population on the Himalayan ecology.

The Indian institute of Astrophysics, Bangalore, studies solar activity while the Indian Institute of Geomagnetism, Bombay, has a programme for the study of atmospheric and solar terrestrial weather relationships.

The Survey of India, Dehra Dun, is responsible, among other things, for tide gauge observations along the Indian coastline and for the study of anticipated problems of sea-level rise and impact on coastal environment.

The Centre for Atmospheric Studies at the Indian Institute of Technology, New Delhi, studies the effect of aerosols on climate change, air pollution over India, and other related issues.

The Department of Science and Technology is also actively involved in the national efforts of the International Geosphere-Biosphere programme.

The practice of scientific forestry in India dates back to over 120 years. Systamatic research and trainign in foresting commenced nearly 70 years ago. Research and forestry education now come under the purview of the Indian Council of Forestry Research and Education, which conducts its programmes through six regional institutions and a number of universitites and other organizations. Its six regional institutions, including the Forest Research Institute at Dehra Dun which is a premier institution in forestry, carry out extensive field and laboratory research. The Indian Institute of Forest Management (IIFM) Bhopal, was established in 1982 to meet the growing need for managerial expertise in forestry and allied sectors. The institute also runs management development programmes for in—service managers of forest departments, forest development corporations, forest based industries, financial institutions and voluntary organizations. In addition, the Institute is involved in applied research and provides consultancy service.

Forest management in the field is planned and implemented by the Indian Forest Service (IFS). Two year postgraduate training in forestry is imparted to IFS officers at the Indira Gandhi National Forest Academy, Dehra Dun. There are also three regional State Forest Service colleges and numerous rangers' colleges for training middle level and field professionals.

NGOs in India have played a vital role in raising awareness about the issues related to environment and development, and in mobilizing people to take action. They have employed a variety of techniques and media. The Kerala Sastra Sahitya Parishat, which was the catelytic agency involved in mobilizing public opinion agaisnt the Silent Valley hydroelectric project, uses traditional and folk media to communicate its messages. The Centre for Science and Environment (CSE), New Delhi, has brought out three widely circulated volumes on the state of India's environment, in addition to several other publication. CSE has also played a key role in bringing in the South perspective in International discussions of environment and development issues. Eklavya, Bhopal, develops innovative and relevant school programmes and material. The Assam Science Society which has a membership of professional and students, attempts to enhance science education.

The Narmada Bachao Andolan has brought together scattered voices of protest against the damming of the river Narmada and has raised awarness not only in the affected area and in the rest of India, but alos among the international community. The Vivekanand Kendra, Tamil Nadu, trains hundreds of workers in the fields of health, education and development.

A major focus of its activities is in Arunachal Pradesh where it runs 14 residential schools for tribal children. The People's Commission on Environment and Development, New Delhi, is a forum creatd to bring together and articulate citizen's concerns to put before the UNCED. Kalpavriksh, New Delhi, organizes awareness programmes and carries out campaigns on specific issues by lobbying, holding demonstrations and fighting legal cases.

The Ministry of Environment and Forests has instituted a number of awards to recognize outstanding contributions of individuals and organizations in various environment related endeavours.

National Awards for Prevention and Control of Pollution have been instituted to recognize the achievements of industries for their contribution in the prevention and control of pollution.

Indira Priyadarshini Vrikshmitra Awards are given to individuals and organizations for outstanding work in the field of afforestation and wastelands development.

Indira Gandhi Paryavaran Puraskar is awarded to either an individual or organization for contribution in the field of environment.

Pitamber Pant National Fellowship recognizes excellence in research in any branch of environmental science.

The Centre for Mining Environment at Dhanbad (Bihar) was establised in 1987 by the Ministry of environment and Forests to generate scientific data for sustainable mining in the country. The Centre conducts postgraduate and doctoral level courses, as well as training programmes for in service professionals. Research areas include land use management, noise and vibration problems in mining areas, air pollution in fire areas and its effects on health.

Remote sensing for survey of resources is carried out by India's earth observation satellite system, the IRS series of satellites. Projections of crop yields, land-use mapping, monitorin of forest cover and biomass, identification of agro-climatic zones are today possible, and provide a basis for micro-level planning. Drought monitoring on a real time basis is also becoming possible, as is the use of remote sensing for mitigating damage due to floods. Detailed remote sensing surveys have also helped to considerably narrow down areas for groundwater exploration. Satellite based glacier inventory of the Himalayan states has been found promising for planning and operating mini and micro hydroelectric stations.

Fishers prospect charts, derived from satellite monitoring of sea surface temperature anamolies, are in regular use. Remote sensing has also been used extensively for forest mapping, in India. It is through this that a correct picture of the extent of forest cover and the relative changes in it have been obtained.

The National Natural Resource Management System of the Ministry of Environment and Forests involves utilization of remote sensing technology for accurate inventory of resources such as land, water, forests, minerals, ocean, etc., and to utilize this information for monitoring changes in ecological systems.

The objective of all development is to add to the economic well-being of the people so that their standard of living can be improved. Development projects are, therefore, taken up to convert the natural resources into goods and services. It is imperative to incorporate environmental aspects into the development projects right at the inception stage to prevent the erosion of the resouces base itself. Impact assessment is a handy tool to assess the environmental compatibility of the projects in terms of their location, suitability of technology, efficiency in resource utilisation and recycling etc. Impact assessment was introduced in 1978 and now covers almost all major projects.

At present environmental impact assessment is being done for the following types of project: (a) (i) river valley; (ii) thermal power; (iii) mining; (iv) industries; (v) atomic power; (vi) rail, road, highways, bridges; (vii) ports and harbours; (viii) airport; (iv) new towns and (x) communication projects, (b) projects which require approval of the Public Investment Board/Planning Commission/Central Electricity Authority; (c) projects referred to the Ministry of Environment and Forests by other ministries; (d) projects which are sensitive and located in environmentally degraded areas; (e) public sector undertakings of the Centre where the project cost is more than Rs. 50 crore. A notification has been issued in January 1994 which makes Environmental Impact Assessement statutory for 29 categories of developmental projects under various sectors such as industrial, mining, irrigation, power, transport, tourism, communication, etc.

The notification contains details aimed at rationalising and standarding the procedure for environmental clearance. Extensive delegations to the stae governments are also provided in this notification. An amendment to this notification stipulates inter alia that all applications complete in every material aspect have to be examined and decision conveyed to the applicants within 30 days in the case of site clearances and 120 days in the case of environmental clearnce of projects. Once an application has been submitted by project authority the preliminary scrutiny of the project is done by the respective technical divisions and the overall appraisal of the projects is undertaken by specially constituted environmental appraisal committees of experts. In addition, special groups/committees and task forces are constituted as and when needed for expert inputs on major projects. After a detailed scrutiny and assessment, the appraisal committee makes its recommendation for approval or rejection of the projects. Depending on the nature of the project, certain safeguards are recommended. For monitoring and timely implementation of safeguards suggested, six regional centres have been set up by the Ministry at Shillong, Bhubaneswar, Chandigarh, Bangalore, Lucknow and Bhopal.

Under the Forests (Conservation) Act, 1980 diversion of forest land for non-forest purpose requires prior approval from the Central Government. While proposals involving forest land less than 20 hectare can be decided by the state forest departments, proposals involving more than that are appriased by the Advisory Committee of the Ministry, constituted under the Forests (Conservation) Act, 1980 as amended in 1988.

When a project requires both environemental and forest clearance, the proposals are simultaneously processed under the Single Window Celearance Scheme. All cases with complete environmental data and action plans are decided within three months. In the case of diversion of forest land, the decision is taken within six months.

Major environmental impacts of river vally projects which need consideration are: (i) degradation of catchment areas; (ii) command area development; (iii) rehabilitation of those affected; (iv) incresed incidence of water-borne diseases; (v) reservoir induced seismicity; and (vi) deforestation and loss of flora and fauna including gene-pool reserves.

Major environmental impacts of mining operations are: (i) degradation of land; (ii) pollution of surface and ground water resources; (iii) pollution of air; (iv) deforestation including loss of flora and fauna; (v) rehabilitation of affected populationincluding tribals; and (vi) impact on historical monuments and religious places. A major component of the mining operations in India is the opencast mining which severely affects land use pattern. Mining operations have serious adverse impact on the growth of vegetation and general landscape. Minerals extracted interact with surface and ground water thus polluting the water resources. Loss of top-soil due to deforestation also depletes ground water resources and results in drying up of perennial sources like springs and streams especially in hill areas.

Major environmental impacts of thermal power projects include; (a) air pollution; (b) water pollution; (c) deforestation; (d) rehabilitation; and (e) land degradation. Flue gases emerging from stacks containing sulphur dioxide, oxides of nitrogen, carbon monoxide, etc., are detrimental to human beings and vegetation. Water pollution from thermal stations can due to release of slurry which is a mixture of flyash and water. Thermal pollution is due to release of cooling water which can affect acquatic life. Solution to disposal of ash problem is in its recycling by converting it into building blocks and its use in other construction works. Another step which helps in abating pollution cuased by ash is stabilisation of ash dumps through suitable vegetation.

Major environmenal impacts of industrial projects include (i) are pollution; (ii) water pollution; and (iii) disposal and utilisation of solid waste. Impacts of projects in specific areas are examined in great detail and suitable control measures suggested. Linkages of project requirements to utilisation of resources in an optimal way is an essential pre-requisite. Concept of recycling, reuse and adoption of clean technologies is increasingly becoming predominant.

Projects considered under the transport sector include laying of railway lines, roads and bridge construction, airport construction and establishing of ports and harbours. The environmental parameters affected by the transport projects have been classified into (i) natural physical resources; (ii) natural ecological resources; (iii) human/economic development resources; and (iv) quality of life values including aesthetic and cultural values. Adverse impacts on above environmental parameters are to be identified and mitigation measures provided for to offset such impacts.

Under the Environment (Protection) Act, 1986, a notification on Coastal Zone Regulation has been issued declaring coastal stretches of seas, bays, estuaries, creaks, rivers and backwater within 500 meter of High Tide line as Coastal Regulation Zones. Setting up of new industries or expansion of existing industies except those directly related to waterfront, manufacturing, handling, storage or disposal of hazardous substances and setting up and expansion of units/mechanisms for disposal of wastes and effluents etc., are prohibited in these Costal Regulation Zone. All the seven coastal states are required to prepare coastal management plans which would provide protection to ecologically fragile coastal areas rich in biological diversity and provide for land use zoning. The Coastal Regulation Zone notification, 1991, has been amended.

In nuclear power plants, safety from radiation during the operation of the plants and after, and disposal of nuclear wastes are of prime concern. Major environmental impacts of nuclear power projects which need consideration are; (i) radio-active contamination of air, water and soil; (ii) thermal pollution due to discharge of cooling water; (iii) deforestation and loss of flora and fauna; (iv) rehabilitation; and (v) radio-active waste disposal. Exposure to radio-active radiations in excess of the prescribed limits are detrimental to human beings, aquatic life, flora and fauna. The long half life periods for radio-active decay necessitate sealing of the reactor vessel and components for a dormant period of about 30 years after decommissioning of the plant.

Afforestation of wastelands through proper financial assitance by various agencies would provide income and employment opportunities to the poor and improve the quality of the environment. The government can play a facilitating role by removing obstacles and simplifying procedures. The lack of ground-level data has affected the afforestation programme. The afforestation of wastelands has now emerged as an important feature in the present socio-economic and political scenario in India, which aims at solving the problems of scarcity of timber, firewood, fodder and other forest produce as well as reclamation of wastelands and degraded forests. India has vast tracts of wastelands, and these lands are mostly owned by government and village Panchayats and are highly degraded. Tree plantation is the socially optimum and ecologically-sound use of such lands. It may not be economically desirable for a farmer to plant trees on good lands which have a very high opportunity cost in terms of value of agricultural production forgone. However, tree planting may be profitable for a farmer in region prone to recurring drought and having unproductive soil which is not fit for growing agricultural crops.

Although the practice of planting trees is as old as cultivation of other crops, the need for government intervation to promote afforestation was articulated by the National Commission on Agriculture (NCA) in 1976. The government of India accepted the NCA's recommendation and subsequently various afforestation programmes like farm forestry, rehabilitation/ reforestation of degraded lands, formation of community woodlots and strip plantation were started in some States in the late seventies. Recent evidences from various parts of the country indicate that the success of afforestation programmes has been remarkable. In India, there is still a vast scope for implementing afforestation programmes in regions which are not yet brought within the fold of tree plantation schemes and in which there is acute shortage of firewood, timber and other forest produce.

In conjunction with technical guidance and financing, availability of wastelands for afforestation is the other crucial component of the wastelands development and afforestation programmes determing their success. There are many constraints which are hampering the implementation of afforestation programmes in various parts of the country. The non-availability of wastelands for afforestation programmes is one of them. In the absence of a comprehensive survey of land use, several estimates have been made about the extent of wastelands in India. One of the estimates of wastelands indicate that about 175 million hectares of (m ha) land fall in this category (Sigh et al, 1981). The other estimate by the Society for the Promotion of Wastelands Development (SPWD) puts it at 129 m ha-93 m ha in non-forest area and 36 m ha in forest area (SPWD, 1984). The National Wastelands Development Board (NWDB, 1989) estimates wastelands to the extent of 120 m ha with 40 m ha in forest lands and 80 m a in agricultural lands. According to Singh (1994), more than half of the geographical area of India consists of degraded lands. The estimates for wastelands range between 38.4 m ha (11.7% of total geographical area of the country, Directorate of Economics & Statistics, GOI, New Delhi 1978-79) to 175 m ha (53.2% of total geographical area of the country, Ministry of Agriculture & Co-operation, New Delhi, 1982) (Gautam and Narayan, 1988:96). However, Bentley (1984) has estimated that 200 m ha of land in India are partially degraded in terms of short-term productivity. According to Khan (1987), the wastelands which may ultimately be available for development would not be more than 80 m ha, bulk of which is degraded forests and marginal agriculatural lands. There are many other estimates of wastelands in India.

The information needed for assessing the potential of non-forest and cultivated lands, like ownership, extent and type of degradation, and present and future uses, has never been collected on a systematic basis for the entire country (Romm, 1981). Recently, some initiatives have been taken to improve the availability of grass roots level data for this purpose. The Government of India has already implemented a National Wastelands Identification Project to identify the extent and type of wastelands in 146 districts in 19 States.

One of the most serious problems threatening the country today is its population growth. Although the foodgrain production in the last few years has kept pace with the population increase, the daunting task of feeding each and everyone in the next century is the biggest challenge before us. In our attempts to meet such increasing demands, the improper and over—use of chemical inputs had deteriorated the agro—ecosystems to a considerable extent. Moreover, the pressure due to growing human and cattle population on the land has added to the deterioration of land status of the country. The increasing deterioration of land due to soil—erosion, injudicious use of chemical fertilizers, water logging, salinity/alkalinity, shifting cultivation, etc. necessitates a more scientific approach towards the utilisation of these lands, often termed as degraded or waste—lands. The growing awareness world over on the environment conservation and the emphasis on the concept of 'sustainability' has focussed on the area of 'wasteland utilization' as an important component of 'sustainable development.'

There are various aerial estimates of wastelands in the country varying from one—third to one half of the country's total area. The primary reason of the variation in such estimates could be ascribed to the fact that until recently, wastelands had neither been systematically defined nor identified. The first comprehensive attempt to map out such areas and categories them, was done by the National Commission on Agriculture (1976), which estimated different types of wastelands and suggested guidelines for reclaiming and developing such land. The Commission had estimated the extent of wastelands in the country to be 175 million hectares which is more than half the total geographical area in he country. However, this estimate was not based on scientific data. As per an estimate by the Society for Promotion of Wastelands Development (1993), the area under wastelands is around 129 million hectares or about one—third of country's total geographical area.

According to the statistics presented, the state with the greatest expanse of wastelands in the country is Madhya Pradesh with 20.14 million ha very closely followed by Rajasthan with 19.93 million ha. The states with over 10 million ha of wastelands each are Andhra Pradesh and Maharashtra. Gujarat, Karnataka and Uttar Pradesh have each approximately 9 million ha of wastelands.

To a layman, wasteland is a piece of land which is lying uninhabited or uncultivated. These lands are also commonly perceived to produce much less than their potential. Despleted of the green cover and productivity, such lands are often in a critical condition.

Boradly, wastelands may be defined as land where the production of biomass is less than its opotimum productivity. Wasteland also refers to lands which are economically unproductive, ecologically unstable and subject to environmental deterioration.

According to the Technical Task Group, constituted by the Planning Commisison and NWDB (National Wastelands Development Board), wasteland is defined as that land which is degraded and is presently lying unutilised except as current fallows due to different constraints.

Wastelands have been classified by NWDB into culturable and unculturable wastelands.

Culturable Wastelands: Land which is capable of or has the potential for the development of vegetative cover and is not being used due to different constraints of varying degree is termed as culturable wasteland. The culturable wastelands comprise the following categories:

— Gullied and/or ravinous land;

— Undulating upland with or without scrub;

— Surface–waterlogged lands and marsh;

— Salt–affected land;

— Shifting—cultivation area;

— Degraded forest—lands;

— Degraded pastures/grazing—lands;

— Degraded non forest—plantation land;

— Strip—land;

— Sands; and

— Mining/industrial wastelands.

Unculturable Wastelands: Lands, which can not be developed for vegetative cover, are defined as unculturable wastelands. The unculturable wastelands comprise the following categories:

— Baren rocky/Stony wastes/Sheet–rock area;

— Steep–sloping area; and

— Snow–covered and/or glacial area.

Besides the above categories of wastelands, the following could also be included:

— Over cultivated soils leading to depletion of micro–nutrients;

— Acidic soils; and

— Land overgrown with aggressive weeds.

The major causes of land being rendered waste include—deforestation, overgrazing, faulty water management practices, extensive mining activities, etc. Deforestation and overgrazing distinctly hastens the process of soil erosion and land degradation. Faulty water managemnt practices lead to problems such as water logging, soil salinity/alkalinity, etc. Deforestation has often been described as the most primary reason of land degradation and the factors in deforestation are—conversion of forest land into agricultural land, the urban and industrial demand for forest products, indiscriminate quarrying for mineral resources, etc. Besides the above mentioned casuses, the environmental factors like slope, intensity of rainfall and the pedogenic characteristics of a particular area interact to increase the formation of wastelands.

Our forest cover has dwindled notwithstanding three successive National Forest Policies. A scientific land use policy alone can ensure sustained production, ecological balance and environmental benefits. It is time that the Forest Policy is reviewed and a new strategy adopted keeping in view that conservation includes preservation, maintenance, sustainable utilization, restoration and enrichment of the environment.

Man depends on natural resources from his forest environment for all his basic needs. No doubt, the majority in the industrialized countries is no longer dependent on the natural living resources but the bulk of the rural and a section of the urban population in India and the rest of the developing world continue this dependence, especially for their fuel, fodder and timber needs. The forest serves many valuable functions as has been reflected in the national forest policies. Moreover, forest plays an active role as a storehouse of living organisms of potential use and as a regulator of rainfall, soil and water regime, source of many basic needs of the weaker sections of the rural population. The relationship between land, climate and forest is such that if the soil is allowed to deteriorate or lost, degradation of both land and vegetation becomes inevitable. Unfortunately, in the developing countries like India, biotic pressures are intense.

The situation is worsening in spite of the lofty aims propagated by the three successive national forest policies. In India, although the first policy is nearly a century old, the present forest cover is worse than when it was originally proposed. The failure of the national forest policies is perhaps due to their focus on government forests rather than to the land and soil in general. There has been a lack, of scientific land use policy having legal backing and public support. For these reasons, the definition of 'forest' has come to imply land area constituted as reserve forests and not general tree cover.

Biotic Pressure: The tremendous increase in human population, the resultant poverty nd the heavy dependence on agriculture have resulted in the use of wood as the main fuel. India's ecology is today no better with the deficit of firewood at 145 million m^3 and 43 million ha of land brought under the plough between 1951 and 1976 for the extension of agriculture. The loss of forest area for various purposes during 1951-76 was substantial.

The situation has still remained the same and the condition has not changed as is evident from the cases of some of the States. The problem has worsened due to excessive grazing coupled with forest fire. About 52 per cent of India's forests are incapable of regenration largely due to the combined effects of biotic pressures.

In a developing country like India, forests have suffered badly because of the failure in land management practices. To what extent can we put the blame on forest policies? Are the policies wrong or inconsistent or is it that the policies have remained merely ceremonial documents devoid of the will to implement or people's support? An analysis of the forest policies of India would reveal that the main cause of failure has been, perhaps, viewing forests in isolation rather than taking into consideration the country's soil as a whole. It is after all the soil which supports all kinds of plant life in the biosphere.

Forests are a renewable source and contribute substantially to economic development. They play major role in enhancing the quality of environment. The country has an area of 752.3 lakh hectare notified as forests, of which 406.1 lakh hectare is classified as reserved and 215.1 lakh hectare as protected. Unclassified forest area is spread over 131.1 lakh hectare. About 19.47 per cent of the total geographical area of the country is under actual forest cover.

India is one of the few countries which ahs a forest policy since 1894. It was revised in 1952 and again in 1988. Main plank of the revised forest policy of 1988 is protection, conservation and development of forests. Its aims are: (i) maintenance of environmental stability through preservation and restoration of ecological balance; (ii) conservation of natural heritage; (iii) check on soil erosion and denudation in catchment area of rivers, lakes and reservoirs; (iv) check on extension of sand dunes in desert areas of Rajasthan and along coastal tracts; (v) substantial increase in forest/tree cover through massive afforestation and social forestry programmes; (vi) steps to meet requirements of fuel wood, fodder, minor forest produce and soil timber of rural and tribal populations; (vii) increase in productivity of forest to meet the national needs; (viii) encouragement of efficient utilisation of forest produce and optimum substitution of wood, and (ix) steps to create massive people's movement with involvement of women to achieve the objectives and minimise pressure on existing forests.

The entire gamut of forest activities are being given a new orientation in the light of the National Forest Policy of 1988. Some of the important areas for immediate and effective protection of forests include afforestation and development of wastelands, reforestation and replantation in existing forests, settlement, restriction on grazing, encouragement for wood substitutes and supply of other kinds of fuel, elimation of forest contractors, discouragement of monoculture practice etc.

Increasing destruction and degradation of forests and treelands especially in the Himalayas and other hilly areas, is contributing to heavy erosion of top soil, erratic rainfall and recurring floods. It is also causing acute shortage of firewood and loos of productivity due to eroded and degraded lands. The Forest (Conservation) Act, 1980 enacted to check indiscriminate deforestation/ diversion of forest lands for non-forestry purpose was amended in 1988 to make it more stringent by prescribing punishment for violations.

Another area of concern has been degradation of forests due to biotic pressure. Guidelines have been framed for preparation of working plans and felling in forests. Some of the salient features are: (i) working plans shoudl be up-to-date and stress conservation; (ii) preliminary working plan should have multi-disciplinary approach; (iii) tribal rights and concessions should be highlighted and with control mechanisms; (iv) grazing should be studied in detail and specific prescriptions should cover fodder propagation; (v) shifting cultivation and encroachments need to be controlled; (vi) clear-felling with artificial regeneration should be avoided as far as possible and clear felling blocks should not exceed 10 hectare in hills and 25 hectare area in plains, and (vii) banning all felling above 1,000 metre altitude for a few years should be considered to allow these areas to recover. Critical areas in hills and catchment areas prone to landslides, erosion etc., should be totally protected and quickly afforested.

Guidelines have been issued in June 1990 to state governments for involving village communities and voluntary agencies for regeneration of degraded forest lands on usufruct shraing basis. As a follow up of these guidelines, 14 states have issued appropriate orders. These states are: West Bengal, Orissa, Bihar, Madhya Pradesh, Rajasthan, Gujarat, Maharashtra, Tripura, Himachal Pradesh, Haryana, Jammu and Kashmir, Andhra Pradesh, Karnataka and Tamil Nadu. Other states are being persuaded to issued such orders.

Firewood occupies a predominant place as an energy source in rural areas. As against the estimated requirement of about 15.7 crore tonnes of fuelwood per annum, recorded production is only 5.8 crore tonnes. Due to scarcity of firewood, considerable quantities of cowdung and agricultural residues are burnt as fuel leading to air pollution. It is expected that programmes of renewable energy sources and augmenting fuel growth in wastelands will help in closing the gap.

Fire is one of the major factors responsible for destruction of forests in the country. In India, most of the fires are man-made and are generally deliberate and on rare occasions accidental. The causes of deliberate fire incidences are grazing, mahua seed and flower collections, tendu leaf collection, poaching and shifting cultivation, etc. In order to reduce the incidents of fire in India, the following steps have been undertaken by the forest department: (i) development of firelines and (ii) establishment of watch towers besides employing fire watchers during fire seasons. In order to develop the techniques for detection, prevention and suppression of fire in the country, a UNDP assisted Modern Forests Fire Control Project was initiated in 1984 in Chandrapur, Maharashtra and Haldwani/Nainital, U.P. Techniques like development of better communication network and effective use of hand tools and other equipments developed under the projects have proved successful in reducing the fire damage. In addition, fire danger rating system, wireless network, fire reporting system and hand tools etc., were designed. This scheme is being continued in 11 states of the country.

The National Wildlife Action Plan adopted in 1983 provides the framework of strategy as well as programme for conservation of wildlife. At present the protected area network comprises 80 national parks and 441 sanctuaries covering 4.5 per cent of the total geographical area of the country. The Wildlife (Protection) Act, 1972 adopted by all states except Jammu and Kashmir (which has its own Act), governs wildlife conservation and protection of endangered species. The Act prohibits trade in rare and endangered species. India is also a signatory to the Convention on International Trade in Endangered Species of Wild Flora and Fauna. Under this, export or import of endangered species and their products is subject to strict control. Commercial exploitation of such species is prohibited.

The Centre provides finanacial and technical assistance to states for: (i) development and improved management of national parks (ii) protection of wildlife and control of poaching and illegal trade in wildlife products; (iii) eco-development in areas around national parks and sanctuaries; (iv) conservation of elephant and its habitat; and (v) conservation of rhinos in Assam. The Wildlife (Protection) Act, 1972 has been amended to make the provisions more effective.

Endangered species of plants and animals have been brought under the purview of the Act. A Central Zoo Authority has been set up to look after the management of zoological parks in the country. The Authority has since notified rules for recognition of zoos which stipulates the standards for upkeep, maintenance and veterinary care of animals. It coordinates the activities of over 200 existing zoos and also supervises the exchange of animals on a scientific basis. Project Tiger, one of the premeir conservation efforts of the country has completed 20 years in April 1993. Under this scheme 21 Tiger Reserves have been set up all over the country. A Global Tiger Forum has been set up for Tiger Range countries and an interim secretariat has been set up at New Delhi. A Tiger Crisis Cell has been set up to obtain all the information essential for conservation of the tiger.

The Animal Welfare Board of India, established in 1962 under the provisions of the Prevention of Cruelty to Animals Act, 1960 is an autonomous organisation of the Ministry of Environment and Forests working for the cause of animal welfare in the country. A series of camps for training the members of SPCAs and Animal Welfare Organisations are being held all over the country, in collaboration with the Royal Society for Prevention of Cruelty to Animals, London. The Board also celebrates Animal Welfare Fortnight from 14 January every year.

At the time of India's Independence, our priority was the provision of the basic human needs of food, fuel, shelter, health, employment, etc., to our vast population. As such the focus of our Five Year Plans was on agriculture, health, family welfare etc. In the Fourth Five Year Plan, problems related to environment received direct attention and a Committee was set up in 1972 to look into these problems and suggest a solution in consulation with experts and concerned minstries/ departments of the government. Another Committee was set up in January 1980, for reviewing the existing legislative measures and administrative machinery for ensuring environmental protection and for recommending ways to strengthen them. On the recommendation of this high-powered Committee, the Department of Environment was set up in 1980. Consequently in 1985, it was upgraded to a full-fledged Ministry of Environment and Forests to serve as the focal point in the administrative structure for the planning, promotion and coordination of environmental and forestry programmes.

Environmental problem in India can be classified into two broad categories: (a) those arising as negative effects of the very process of development and (b) those arising from conditions of poverty and under-development. The first category has to do with the impact of efforts to achieve rapid economic growth and development. Poorly planned developmental projects are usually environmentally destructive. The second category has to do with the impact on the health and integrity of our natural resources such as land, soil, water, forests, wildlife, space, etc., as a result of proverty.

There are about 30 major enactments related to protection of environment now being administered by the Central and state governments. Prominent among these are: Wildlife (Protection) Act, 1972; The Forest (Conservation) Act, 1980; The Water (Prevention and Control of Pollution) Act, 1974; The Air (Prevention and Control of Pollution) Act, 1981; The Water (Prevention and Control of Pollution) Cess Act, 1977; The Environment (Protection) Act, 1986; The Public Liability Insurance Act; 1991; The Motor Vehicle Act, 1938 as amended in 1988; The Factories Act and the Insecticides Act. These are implemented through several organisations like Central and state pollution control boards, chief inspectors of factories and insecticides inspectors of agriculture departments, etc.

The Environment (Protection) Act, 1986, brought into force from 19 November 1986 is a landmark legislation as it is an umbrella Act for the protection of environment and aims at plugging the loopholes in the other related Acts. The salient features of this Act are as follows: (a) conferring powers on the Central

Government to; (i) take all necessary measures for protecting quality of environment; (ii) coordinate activities of states, officers and other authorities under the Act or under any other law related to the objects of this Act; (iii) Plan and execute a nationwide programme for prevention, control and abatement of environmental pollution; (iv) lay down standards for discharge of environmental pollutant; (v) empower any person to enter, inspect, take samples and test; (vi) establish or recognise environmental laboratories; (vii) appoint or recognise analysts; (viii) lay down standards for quality of environment; (ix) restrict areas in which industries, operations or process may not be carried out or shall be carried out subject to certain safeguards; (x) lay down safeguards for prevention of accidents and take remedial measures in case of such accidents; (xi) lay down procedures and safeguards for handling hazardous substances; (xii) constitute an authority or authorities for exercising powers; (xiii) issue directions to any person, officer or authority including the power direct closure, prohibition or regulation of any industry, operation or process or stoppage or regulations of supply of electricity, water or any other services; (xiv) require any person, officer, state government or authority to furnish any prescribed information; and (xv) delegate powers to any of a state or authority; (b) it confers powers on persons to complain to courts regarding any violation of the provisions of the Act, after a notice of 60 days to prescribed authorities; (c) the Act makes it obligatory for the person incharge of a place to inform the prescribed authorities regarding any accidental discharge or apprehended discharge of any pollutant in excess of prescribed standards. Authorities on receipt of such information or otherwise shall take remedial measures are recoverable with inerest from the pollute; (d) it prescribes penalties for violation of the provisions of the Act. No distinction is shown between government of the

Act. These include issue of rules, notification of standards, action regarding environmental laboratories, strengthening of state departments of environment and pollution control boards, delegation of powers, identification of agencies for carrying out various activities for hazardous chemical management and setting up of environemtn protection councils in the states. The Water (Prevention and Control of Pollution) Act, 1974 and the Air (Prevention and Control of Pollution) Act, 1981, have been made more stringent. Steps have been taken to: (i) prevent pollution at source; (ii) encourage, develop and apply the best available practicable and technical solutions; (iii) ensure that the polluter pays for the pollution and control arrangements; (iv) focus protection on heavily polluted areas and river stretches; and (v) involve the public in decision-making.

The rapid increase in industrialisation and urbanisation has exerted extra pressure on the infrastructural facilities of human settlements manifesting in environment problems like increased incidence of air, water and noise pollution.

The ambient aire quality major towns and cities in the country is being monitored under the National Ambient Air Quality Monitoring (NAAQM) programme. The monitoring results indicate that Sulphur Dioxide and Nitrogen dioxide levels are mostly within the permissible limits whereas Suspended Particulate Matter (SPM) values are higher than the prescribed limits at some places due to vehicular and air pollution, burning of fossil fuel and natural dusty conditions.

The pollution caused by vehicles contributes significantly towards air pollution. The problem of suspended particulate matter is more acute during the summer due to local dusty conditions. During the winter months, lower ambient temperatures, lower mixing depth temperature inversion, higher traffic density, higher consumption of domestic fuels, aggravate the pollution problems.

The data on ambient water quality of rivers indicates that levels of coliform count and Biological Oxygen Demand (BOD) are generally high resulting in deterioration of water quality. This is primarily due to inadequate sanitation facilities and discharge of waste water into the surface water bodies without proper treatment.

Urban noise levels in major cities also indicate and incresing trend due to rise in human population, automobiles and industrial activities. Specific studies reveal that noise levels in industrial areas are generally within the prescribed limits but exceed the standards in respect of commercial, residential and silence zones during certain hours. The problem is more conspicuous near the traffic intersections and commercial centres.

The on-going initiatives of Government to improve environment include preventive as well as promotive measures. Fiscal incentives are provided by the Government to encourage the installation of appropriate pollution abatement equipment in the form of custom waive off and soft loans. While the industries are encouraged and the fiscal incentives are provided for installing equipment for control of pollution, punitive measures including legal action is taken against the defaulting units.

To achieve the goal pollution abatement, emission and effluent standards for air, water and noise have been notified. Regular monitoring is carried out and the enforcement efforts have been intensified. At present, a majority of identified units have already installed the requisite pollution control equipment. According to the data collected by the Central Pollution Control Board

(CPCB) on September 30, 1996, out of 1,551 units belonging to 17 categories of highly polluting industries, 1,259 units had facilities to comply with the environmental standards, 112 were closed and 180 were not having adequate facilities. Show cause notices under Section 5 of the Environment (Protection) Act 1986 have been issued to all the defaulting units.

Apart from notifications of effluent and emission standards for the major categories of polluting industries, national ambient air quality standards including ambient noise standards have been notified. Industries have been directed to instal necessary pollution control equipment within a stipulated time frame. More stringent norms for vehicular emissions have been notified under the Central Motor Vehicles Rules which have come into effect from April, 1996. Supply of unleaded petrol in four metropolitan cities of Mumbai, Calcutta, Delhi and Chennal has been introduced with effect from April 1, 1995 for use in four wheel vehicles fitted with catalytic converters. The use of unleaded petrol will be gradually expanded to other cities in the country.

Twenty-four critically polluted areas in the country have been identified and action plans have been drawn up to improve the quality of environment in these areas. Adoption of clean technologies of production and formation of Waste Minimisation Circles is being encouraged to minimise environmental pollution. Under the World Bank aided Industrial Pollution Control Project, technical and financial assistance is provided for setting up Common Effluent Treatment Plants (CETPs) in clusters of small scale industrial units. An "Eco-Mark" scheme has been launched to certify various products of the industries which fulfil the prescribed pollution control standards to achieve the objective of environment-friendly production, packaging and waste disposal. To increase public awareness and participation, several public awareness campaigns on effects of pollution and measures to control it have been launched.

The Polity Statement for Abatement of Pollution indicates adoption of best available clean and practicable technologies, rather than end-of-the-pipe treatment, as the key elements for pollution prevention. As a part of this thrust, the Ministry of Environment & Forests has set up a Clean Technologies Division for identifying cleaner technologies that can be introduced in different development sectors. Techniques like coal beneficiation are being promoted. The programme envisages setting up a National Clearing House for cleaner technologies as the overall co-ordinating agency and sectoral centres in different areas of development to focus on their activities. Another initiative taken to motivate environmentally oriented technologies and practices is mandatory submission of Annual Environmental Statements which would be subsequently evolved into environmental audit.

Prior environmental clearance of development projects based on impact assessment is being increasingly emphasised. Such clearance has been made mandatory for 29 specified categories of development projects through a statutory notification issued in January, 1994. This has been done with a view to mitigating the adverse environmental effects of these projects and in integrating the environmental concerns into development. This mechanism is also of help in catalysing the process of inducing cleaner environment-friendly technologies into the developmental process.

The success of the Ganga Action Plan has encouraged its replication for water pollution abatement in tributaries of the Ganga (Yamuna, Gomati and Damodar) under Ganga Action Plan Phase-II. A wider scheme called the National River conservation Plan covering pollution abatement works for grossly polluted stretches in 18 major rivers in 10 States of the country has also been initiated. Further, a programme for conservation of selected lakes has also been formulated by the Ministry.

The National Environmental Tribunal Act, providing relief, compensation and restitution to victims of accidents while handling hazardous substances, and for environmental damages, came into force from 17 June, 1995. The Act provides (i) strict liabilitiy for damages arising out of any accident occurring while handling any hazardous substances and (ii) Establishment of National Environmental Tribunal for effective and expenditious disposals of cases arising from such accidents with a view to give relief and compensation for damage to persons, property and the environment and (iii) matters connected therewith or incidental thereto.

The National Environment Appellate Authority (NEAA) has been set up by the Government in January 1997. Public hearings have now been built into the environment impact assessment. The machinary for hearing appeals against environment pollution impact assessment is also being set up. The measures are to ensure greater transparency and faster decision-making in matters concerning the environmental impact of industrial projects.

As per the Policy Statement of Abatement of Pollution announced in February 1992, the key elements for pollution prevention are adoption of the best available clean and praticable technologies rather than end of the pipe treatment. The focus is on source reduction and substitution of chemicals, with safe alternatives. The thrust has, therefore, been made for considering process changes which involve significant improvements in energy and water conservation. To follow up on the various issues covered in the Policy

Statement for Abatement of Pollution, the National Conservation Strategy and the Forest Policy Statement, several new programmes and studies have been initiated and commissioned. An Environment Action Programme has been formulated covering a wide ambit of subjects such as clean and low-waste technologies, improvement of water quality, institutional and human resources development, forestry and natural resources accouning.

To integrate natural resource accounting into the national accounting process, collection and analysis of environmental data has been initiated. It is proposed to produce a computerised map of the critically polluted areas through digitisation, on a format based on Geographic Information System. Base thematic maps on 1.6 M scale have been prepared for the country on the following themes: (i) major river basins and drainage network; (ii) administrative divisions; (iii) designated best use classification of streams; (iv) location of water and air pollution monitoring stations; (v) location of critically polluted areas; and (vi) major cities of India (above one lakh population).

The gazette notification on environmental audit issued in 1992 has been amended and now applies to all units seeking environmental clearance, and such units are required to submit environmental statements for the period ending 31 March on or before 30 September every year beginning from 1993 To facilitate industries in preparing environmental statements, model environmental statement reports for six categories of industries have been prepared. A booklet titled "Environmental Statement as part of environmental audit" has also been prepared by the Ministry. A software package 'Paryavaran' along with a user manual, has been prepared for analysis of information submitted in these environmental statements and is being distributed to all the SPCBs.

An 'Eco-Mark' label has been introduced to label consumer products that are environment friendly. Sixteen products have been identified for labelling and standards for toilet soaps and detergents, paper, paints, architectural paints and laundry soaps have been notified for awarding this label. The procedure for granting consent to small scale industries has been simplified. A new format for the consent application and for authorisation required under the Environment (Protection) Act, 1986 has been developed and notified. Under the scheme "Adoption of clean technology in the small scale industries and to extend necessary technical support", training and awareness programmes for personnel in small Industry Development Organisation and entrepreneurs are being organised. A manual "From Waste to Profits" giving guidelines for waste minimisation has been prepared.

The Central Pollution Control Board (CPCB) is the national apex body for assessment, monitoring and control of water and air pollution. The executive responsibilities for enforcement of the Acts for Prevention and Control of Pollution of Water (1974) and Air (1981) and also of the Water (Cess) Act, 1977 are carried out through are Board. Twenty three states and union territories have already adopted the Act and respective state pollution control boards have been constituted. These states are Andhra Pradesh, Assam, Bihar, Goa, Gujarat, Haryana, Himachal Pradesh, Jammu and Kashmir, Karnataka, Kerala, Madhya Pradesh, Maharashtra, Meghalaya, Mizoram, Orissa, Punjab, Rajasthan, Sikkim, Tamil Nadu, Tripura, Uttar Pradesh, West Bengal, Delhi and Pondicherry. Arunachal Pradesh has adopted the Act, but is yet to constitute the board. Enactment of the Enviornment (Protection) Act, 1986 has further extended the scope of the activities of the Board. Under the Environment (Protection) Act, 1986, effluent and emission standards in respect of 61 categories of industries have been notified. So far, 84 laboratories have been recognised as environmental laboratories. Minimum National Standards (MINAS) for effluents and emissions from specific industries have been formulated and control measures are being implemented in a phased manner. A notification consolidating all the environmental standards including general effluent, emission and noise standards has been issued. It also includes standards for waste water generation in respect of 11 categories of industries. Further mass emission norms which would come into effect from 1 April 1996 have also been issued for petrol and diesel driven vehicles under the Central Motor Vehicles Rules of the Ministry of Surface Transport. Unleaded petrol of Delhi, Bombay, Madras and Calcutta from 1 April 1995. Petrol with a maximum lead content of 0.15 g/l has been introduced at all the retail outlets of these four metro cities since June 1994.

Seventeen categories of heavily polluting industries have been identified namely, cement, thermal powre plants, distilleries, sugar, fertilizer, integrated iron and steel, oil refineries, pulp and paper, petrochemicals, pesticides, tanneries, basic drugs and pharmaceuticals, dye and dye intermediates, caustic soda, zinc smelter, copper smelter and aluminium smelter. Action is taken against the defaulting units in these categories on priority. On the basis of the designated best use of criteria CPCB has identified 13 grossly polluted stretches of Sabarmati, Subernarekha, Godavari, Krishna, Indus (tributaries), Sutlej, Ganga (tributaries), Yamuna, Hindon, Chambal, Damodar, Gomati, and Kali rivers to formulate short-term result oriented programmes. The CPCB, in consultation with SPCBs has identified 22 critically polluted areas in the country which need special attention for control of pollution. These are Vapi (Gujarat), Singrauli (U.P.), Korba, Ratlam, Nagoda

(Madhya Pradesh), Digboi (Assam), Talcher (Orissa), Bhadravati (Karnataka), Howrah (West Bengal), Dhanbad (Bihar), Pali and * Pataucheru (Andhra Pradesh), Chembur (Maharashtra), Najafgarh (Delhi), Govindhgarh (Punjab), Udyog Mandal (Kerala) and Parwanoo and Kala Amb (HP). The progress in abatement of pollution in these areas is being reviewed. A Bill has been introduced in the Parliament for establishing a National Environment Tribunal.

There are a host of human interventions including development activities which have resulted in considerable environmental degration. Major human interventions in forests are deforestation, commercial logging, setting up protected area, partial closure of forests, etc which are described below:

— There is increasing deforestation due to commercial exploitation, building of dams, mining and construction activities. Of the world's estimated 8.4 billion hectares of forests in 1990, tropical forests covered 1.76 billion ha. During 1981-90, tropical forests were lost at the rate of 0.8 per cent (15.4 million ha) a year, as per estimates of the World Resources Institute. The net annual deforestation during 1981-90 exceeded two per cent in 10 tropical countries of Asia and Africa.

— Commercial logging for industrial activities is increasing rapidly. Eighty-four per cent of such logging took place in closed tropical broadleaf forests in primary (undisturbed forests) during the 1980s. Logging activity is a causal factor for forest degradation and is reflected in rough wood production which increased by 19 per cent between 1979-81 to 1989-91. Globally, almost 50 per cent of such rough wood is used for industrial purposes, the rest for heating and cooking.

— Setting up of protected areas for conservation purposes has led to complications and conflict-situation with indigenous communities and also denial of many of their rights and privileges.

— Closure of parts of forests for setting up of industries or agro-based activities for private, semi-private lands, construction of railways, roads and new settlements has led to shrinkage of forest cover and increased hardship for local communities in their day-to-day existence.

— Interventions for adhering to international agreements have also alienated many local communities and some of their practices, eg, tribal hunting of wild animals which goes against biodiversity agreements.

— Policies of economic liberalization, privatization and globalization have both, directly and indirectly, led to reduction of forest cover and cuts in subsidies and grants affecting food subsidies and other welfare schemes involving poor and marginalized communities.

The environmental research programme aims to develop strategies for sustainable resource management and create facilities and trained manpower to conduct research in priority areas. Research projects are supported under three main schemes: (a) Man and Biosphere Programme; (b) Environment Research Programme; and (c) Action-oriented research programme for Eastern and Western Ghats. A number of small, specific research projects are also beng supported. Expert committees and expert working groups make recommendations for undertaking research in priority areas, scrutinise proposals, evaluate progress and recommend suitable mechanisms for implementation of the research projects. Priority areas of research are identified in five fundamental elements viz., land, water, air, space and energy. To strengthen the environmental research and training base, the following Centres of Excellence have been set up: Ecological Research and Training Centre, Bangalore: Centre for Mining Environment, Dhanbad: Centre for Environmental Education, Ahmadabad: CPR Environment Education Centre, Madras and the Salim Ali Centre for Orinthology and Natural History, Coimbatore.

This Institute, established in 1988, is an autonomous organisation of the Ministry of Environment and Forests for developing strategies, technologies and knowledge base for ecologically sound developoment of the Himalayan region. Besides undertaking action-oriented research projects the Institute has also installed three weather monitoring stations for collecting and analysing climatic data for the Himalayan region. Units of the Institute are also located at UP, Sikkim, Nagaland and Himachal Pradesh.

Forestry research is the primary responsibility of the Indian Council of Forestry Research and Education. It has the following forestry research institutes and centres under it: (i) Forest Research Institute, Dehra Dun; (ii) Institute of Arid Zone Forestry Research, Jodhpur; (iii) Institute of Rain and Moist Deciduous Forests, Jorhat; (iv) Institute of Wood Science and Technology, Bangalore; (v) Tropical Forestry Research Institute, Jabalpur; (vi) Institute of Forest Genetics and Tree Breeding, Coimbatore; (vii) Temperate Forest Research Centre, Shimla (viii) Centre for Forest productivity, Ranchi and (ix) Centre for Social Forestry and Environment, Allahabad. In addition, the Indian Plywood Industries Research and Training Institute, Bangalore, has been transferred to the Ministry of Environment and Forests from the Ministry of Industry. Besides forestry research in wood panel products, this Institute imparts training to workers in optimum utilisation of timber.

Research programmes in wildlife are carried out by the Wildlife Institute of India, Dehra Dun and the Salim Ali Centre for Orinthology and Natural History, Coimbatore. Several projects on habitat evolution, elephant movement, ecology of gharial and turtles, status of endangered species behavioural ecology, bio-diversity, resource study, conservation, ecology and management of specific animals etc., are being carried out by both these institutes.

Priority is accorded by the Ministry of Environment and Forests to promote evironmental educat on, create environmental awareness among various age groups and to disseminate information through Environmental Information System (ENVIS) network to all concerned. Special emphasis is given to non-formal environmental education through seminars/symposia/workshops, training programmes, eco-camps, audio-visual shows etc. The Ministry has been organising a National Environment Awareness Campaign (NEAC) since July 1986. As a part of this Capaign, 19 Novmber to 18 December every year is observed as the National Environment Month. Students/youth, techers, women, tribals, administrators, professionals, legislators, industrial workers, Armed Forces and the general public are covered under this Campaign. During 1994-95 about 2,200 organisations have been granted financial assistance by the Ministry to organise various activities for creating environmental awareness. The Ministry also provides financial support for setting up eco-clubs at schools and for production on films on environment.

A new scheme "Paryavaran Vahini" has been launched during 1992-93 to create environmental awareness and to ensure active public participations by involving the local people in activities relating to environmental protection. Parayavaran Vahinis are proposed to be constituted in 183 selected districts all over the country which have high incidence of pollution and density of tribal and forest population. The Vahinis also play a watch dog role by reporting instances of environmental pollution, deforestation, poaching, etc. They function under the charge of District Collectors with active cooperation of the state/union territory governments. this scheme is entirely financed by the Ministry of Environment and Forests.

The National Museum of Natural History (NMNH) set up in New Delhi in 1978, is concerned with the promotion of non-formal education in the area of environment and conservation. Besides permanent exhibit galleries on various aspects of environment, the museum also conducts temporary exhibitions and a large number of educational programmes and activities for school children, college youth and the general public. A Regional Museum of Natural History has been established at Mysore and two more and planned at Bhopal and Bhubaneswar.

The Indian Council for Forestry Research and Education is the focal point for forestry education and extension developmnet in the country. Indira Gandhi National Forest Academy, Dehra Dun imparts in-service professional training to Indian Forest Service (IFS) professionals. State forest service colleges provide training to the officers of the State Forest Service (SFS). The Indian Plywood Industries Research and Training Institute, Bangalore organises short-term courses in the area of wood science.

The Indian Institute of Forest Management, Bhopal, also provides training in forest management and allied subjects to persons from the Indian Forest Service, forest development corporations and forest related industries to develop forestry management skills. The Wildlife Institute of India, Dehra Dun conducts various programmes to provide in-service training in wildlife management for forest officers, wildlife ecologists and other professionals.

Environmental Information System (ENVIS) has been set up by the Ministry in 1982 as a decentralised information system network for collection, storage, retrieval and dissemination of environmental information to decision makers, policy planners, scientists, engineers, environmentalists, research workers and the general public all over the country. Besides the Focal Point in the Ministry, the ENVIS network presently consists of 20 subject oriented centres known as ENVIS centres, set up in various institutions/organisations of the country on priority areas of environment such as environmentally sound and appropriate technology, bio-degradation of wastes, desertification, estuary, mangroves, corals and lagoons, media and environment, environmental education, solid wastes disposal, animal ecology, Himalayan ecology, etc. The Focal Point brings out a quarterly abstracting journal "Paryavaran Abstracts" containing information about environmental research in the Indian context.

ENVIS has been designated as National Focal Point (NFP) and Regional Service Centre (RSC) for South Asia sub-regional countries by INFORTERRA (an international referral system for sources of information on environment) of United Nations Environment Programme (UNEP). As NEP, ENVIS updated more than 250 Indian Potential Sources in the International Directory of UNEP for providing information in the field of environment and its related areas.

The Ministry functions as a nodal agency for United Nations Environment Programme (UNEP), South Asia Cooperation Environment Programme (SACEP) and International Centre for Integrated Mountain and

Development (ICIMOD) and various international agencies, regional bodies and multilateral institutions. In coordinates all bilateral cooperation in the field of invironment. India has such cooperation programmes with the Netherlands, Norway, Sweden, Denmark, Great Britain, USA, the Russian Federation, Canada, Japan and FRG in addition to forestry programmes with external assistance.

India is signatory to the following important international treaties/agreements in the field of environment: (i) International Convention for the regulation of Whaling; (ii) International Plant Protection Convention; (iii) The Antarctic Treaty; (iv) Conventon on Wetlands of internatonal importance especially as waterfowl habitat; (v) International Convention on international trade in endangered species of wild flora and fauna; (vi) Protocol of 1978 relating to the international convention for the prevention of pollution from ships, 1973; (vii) Vienna Convention for the protection of the ozone layer; (viii) Convention on Migratory Species; (ix) Basel Convention on trans-boundary movement of hazardous substances; (x) Framework Convention on climatic change; (xi) convention on conservation of bio-diversity; (xii) Montreal Protocol on the substances that deplete the ozone layer and (xiii) International Convention for Combating Desertification.

Instituted in 1987, the Indira Gandhi Prayavaran Puraskar, consisting of a cash component of rupees one lakh, a silver trophy and a citation, is awarded every year to an organisation and to an individual for significant contributions in the field of environment.

The Indira Priyadarshini Vrikshamitra Awards have been constituted by the Ministry of Environment and Forests in 1986 to recognise outstanding contributions of individuals and organisations in the field of afforestation and wastelands development. Ten awards are given every year to individuals, educational institutes, Panchayats, voluntary agencies and government agencies. Each award carries a medallion, a citation and a cash component of Rs. 50,000.

The Maha Vriksha Puraskar, instituted by the NAEB during 1993-94 will be given every year to individuals/ organisations for trees of notified species having the largest girth and height and in good health and vigour. These awards would consist of a cash prize of Rs. 25,000, a plaque and a citation.

Since 1991, national awards are being presented every year to eligible industries in recognition of their contributions to the prevention and control of evnvironmental pollution.

Human activities have pushed our planet to the brink of disaster necessitating a comprehensive global action to retrieve the situation. While exploring newer forms of renewable sources of energy to address the environmental malady, our planners and administrators need to address the most urgent task of improving energy efficiency. The rural areas should depend on minihydel projects and bioenergy as far as possible. A serious and lasting government commitment to the development and use of energy efficient and renewable technologies is the need of the hour. Like it or not, we find ourselves in a world where we are responsible for each other's well-being. In the last few years of this millennium, difficult questions of social equality, national sovereignty, and individual rights and responsibilities are emerging. A person may be able to afford a large, energy-consumptive automobile, but can the planet afford it? Indeed, the larger question boils down as to how many carbon-emitting automobilies can the planet tolerate without the habitability of the earth being disturbed. At a more mundane level, a couple may desire and be able to support several children, but can the planet afford several children per family? Does our generation have the right to extinguish plant and animal species that have evolved over millions of years? Do we not have the obligation to preserve our biological heritage for our future generations?

An affirmative answer to these questions depends on restoring and prserving the conditions that make the earth habitable, a place capable of supporting a diversity of life and modern civilization. Human activities have pushed the planet to the brink of disaster.

A comprehensive global action plan to remedy the situation should include: developing energy strategies that have climate protection as their cornerstone; expanding the earth's forest cover so as to prevent global warming; doubling the per capita grain production and lastly, breaking the momentum of population growth.

While these are the macro-level targets for making this globe a sustainable one in the forthcoming century, at the micro-level it amounts to a severe test on the capacity of world leaders as well as the local ones in their efforts in ecological economic betterment of the populations under their jurisdiction.

It is no wonder that the modes of energy production that are in vogue around the world are primarily responsible for the change in the earth's climate. The huge quantities of oil, coal and natural gas that fuel the global economy account for most of the carbon dioxide emissions responsible for global warming through the greenhouse effect. Producing less carbon dioxide requires using less fuel from among the traditional category. This in turn means exploring other non-conventional energy sources, enough to substitute the fossil sources.

Even though India is one of the few Third World countries which has constitutionalized protection and improvement of environment, the various enactment suffer from several lacunae including the non-recognition of the crucial role that PRIs can play in the endeavour. The involvement of PRIs as the watch-dog of environmental protection at the grass roots level needs to be duty recognized. The Constitution (73rd Amendment) Act 1992 now provides these institutions an opportunity to play their legitimate role. Environment protection represents one of the more recent and yet one of the more profound aspects new public affairs dimension in public administration.

Environmental issues have aroused too much intellectual and academic interest both in developing and underdeveloped nations. They include envioronmental degradation, deforestation and desertification, atmospheric pollution and imbalances as well as disertifications in ecology resulting from the way natural resources—land, water, forests, minerals, etc are harnessed for fulfilment of human needs. The UN Conference on Human Environment in 1972 proclaimed that the defence and improvement of human environment both natural and man-made had become an imperative good for mankind, to be pursued together with fundamental goals of peace and worldwide economic and social development.

The achievement of these goals was the responsibility of citizens, communities, enterprises and institutions at every level. Later on, the World Conservation Strategy (1980) and the Brundthland Report also noted the irreversible destruction of ecosystems of the poor countries and the implicit threat to the world security and the consequent political instability and social problems. The problem of environmental crises of the developing countries is different from that of the developed countries. The establishment of viable community-based institutions for environment protection was suggested with full legal, administrative and technical support. These institutions should be empowered to plan, to work out the modality and to implement the various measures for environment protection and conservation. The Panchayati Raj as an institution of local rural government is the excellent model for it in rural India.

Among the developing countries, india is also facing environmental problems and crises. The enormous increase in population is the most potent cause for acceleration of the overutilization of productive resources and downgrading the quality of environment.

India has a domesticated animal population of nearly 500 million. Considering that only 3.5 per cent of the land area are under grass, the population is supported by the forest and agriculture residues which are thereby diverted from agricultural land. Out of the total cultivable land, 175 million ha are degraded needing special treatment to restore productivity. Of the 75 million ha designated as forest land, only 35 million ha are close forest. Despite all efforts, India has continued to lose forest cover. The deforestation causes loss in bivodiversity. Over 1,500 species of plants and animals are on the endangered list. Levels of air and water pollution are much beyond acceptable limits. These challenges disturb the environment equilibrium and the life of mankind.

The basic aim of our National Forest Policy must be to ensure environmental stability and maintenance of ecological balance including atmospheric which are vital for the sustenance of all forms of life—human, animal and plant. Rural India has different kinds of environmental crises compared to other countries. The rapid growth of rural population has placed inexorable burden on farm as well as on other land resources, on forests, on water resources and worsened the quality of life of the rural poor in respect of housing, health, ecological surroundings and other essentials.

The Un Declaration on Human Environment in 1972 signalled India to initiate positive steps in the direction towards environment improvement. The Constitution of India has conceptualized its thinking on environment in the form of the Directive Principles of State Policy in favour of protection and improvement of environment, and safeguarding of forests and wildlife (Article 48A), a fundamental duty to protect and improve the natural environment including forests, lakes, rivers and wildlife and to have compassion for living creatures [Article 51A(g)], and a subject in the Consurrent List in its Seventh Schedule (Item 17A and 17B). Both the Directive principles and Fundamental Duty are non-justiciable, but these provide the necessary constitutional sanction if the State intends to adopt a law in the matter.

The other component of the infrastructure for environment improvement and protection is provided by the existing legislation. There are 30 major enactments such as Water Cess Act, Forest Act, Forest Conservation Act, Wildlife Protection Act, Environment Protection Act, of Union and State Governments.

Administrative actions—regulatory, negotiational and persuasive—under these enactments are mainly taken by the Central and State administrative organizations—the Central Ministry of Environment and Forests, the Central Pollution Control Board and the State Departments of Environment and State Pollution Control Boards. Besides this, there also exist the other administrative mechanisms concerned with the implementation of policies on environment. The

Panchayati Raj institutions have also become important instruments in rural India for environment protection and improvement.

There is no end to the debate on environment and development. However, instances of the preservationist approach is to be found in the local indigenous communities living in and around forests. In real life, such communities have been seriously affected as a result of both degradation of forest land and their reduced accessibility to forest resources on account of strict forest laws. Degradation of surrounding environment and rigid forestlaws have adversely affected food accessibility, livelihood options and quality of life of local indigenous communities. Such degradation has often caused periodic phases of hunger and malnutrition in the absence of supportive means of livelihood for acquiring basic essentials of life.

Forest plantations of eucalyptus and other species no longer provide the rich biodiversity available earlier in natural forests. Common property resources, in which groups of local people have co-equal use rights, such as community pastures, community forests, wastelands, village ponds, rivers, etc have declined at a rapid pace. Such phenomenon has led to a diminished role of local natural resources which have traditionally constituted invaluable asset-base for meeting basic needs and livelihood requirements of indigenous communities.

Such relatively undisturbed lands include forests, grasslands, wetlands, water bodies, etc which constitue habitat for indigenous communities, plants and animal species and thus contribute to maintenance of human and biological diversity. Such lands perform important environmental functions and also constitute essential means of livelihood. As far as fragility of such ecosystems is concerned, the indigenous communities have traditionally presented little threat to sensitive ecological zones, because their production systems have been sustainable, scattered over a large area, and they have traditionally kept encroachers, poachers and others out of the area.

The benefits provided by forests, trees and common property resources are basic to such communities and amongst direct benefits, the following are included:

— food such as nuts, wild fruits, vegetables, leaves, flowers, roots, stems honey, wild animals insects, etc;

— habitat and shelter;

— raw materials like bamboo, canes, fibres, oils, bhabbar grass, waxes, resins, gums, dyes and wood for furniture and capital equipment for agriculture, artisanship, etc;

— wood for building, fencing, tool making, etc;

— firewood;

— medicines and drugs;

— fodder such as grass, branches, twigs and leaves, grazing sites;

— means of livelihood, both seasonal and annual;

— shade;

— ornaments, religious items and cultural symbols; and

— drought relief.

Apart from direct benefits, forests, trees and common property resources also provide indirect benefits, such as preventing erosion, conserving moisture, conserving water, recycling nutrient, preventing drought or reducing its impact, providing leaf manure, fixing nitrogen by leguminous trees, regulating climate and rainfall, providing greenery and beauty and reducing pollution.

Forests as safety net: In short, forests, trees and common property resources provide safety nets to the local indigenous communities. In the presence of spiraling prices, reduced wages in real terms, unemployment, sickness, reduced productivity from land, and recurring shortages, forests, trees and common property resources act as a kind of safety net for local communities, protecting them from the harshness of market forces. They come to the rescue by providing a safety net against food and livelihood insecurity, drought attacks, pest attacks, illness, pollution, high prices, high rents, etc. They play a dominant role in providing alternative sources of livelihood and in offering coping strategies to local communities.

The strategy for development of the Scheduled Tribes is based on the TSP (tribal sub-plan) approach which came into operation since 1974-75 (V Plan) in 16 States (now 18 States) and two Union territories. The main objective of the tribal sub-plan is to (i) raise the socio-economic condition of the tribal population and strengthen infrastructure in the tribal areas, and (ii) to protect and promote tribal interests through legal and administrative support.

The programmes are now being implemented through (i) 194 Integrated Tribal Development Projects (ITDPs) comprising generally blocks/tehsils with 50 per cent or more Scheduled Tribe population; (ii) 277 pockets of tribal concentration (Modified Area Development Approach Projects) having a total population of 10,000 or more, and Scheduled Tribe population of 50 per cent or more; and (iii) 90 primitive tribe projects or micro-projects.

The tribal sub-plan has a two-fold thrust, viz (i) socio-economic development of the tribal areas, and (ii) socio-economic development of the tribal families.

It was expected that during the Seventh Plan period, there would be cent per cent coverage of Scheduled Tribe population under the tribal sub-plan. Benefits were also proposed to be extended to the scattered Scheduled Tribe population which was not covered by any specific project through family-oriented programmes. It may be mentioned that the tribal population coverage during the Sixth Plan period was only 75 per cent. During the Seventh Plan, the following were the objectives under tribal sub-plan approach: (i) taking up family beneficiary programme through raising productivity-level of the beneficiary families in the field of agriculture, horticulture, animal husbandry, small industry, etc. (ii) elimination of exploration of the tribals in the sphere of alienation of land, money-lending, debt bondage, forest, etc. (iii) human resource development through education and training programmes, (vi) infrastructure development, (v) development of vulnerable tribal areas and groups like, forest villagers, displaced tribes and tribal women; and (vi) upgradation of environment of tribal areas.

For the year 1985-86, the target of tribal families to be economically assisted was fixed at 8.35 lakh, and the achievement reported was 8.3 lakh families. For 1986-87, the target fixed was 8.35 lakh tribal families and for 1987-88, a tentative target of assisting 8.50 lakh tribal families had been kept.

Special Central Assistance: Under tribal development, Special Central Assistance (SCA) is an additive to the State Plan efforts for Scheduled Tribes. The Eighth Plan had a target to cover 46.50 lakh families. Against this, 28.69 lakh families were covered during the first three years of the Plan (8.88 lakh in 1992-93; 10.42 lakh in 1993-94; and 9.39 lakh in 1994-95). This constituted 61.7 per cent of the target. To improve the literacy rate among tribal women, a new scheme was introduced since 1992-93, and is being implemented through non-governmental organizations in 48 districts with tribal concentration where female population is less than two per cent.

Financing tribal sub-plan: There are four sources for financing tribal sub-plan programmes: (i) Special Central Assistance (SCA) administered by Ministry of Welfare, (ii) State Plan funds, (iii) centrally-sponsored schemes, and (vi) institutional finance.

Since the V Plan period, with the launching of the tribal sub-plan approach, special programmes for extremely backward tribe groups had been taken up. These were micro-projects or projects for primitive tribal groups. These primitive tribal groups had three criteria for their identification: (i) almost stagnant population, or extremely low growth rate facing the danger of extinction, (ii) having are pre-agricultural level of technology, and (iii) extremely low level of literacy.

Another important factor was the ecosystem in which they lived. There were also other factors which entered into the situation of each of these tribal groups calling for a sensitive and in-depth study of each, precedent to enforcement of any action plan.

The Planning Commission also mentioned that particular care need to be taken of the small primitive tribal groups, some of which were on the verge of extinction.

The Dhebar Commission (1961) alluded to them as the 'lowest layer}, and listed 50 tribes in various States which were in an extremely underdeveloped state. During the V Plan period, the Ministry of Home Affairs identified 52 tribal communities as primitive, their estimated population being 10 lakhs. During the VI Plan period, an additional 20 tribal groups were identified raising their total number to 72 with an estimated population of 14 lakhs. Now the clusters of tribal concentration have gone up to 90.

There had been emphasis since the V Plan period on preparation of a project report for each of these groups relative to its situation. Nevertheless, there had been considerable neglect in this regard. Apart form the continued misery of conditions in which they lived, the risk of extinction of some of these tribes was also great.

One in every seven persons on this planet lives in India. With 16 per cent of the world's population and only 2.4 per cent of its land area, there is obviously a great demand on the natural resources including land. This is so in spite of the fact that an average Indian consumes a much lower quantum of resources than a person in the developed world. If an average person in the South were to consume as much as an average person in a developed country, the environmental crisis would be unimaginable. While, to a large extent, the lower per capita consumption is due to poverty, an :mportant reason is also that a majority of the population in India follows a sustainable lifestyle which is based on environmentally sound practices evolved over thousands of years.

The environmental problem today is being precipitated partly because practices which were appropriate earlier, like shifting cultivation and unrestricted cattle grazing, are not so anymore. For instance, as a result of increasing population and decreasing availability of land, crop-fallow cycles in shifting cultivation have been reduced to a mere five years from a more sustainable 20-40 years in the past.

But just as there were learnings and difficulties with regard to traditional practices, so was the case with newly introduced technologies. Many measures, at one time seen as solutions, are today extracting an unanticipated price. The Green Revolution of the 1960s met India's growing demand for food. While it helped India to dramatically increase foodgrain production, what was not fully appreciated then was that the Green Revolution would on the one hand affect the country's natural resource capital, and on the other, create dependencies on inputs such as chemical fertilizers and pesticides. There are indications of soil health problems such as deficiency of micronutrients and organic matter, incidence of soil salinity and damage to the physical structure of the soil, apart from increasing dependence on chemical inputs, many of which are imported.

Today there is widespread realization that there can be no readymade solutions, that technology alone cannot solve problems, that we have to use all our ingenuity to find solutions which combine the best of the old practices with the benefits that modern science and technology can offer.

The challenges are staggering in number, scale and complexity. We need to develop and to modernize in less wasteful ways than is the current paradigm, but not lose our sound traditional values and practices. India will have to leap-frog over wasteful and polluting technologies and go for technologies which are the most environmentally sound, and are based on maximizing recycling and efficient use of resources practices which are inherent in India's traditions. It is when such development comes about that the population pressures will ease, as development brings down demographic growth rates.

The task is stupendous. For while the challenge of development might seem to be 'how to get there' the real challenges is 'how not to get there'. Urbanization, industrial growth, transportation systems, agriculture, housing... all have to stop imitating practices that are already being phased out in the developed world. With the North becoming more conscious about the condition of their own environment, 'dirty' factories are moving South. To cite only one example, the production of harmful and toxic dyestuff intermediates such as H-acid, K-acid, gamma acid and metanilic acid taken up in the 60s stands at over 41,000 tonnes in the country today, with an estimated Rs. 6 billion worth for export to the developed countries.

The forces which are taking India, and much of the developing world, on the conventional and largely imitative and unimaginative development path are many. But this path is not sustainable—for India or for the world. As Mahatma Gandhi remarked over 60 years ago. "God forbid that India should ever take to industrialism after the manner of the West. The economic imperialism of a single, tiny kingdom is today keeping the world in chains. If an entire nation of 300 million took to similar economic exploitation, it would strip the world bare like locusts.

When the West developed, it did so perhaps in ignorance of the environmental impact of its activities. Today we know that such a path is neither practicable nor desirable for countries which are raising their standards of living. We, along with other developing countries, have to find alternative paths to an alternative goal.

A goal which ultimately is the true goal of development—an environmentaly sound and sustainable quality of life, which is socially just and equitable. A goal that must be common to all citizens of the planet. A goal that is perhaps as distant from the developing world as it is from the over-consuming, wasteful societies of what is currently referred to as the 'developed' world.

It is this goal of development that we seek together as people, as organizations and as governments at the United Nations Conference on Environment and Development. It is this intermeshing of environmental and developmental concerns that must form the goal of humankind.

The world is rapidly realizing that environmental issues such as global warming and ozone depletion, acid rain, marine pollution and the threat to biodiversity are global and not merely national issues. But in a world where per capita GNP varies from US $ 80 in Mozambique to US $ 29,880 in Switzerland; where life expectancy at birth varies from 42 years in Sierra Leone to 79 years in Japan; and where literacy rates vary from about 12 per cent in Somalia to over 95 per cent in the United States, what is not as explicitly understood is that development too is a global issue. And perhaps even less understood is the fact that a sustainable and viable planet requires that development be global. As Mrs. Indira Gandhi, then Prime Minister of India and the only visiting head of government to attend the UN Conference on the Human Environment in Stockholm in 1972, said, the removal of poverty is an integral part of the goal of an environmental strategy for the world.

3

National Water Development Agency

Agency and its objectives

The National Water Development Agency (NWDA) was established in July, 1982 as an autonomous Society under the Societies Registration Act, 1860 under the Ministry of Water Resources. The Agency functions with the following main objectives:

(a) To promote scientific development for optimum utilisation of water resources in the country.

(b) To carry out detailed field surveys and investigations of the possible sites for storage reservoirs and inter connecting links in order to establish feasibility of the components of the development of Peninsular and Himalayan Rivers according to the National Perspective for Water Resources Development

(c) To carry out detailed studies about the quantum of water in various Peninsular and Himalayan River Systems, which can be transferred to other basins/ States after meeting the reasonable needs to basin States in the foreseeable future.

(d) To prepare feasibility reports of various components of the development of the Peninsular and Himalayan Rivers.

(e) To carry out such other activities, the Society may consider necessary, incidental, supplementary or conducive to the attainment of above objectives. The Agency is headed by a Director General who is the Principal Executive Officer of the Society.

The Agency has two field organisations, each headed by a Chief Engineer, 5 Circles each headed by a Superintending Engineer and IS Divisions each headed by an Executive Engineer. National Water Development Agency Society, the apex body of National Water Development Agency meets at least once in a year with the Union Minister of Water Resources as its President, to review the progress and performance of the Agency.

The Governing Body of the Society under the Chairmanship of the Secretary, Ministry of Water Resources, manages, administers, directs and controls the affairs and funds of the Society.

Financial aspects

The budget allocation for the year 1998-99 is Rs. 10.00 crore and revised budget estimate is Rs. 12.50 crore. The actual expenditure incurred during the year 1998-99 up to December, 1998 was Rs 8.3 3 crore.

Inter basin transfer of water

Proposals of the national perspective plan

The National Water Development Agency has been carrying out the studies in accordance with the National Perspective Plan for the development of water resources. The proposal comprises two components, namely Peninsular Component and Himalayan Component.

Peninsular component

The Peninsular Rivers Development is divided in the following four parts:

(i) Interlinking of the Mahanadi-Godavari-Kdshna-Pennar-Cauvery.

(ii) Interlinking of the west flowing rivers north of Bombay and south of Tapti

(iii) Interlinking of the river Ken with Chambal

(iv) Diversion of the west flowing rivers of Kerala and Karnataka to the east.

The work under this Component comprises Water balance studies of 137 basins/ sub-basins and at 49 identified diversion points, studies of 58 identified storages, toposheet studies of 18 links including identifications of command area enroute, preparation of prefeasibility reports of 17 links and survey and investigations of 15 water transfer links for preparing feasibility reports.

Under the Peninsular Component, National Water Development Agency has completed the collection of data for all the 137 basins/ sub-basins, water balance studies of 137 basins/ sub-basins and 52 identified diversion points, 58 studies of identified storages, toposheet studies of 18 links and prepared prefeasibillry reports of all the 17 water transfer links. The feasibility reports of 5 links will be completed by March 1999. Survey and investigations of 8 more links, namely (I) Mahanadi (Manibhadra) - Godavari (Dowlaiswarm) link, (ii) Krishna (Almatti) -Pennar link, (iii) Krishna (Nagadunasagar)-Pennar (Somasila) link, (iv) Damanganga- Pinjal link (v) Parbati-Kalisindh-Chambal link, (vi) Inchampalli Low Dam - Nagarjunasagar Tail Pond link, NO Pennar (somasila) - Cauvery (Grand Anicut) link and (viii) Cauvery (Kattalai) - Vaigai-Gundar link for the preparation of feasibility reports were continued during 1998-99.

Himalayan component

The component of the Himalayan Rivers Development envisages contstruction of storage reservoirs on the principal tributaries of Ganga and Brahmaputra in India and Nepal, along with interlinking canal systems to, transfer surplus flows of the eastern tributaries of Ganga to the West, apart from linking of the main Brahmaputra and its tributaries with Ganga and Ganga to Mahanadi. It would also provide the necessary augmentation of flows at Farakka to flush the Calcutta Port and the inland navigation facilities across the country. The work under this Component comprises water balance studies at 19 diversion points, toposheet studies of 16 reservoirs, toposheet studies of 19 water transfer links, preparation of prefeasibility report of 14 water transfer links and survey and investigations of 11 water transfer links for preparation of feasibility reports. Up to the end of March 1998, water balance studies at 19 diversion points, toposheet studies of 16 storages, toposheet studies of 19 water transfer links and prefeasibility report of 14 links were completed.

The survey and investigation of 6 links, namely (i) Manas-Sankosh-tista-Ganga link, (ii) Sarda-Yamuna link, (iii) Ghagra-Yamuna link, (iv) Ganga-Damodar-Subamrekha link, (v) Yamuna-Rajasthan link and (vi) Chunar-Sone Barrage link for preparation of feasibility reports were continued during 1998-99.

Sanding committees of NWDA

Technical advisory committee

The Technical Advisory Committee (TAC) of National Water Development Agency under the Chairman, Central Water Commission, examines and scrutinises various technical proposals framed by National Water Development Agency. The TAC meets twice a year.

National commission for integrated water resources development plan

Ministry of Water Resources has set up a National

Commission for Integrated Water Resources Development Plan under the Chairmanship of Dr. S. R. Hashim, Member Secretary, Planning Commission with Director General, NWDA as its Member-Secretary. The secretarial services to the Commission are being provided by NWDA. The Commission has held nine meetings so far. Nine working Groups, each headed by a Member of the National Commission, have been constituted to assist the National Commission in the preparation of the report. The Commission is scheduled to submit its report to the Government of India by June, 1999.

Progressive use of Hindi

There has been continuous progress of the use of Hindi in official work. Hindi month was celebrated in NWDA (HQ) from 14.8.1998 to 14.9.1998. Various programmes and competitions were organised during this period. The programme also included an item on self evaluation of various units about the use of Hindi in their official work which was done for the first time. All the officers and staff members of NWDA actively participated in the programme and competitions.

A Rajbhasa Sangosthi entitled "Hamara Sangathan Aur Rajbhasa Hindi-Dasha Aur Disha" was organised on 7.9.1998. The Sangoshthi was inaugurated by Secretary, Ministry of Water Resources, who appreciated the efforts made by NWDA in the propagation and promotion of the official language.

Three incentive schemes namely i) Original noting/ drafting incentive scheme ii) Hindi technical articles incentive scheme and iii) Hindi dictation incentive scheme were continued for encouraging officials to do more work in Hindi. Though most of the regional offices of NWDA are located in region 'B' and 'C' category, sincere efforts have been made by them to implement the official language rules to improve its use. Nine of the regional offices have already been inspected by the officers from the headquarters. Suggestions and instructions to improve the use of Hindi have also been issued. Hindi Divas and Hindi Pakhwara were also organised in the regional offices and competitions held and prizes were given.

The NWDA has been awarded second prize of Northern Region by the Kshetriya Karyanvayan Karyalay (Delhi) of the Official Language Department, Home Ministry for giving excellent performance in the implementation of Hindi in the office. The performance of about 3 50 offices was evaluated for the prize. The prize was given in a function held on 12.1.1999 at Agra.

Vigilance activities

During the year 1998-99, one Vigilance case continued from previous year and two disciplinary cases were initiated.

4

Commission Board and Research Stations

Internal cooperation

Indo-Bangladesh joint rivers commission

A new chapter in the Indo-Bangladesh relations opened with the signing of the Indo-Bangladesh Treaty by the Prime Ministers of India and Bangladesh on 12th December, 1996 on the sharing of Ganga Waters for a period of thirty years. Under this treaty, both countries will be benefitted. The new treaty is a definite improvement over the agreement signed in 1977, which expired in 1988. Under this treaty, the interests of Calcutta Port and also the interests of Bangladesh have been duly recognised and taken care of. As a follow up of the treaty, Joint Committees have been set up on both sides for monitoring its implementation. During 1998-99, four meetings of these Committee have been held.

As a follow up, thirty second meeting of Indo-Bangladesh joint Rivers Commission (JRC) took place in July 1997 and first meeting of Joint Committee of Experts (JCE) was held in August, 1997 for discussing issues related to the sharing of Teesta Water and other six common rivers.

Two meetings of Standing Committee of JRC took place between November 1997 and November 1998 in which the issues concerning the closure of the gap of right embankment of Teesta river by both sides at the

Indo-Bangladesh border; exchange of data of common rivers between the two counties and Back Water effect on Indian territory due to construction of Teesta Barrage in Bangladesh were discussed. The work on the tying of the right embankment of the River Teesta at the Indo-Bangladesh border has since been completed.

Two meetings of Indo-Bangladesh Experts on flood forecasting and warning was held between November 1997 and November 1998 in which discussions about the transmission of data of flood forecasting and warning on the major rivers like Ganga, Teesta, Brahmaputra and Barak during monsoon season of 1997 and 1998 were discussed.

Two meetings of Indo-Bangladesh joint Scientific Study team to determine the reasons for discrepancies in the release of Ganga waters from Farakka and arrivals at Hardinge Bridge in Bangladesh, took place during June and November 1998. In these meetings modalities for the scientific study to be taken up were finalised.

Indo-Bhutan projects

The co-operation with Royal Government of Bhutan continued in respect of the works for hydro-power development and establishment of hydrometeorological and flood forecasting network on the rivers, common to India and Bhutan.

For the Sankosh Multipurpose Project, the Detailed Project Report was completed in December, 1995. The studies for Environment Impact Assessment and Socioeconomic aspects of the project have also been completed.

Indo-Nepal co-operation

There is considerable scope for cooperation between India and Nepal in the field of water resources particularly in the field of hydropower development utilising the abundant potential of northern tributaries of Ganga flowing from Nepal to India. Several projects have been identified and negotiations have been going on for a long time. With the signing of the Treaty on integrated development of Mahakali river in February, 1996, which came into force from June 1997, negotiations for implementation of Pancheshwar multipurpose project gained momentum during 1997-98. However, during 1998-99 there has not been much progress due to some unresolved contentious issues in the Treaty. This has also settled the negotiations on other projects like Sapta Kosi High Dam. Implementation of certain provisions of the Treaty about providing water and power to Nepal from the existing Sarada and Tanakpur barrages could, however, make considerable progress during the current year.

Indo-Pakistan co-operation

Under the Indus Waters Treaty, 1960, India and Pakistan have created two permanent posts of Commissioners for Indus Waters, one each in India and Pakistan. Each Commissioner is representative of his Government for all matters arising out of the Treaty and serves as the regular channel of communication on all matters relating to implementation of the Treaty. The two Commissioners together form the Permanent Indus Commission. During 1998, the Commission undertook one general tour of inspection in Pakistan in March and also held a meeting in Pakistan in May. Flood warning arrangements were made by India through priority telegrams, telephones and radio broadcasts for the benefit of Pakistan from first July to tenth October, 1998 for the Indus system of rivers. As part of the composite and integrated dialogue between India and Pakistan, Secretary level talks were also held on fifth November, 1998 on Tulbal Navigation Project with a view to finding a solution to the issue consistant with the provisions of the Treaty.

Inter-state water disputes and tribunals

Cauvery water dispute

The Cauvery Basin is an inter-state basin covering areas in Kerala, Karnataka, Tamil Nadu and Karaikal region of Union Territory of Pondicherry. Use and development of Cauvery waters was regulated by agreements of 1892 and 1924 between the erstwhile Princely State of Mysore and Province of Madras. The State of Kerala was not a party to this agreement. The 1924 Agreement was to expire at the end of 50 year-, and became open for review in the light of experience gained and further possibility of extension of irrigation etc.

With the re-organisation of States in 1956, the former princely State of Coorg, which was partly in the Cauvery basin, became part of Karnataka and some areas of Malabar in Madras State in the Cauvery basin, became part of Kerala. The then French territory of Pondicherry, which is also served by Cauvery, became a Union Territory. Thus, presently, Kerala, Karnataka, Tamil Nadu and Pondicherry are interested States for using Cauvery Water.

For more than two decades, sharing of Cauvery water among the basin States has been discussed/ negotiated bilaterally between Karnataka and Tamil Nadu with mediation by Centre, but there has been no breakthrough.

The Government of Tamil Nadu made a formal request in July 1986 under the provisions of Inter State Water Disputes Act, 1956 for constitution of a Tribunal.

In view of the uncompromising attitude adopted by the concerned States and the directions given by the Supreme Court, Central Government considered the matter in totality and came to the conclusion that there was no possibility of resolving the dispute by continuing the negotiations. In accordance with Section 4 of the Inter State Water Disputes Act, 1956, Central Government considered the request received from Tamil Nadu under Section 3 of the Act and decided to constitute a Tribunal for adjudication of the Cauvery Water Dispute and to refer the complaint of Government of Tamil Nadu to It for adjudication. Notification to this effect was issued on second June, 1990.

In pursuance of the direction given by the Supreme Court, the Tribunal heard the matter and passed an interim order in June, I, 99 1. The brief contents of the interim order are as under :-

(i) The State of Karnataka to release water from its reservoirs in Karnataka so as to ensure that 205 TMC of water is available in Tamil Nadu's Mettur Reservoir in a year from June to May. This will be effective from first July, 1991.

(ii) The State of Karnataka shall regulate the releases from their reservoirs during the year to ensure monthly inflows into Mettur reservoir as given in the order.

(iii) In respect of each month the releases are to be made in four weeks in four equal instalments.

(iv) Six TMC of water for Karaikal region of the Union Territory of Pondicherry will be delivered by the State of Tamil Nadu in a regulated manner.

(v) The State of Karnataka shall not increase its area under irrigation by the waters of river Cauvery beyond the existing 11.2 lakh acres.

(vi) The Order will remain operative till the final adjudication of the Dispute, referred to the Tribunal.

After obtaining opinion of the Supreme Court the interim order was gazetted on 10. 12.1991.

In May 1992, Government of Tamil Nadu filed an Original Suit No. I of 1992 in the Supreme Court on the grounds that Karnataka was not following the directives given by the Cauvery Water Disputes Tribunal in its interim order dated 25.6.1991 and prayed, inter-alia, to pass a decree of mandatory injunction directing the Union of India to frame a scheme making provisions for all matters necessary to give effect to the decisions of the Tribunal and to issue a notification thereof in the Official Gazette.

Preparation of a scheme by the Central Government for effective implementation of the interim order of the Cauvery Water Disputes Tribunal dated 2 5.6.1991 was being monitored regularly by the Supreme Court (Suit No. 1/92 -State of Tamil Nadu Vs. State of Karnataka and Others). After the hearing on 9.4.199 7 when the Supreme Court directed the Central Government to frame a scheme, there have been regular hearings on 20.8.1997, 30.9.1997, 11.11.1997, 6.1.1 9981, 31.3.1998, 28.4.1998 and 21.7.1998 in the Supreme Court.

Subsequently, at the instance of the Prime Minister, the Cabinet Secretary took meetings to discuss the draft scheme With the Chief Secretaries of the Cauvery basin States on 29.7.1998 and 4.8.1998. Thereafter, the Prime Minister met the Chief Ministers of the basin States/ U.T. on 6.8.1998 and 7.8.1998 and, based on the consensus, a scheme was finalised for implementation of the interim order of the CWDT dated 25.6.1991 and all related subsequent orders of the Tribunal. The same was notified in the official gazette on 11. 8.1998. The components of the Scheme are as under :

(i) This Scheme may be called the Cauvery Water (Implementation of the Order of 1991 and all subsequent related orders of the Tribunal) Scheme, 1998.

(ii) It shall come into force on the, date of its publication in the Official Gazette.

Constitution of the cauvery river authority

There shall be an Authority under this scheme to be known as the Cauvery River Authority (hereinafter referred to as the Authority).

The Authority shall consists of the following:

(a)	Prime Minister of India	Chairperson
(b)	Chief Minister of Karnataka	Member
(c)	Chief Minister of Kerala	Member
(d)	Chief Minister of Tamil Nadu	Member
(e)	Chief Minister of Pondicherry	Member

The Secretary in-charge of the Ministry of the Central Government dealing with water resources "I be the Secretary of the Authority.

Powers and functions of the authority

(i) The role of the Authority shall be to give effect to the implementation of the interim order dated twenty fifth June, 1991 of the Tribunal and all its related subsequent orders.

(ii) The Authority shall frame rules and regulations for the conduct of its business.

(iii) The Authority may convene meetings as and when necessary.

Monitoring committee

Under the Authority, there shall be a Monitor! Committee with the following composition:-

(a)	Secretary-in-charge of the Ministry of Central Government dealing With Water Resources	Chairman

(b)	The Chief Secretaries to the Governments of Karnataka, Kerala, Tamil Nadu and the Union Territory of Pondicherry	Members
(c)	Chairman, Central Water Commission	Member
(d)	One officer each, not below the rank of a Chief Engineer, to represent the States of Karnataka, Kerala and Tamil Nadu and the Union Territory of Pondicherry to be nominated by the Respective State Governments or the Union territory administration	Members
(e)	Chief Engineer, Central Water commission	Member-Secretary

Role and functions of the monitoring committee

(i) The role of the Monitoring Committee will be to render assistance to the Authority to enable it to take decisions on the issues under consideration.

(ii) The Monitoring Committee shall assist the Authority in collecting information and data.

(iii) The Monitoring Committee shall assist the Authority in monitoring the implementation of the decisions of the Authority. In case, any difficulty arises in implementation, the Monitoring Committee shall report the position to the Authority.

(iv) The Monitoring Committee shall assist the Authority in setting up a well designed hydro meteorological network in Cauvery basin along with a modern communication system for transmission of data and a computer based control room for data processing to determine the hydrological conditions.

Meetings of the monitoring committee

The Monitoring Committee shall meet at least once in three months but it may meet as often as necessary.

Headquarters of the authority

The Headquarters of the Authority shall be at New Delhi.

Financial provisions

All the capital and revenue expenditure required to be incurred by the Authority shall be borne by the Central Government initially till the issue of sharing of cost among the party States or the Union territory is either decided by them through mutual discussions or till the Tribunal takes a decision on the above matter.

The accounts of the Authority shall be maintained and audited in such manner as may be provided in rules made by the Central Government, in consultation with the Comptroller and Auditor General of India, in this behalf.

The Supreme Court has thereafter disposed off the suit no. 1/92 in view of the above action taken by the Central Government.

The Monitoring Committee of Cauvery River Authority held its first meeting on 7.10.1998. Subsequently, Cauvery River Authority held its first meeting on 2 8.10.1998.

Sone water dispute

The annual flow of River Sone at the time of Bansagar Agreement 1973 was assessed to be 14.2 5 MAF out of which Uttar Pradesh was given 1.2 5 MAF, Madhya Pradesh 5.25 MAF and Bihar 7.75 MAF of water. Later, the Sone River Commission was set up in 1980 which gave its report in 198 7 in which the availability of water in Sone Basin was assessed to be 16.3 7 MAF at 75 per cent dependability. Subsequently, a High Level Technical

Committee (HLTC) was constituted by the Ministry of Water Resources in 1990. The HLTC submitted its report in 1993, which was accepted by the Sone River Commission. However, the Government of Bihar does not agree with the methodology adopted by the Sone River Commission. It has suggested that, pending further hydrological studies, using up to date hydrological data, the earlier figure of 14.25 MAF adopted, in the Bansagar Agreement of 19 73 may not be changed.

Ravi and Beas water tribunal

The Ravi and Beas Waters Tribunal which was constituted in April, 1986 submitted its report in January, 1987. The Report was circulated in May, 198 7. A further reference was made to the Tribunal comprising a suo-moto reference by the Central Government and reference received from the Governments of Punjab, Haryana and Rajasthan seeking explanation/ guidance on certain points of the report. Further, report of the Tribunal giving such explanation/ guidance has yet to be received. The last hearing of the Tribunal was held in July, 1998.

Upper Yamuna river board

Yamuna Water dispute was resolved by signing of a Memorandum of Understanding (MOU) by the Chief Ministers of Himachal Pradesh, Haryana, Uttar Pradesh, Rajasthan and National Capital Territory of Delhi in May, 1994 about allocation of the utilisable surface flows of Yamuna among the co-basin States. Subsequently, separate agreement on construction of Hathnikund Barrage on Yamuna was signed in November, 1994 and agreement on Kishau Dam on Tons river and Renuka Dam on Giri rivers were also signed in November, 1994 by all the co-basin States, except Rajasthan.

The construction of Hathnikund Barrage is in progress. Detailed project Reports on Renuka Dam and

Kishau Dam Projects are being techno-economically appraised in the Central Water Commission and the Central Electricity Authority.

As per the provision in the MOU, the Upper Yamuna River Board (UYRB) with its headquarters at Delhi has been constituted by the Ministry of Water Resources, Government of India, by a resolution of eleventh March, 1995. A Review Committee known as the Upper Yamuna Review Committee (UYRC), constituted under the chairmanship of the Union Minister of Water Resources and the Chief Ministers of all the co-basin States as Members, is supervising the working of the Upper Yamuna River Board to ensure the implementation of the MOU about the allocation of surface flow of Yamuna and to issue directions, as deemed necessary, for proper development and management of the Upper reaches of the Yamuna River Basin up to Okhla.

The Upper Yamuna River Board with representatives from all the five basin States and from the concerned Central Government departments has held fifteen meetings so far, under the Chairmanship of Member (WP&P), Central Water Commission, including two meetings during the year 1998-99, up to November, 1998. In these meetings, the Board took decisions on seasonal distribution of Yamuna Waters up to Okhla. The UYRC has held two meetings so far, the last being in September, 1997.

Amendment in river boards act, 1956

The River Boards Act, 1956 was enacted under Entry 56 of List I of the Constitution of India foe the establishment of River Boards for the regulation and development of Inter-State River and River valleys. The Central Government has, however, not been able to constitute any River Board under this act so far. Moreover, the role of the River Boards as envisaged in the said Act is only advisory in nature. It has, therefore, been felt necessary to make amendments in the said Act and to provide sufficient powers so that the Act can serve the purpose for which it has been enacted.

The Amendment in the River Boards Act, 19 56 is presently under process in this Ministry.

Amendment in inter state water disputes act, 1956

The Inter State Water Disputes Act, 1956 (ISWD Act) (as modified up to 31.12.1980) was enacted by the Parliament under Article 262 of the Constitution for adjudicating of disputes relating to waters of Inter-State rivers or river valleys.

In its report of 198 7, the Sarkaria Commission gave five recommendations under Chapter XVII relating to Inter State River Water Disputes. These recommendations were finally considered by Inter State Council in its fourth meeting held on 28.11.1997.

Progressive use of Hindi and Other Miscellaneous activities

Use of Hindi

Effective measures were taken in the Ministry of Water Resources for the progressive use of Hindi for official purposes. The Official Language Implementation Committee of the Ministry under the Chairmanship of Joint Secretary (Administration) has been meeting regularly. Timely action was taken on the decisions taken in these meetings. Sufficient progress has been made in implementation of Raj bhasa Hindi in the Ministry.

The Hindi Advisory Committee under the Chairmanship of the Prime Minister, who is holding the charge of the Minister of Water Resources, has been reconstituted.

To encourage the staff to work in Hindi, schemes such as (i) dictation scheme for officers, (ii) noting and drifting competitions and (iii) award scheme for original writing in Hindi on Irrigation related topics, have been implemented.

To encourage healthy competition among the organisations under the Ministry for work in Hindi, a Running Shield Scheme (Chal Vaijayanti) was introduced. Under this scheme, this year, first and second prizes were awarded to Water and Power Consultancy Services (India) Limited, New Delhi and Central Water and Power Research Station, Pune respectively.

During the Hindi Fortnight from 1.9.1998 to 15.9.1998, special programmes and competitions were organised. Employees and officers of the Ministry enthusiastically participated in these competitions. The closing ceremony was held on fifteenth September, 1998. Secretary (WR) gave away the cash prizes and certificates to the winners.

Hindi workshops were also organised with a view to promoting official work in Hindi. Deputy Director (OL) and Assistant Director (OL) inspected ten offices to oversee the compliance of official language policy and instructions were given for rectification of the deficiencies pointed out during such inspections. Regular monitoring of the work being done in Hindi in the Ministry and its attached/subordinate offices was done through quarterly reports.

Twenty stenographers and seventeen typists were nominated for the Hindi training during the year.

Detailed check points were issued to various sections for ensuring that the infringement of Official Language Act, 1963 did not take place.

Computerisation in the ministry

The ministry of Water Resources is located in five different buildings, Shram Shakti Bhavan, Shastri Bhavan, Krishi Bhavan, Lok Nayak Bhavan and CGO Complex. Computers have been provided to each and every Wing in the Ministry. NIC Computer Centres have been set up in Krishi Bhavan, Lok Nayak Bhavan and CGO Complex in addition to the main computer centre in Shram Shakti Bhavan. Ninety two computer terminals have been installed in all these buildings for the use of officers and staff, which are linked to the respective computer centres. Personal Computers have also 'been provided to senior Officers and some Sections. Major specific-purpose software such as 'Monitoring of daily gauge and discharge data system', 'Minor Irrigation Census data', 'Physical and Financial Progress of Command Area Development Programme', 'Irrigation Water Management System', 'Crop Productivity Monitoring System', have been developed and implemented to ensure faster retrieval and dissemination of information in various Wings of the Ministry. A Home Page outlining the objectives and activities of the Ministry of Water Resources has been put on the Web accessible at http://www.nic.in/mowr. Radio Frequency link has also been established in the Ministry to improve the communication network and provide Internet mail and browsing facility.

The computer terminals provided by the National Informatic Centre to the various officers and staff in the different Wings are only dumb terminals. Keeping in view the demands of information technology, it has been felt that dumb terminals should be replaced by PCs. The Vittal Committee in its report has also emphasised the need for introduction of Information Technology in the official work and it suggested spending three per cent of the total budget on computerisation. Accordingly a scheme for setting up a Local Area Net Work in the entire Ministry covering all the Wings has since been formulated in consultation with the National Informatic Centre. A Memo for the Standing Finance Committee for procurement of 160 nodes for this purpose during a span of two years has also been prepared. It is likely to be considered after the approval of Planning Commission.

Inspection of reservation rosters

With a view to monitoring the implementation of reservation in services for Scheduled Castes/Scheduled Tribes/Other Backward Classes, various attached/ subordinate offices and organisations were inspected during the year. The organisations have been advised to take immediate follow up action on various recommendations made following the inspections.

Redressal of staff grievances

A Grievances Redressal Cell is in existence in the Ministry of Water Resources which entertains the grievances of staff of ail the organisations under the Ministry. Joint Secretary (Admn.) and Deputy Secretary (Admn.) have been designated as Director of Public Grievances and Director of Staff Grievances respectively.

The inspection of Grievances Redressal Machinery of various organisations under this Ministry is carried out annually. During last year, Central Ground Water Board and Sardar Sarovar Construction Advisory Committee were inspected. In the current year up to January, 1999, Central Water Commission and Central Soil and Materials Research Station have been inspected. Two more organisations are likely to be inspected by the end of March, 1999.

Minority welfare

In accordance with the guidelines issued by the Ministry of Social Justice & Empowerment in March, 1990, the

Ministry is monitoring the recruitment of minority communities and representation of minorities in Selection Commissions/ Boards in the Ministry and the organisations under it.

Monitoring of reservation for physically handicapped

Monitoring of the recruitment of physically handicapped is being done to ensure fulfilment of three percent quota for this category by the Ministry as well as various organisations under it. In all, 93 posts have been identified for filling up from among the physically handicapped, out of which 47 posts have already been filled up. The action to fill up the remaining posts reserved for them is in progress. Periodic reports on the progress made are being sent regularly to the Ministry of Social justice U Empowerment.

Committee for complaints on sexual harassment of women employees

In accordance with the guidelines laid down by the Supreme Court to tackle sexual harassment of women employees, a Committee has been constituted to look into the complaints of the women working in the Ministry of Water Resources. The Committee will submit its findings to the joint Secretary (Admn.) for necessary action. The Committee will also make Annual Report of the complaints received and action suggested by the Committee.

The Committee has held its meetings from time to time and met the women employees in the main Ministry and its organisations in Delhi to find out if they have any complaints regarding sexual harassment. However, during the last one year, not a single complaint came to the notice of the Committee about sexual harassment of women.

Consultative committee of the ministry

During the year, two meetings of the Consultative Committee of the Ministry of Water Resources were held on 2.11.1998 and 20.2.1998.

Vigilance and disciplinary cases

Vigilance activities were continued in the Ministry, its attached and subordinate offices, public sector undertakings and other autonomous organisations with greater emphasis on disposal of old vigilance and disciplinary cases. During the year 102 complaints were received (up to December, 1998) including 21 cases received from the Prime Minister's Office. Prompt action was taken for disposal of references received from PMO. Out of the 21 cases, investigations were completed in 18 cases and 11 of them were finally disposed off. Of the remaining 81 complaints, 36 cases were Finally closed. Five major penalty proceedings and 2 minor penalty proceedings were initiated.

Major penalties were imposed on 2 persons and minor penalties also on 2 persons. Special attention was paid to the submission of statistical quarterly return about complaints and vigilance cases to the Central Vigilance Commission, fortnightly reports to PMO and monthly report to DOPT. Periodic review of vigilance/ disciplinary cases were carried out with the Vigilance Officers/ Chief Vigilance Officers of the organisations under the Control of this Ministry.

Central water commission

Organisation and functions

The Central Water Commission is an attached office of the Ministry of Water Resources. Its headquarters is located in New Delhi. It is the apex technical organisation in the country in area of development of water resources. The Commission is responsible for initiating, coordinating and furthering, in consultation with the State Governments, the schemes for control, conservation, development and utilisation of water resources throughout the country for the purpose of irrigation, flood management, power generation and navigation. The Commission, if so required, also undertakes the construction and execution of projects.

Over the years, the Commission has developed the technological know-how in planning, investigation, appraisal, design, construction of projects for development of water resources, monitoring and management of projects, hydrological observations and flood forecasting. The Commission is headed by a Chairman with the status of Ex-officio Secretary to the Government of India and three Members with the status of Ex-Officio Additional Secretary to the Government of India. The three Members head the three technical Wings namely Design & Research (D&R) Wing, Water Planning 61 Projects (WP&P) Wing and River Management (RM) Wing. There are two units separately for Human Resources Management and Training headed by two Chief Engineers.

Thirteen regional field organisations of the Commission are functioning at Bangalore, Bhopal, Bhubaneshwar, Chandigarh, Coimbatore, Delhi, Hyderabad, Lucknow, Nagpur, Patna, Shillong, Siliguri and Vadodara, each headed by a Chief Engineer, who are responsible for monitoring of major and medium projects and appraisal of medium projects of the region in addition to flood forecasting and hydrological observations.

Monitoring of Command Area Development Programme in certain projects, minor irrigation schemes and other water management activities have also been added to these responsibilities.

Design and research wing

Major activities of the Design and Research Wing include:

— Design of water resources structures Hydrological studies

— Review and planning of safety aspects of dams

— Research, development and training

Design of water resources structures

D&R wing of CWC is actively associated with the design of almost all the major water resources projects either through consultancy or during the process of technical appraisal. The following four design units have been identified to cater to specific requirements and to attend to special design related problems of different regions :

— Design (North and West) unit

— Design (North-West and South) unit

— Design (East and North East) unit

— Design (Narmada Basin)

Each of the units have specialised Directorate such as Hydel Civil Design (HCD) Directorate, Concrete & Masonry Dam Design (CMDD) Directorate, Embankment Design Directorate, Gates Design Directorate and Barrage and Canal Design Directorate etc.

Project appraisal

Detailed Project Report (DPR) in respect of 23 new projects submitted by various State Governments and other agencies have been technically examined in D&R Wing during the year. In addition, examination of replies to comments/ observations and related studies in respect of 33 projects, which were earlier referred and examined in CWC, have also been carried out.

Detailed design and preparation of drawings

Different categories of projects for which detailed designs have been carried out and drawing of various components of different types of hydraulic structures have been prepared on priority basis during the year 1998-99 are as follows:

SI. No.	Category	No. of Projects
1.	Projects at construction stage	65
2.	Project at Pre-construction stage (for which specifications drawings are under preparation)	1
3.	Project at investigation and planning stage (for which detailed project report are being prepared)	17

In addition, specific problems in respect of 30 projects (for which design consultancy etc. were provided earlier) were also referred to D&R Wing time and again. State-wise break up of 113 consultancy projects of D& R wing is shown in Fig. 2. Some of the important projects which are presently being dealt with in D&R wing are as follows:

Pancheswar multipurpose project, Nepal

Under Indo-Nepal bilateral co-operation, the scope of Pancheswar multipurpose project is being actively discussed and defined to enable finalisation of detailed project report. The treaty between His Majesty's Government of Nepal and Government of India as signed in 1996 lays down the framework for integrated development of the Mahakali river including Pancheswar Project, Sarda Barrage Project and Tanakpur Barrage Project.

Tala H.E. project, Bhutan

The project Includes construction of 91 metre high diversion dam across the River Wangchu near Honka (located at about 3 km down stream of the existing Chukha H.E. Project) to divert 142.5 cumecs of water into 22.4 km long head race tunnel to generate 1020 MW (6x 170 MW) power under a design head of 820 m. Specification drawings have since been issued to project authorities for preparation of tender documents. The award of work is under finalisation and works for preparation of construction drawings for diversion tunnel are under progress. Construction drawings in respect of various portals for Adits to head race tunnel have already been prepared and Issued to project authorities.

Other projects in Bhutan

D&R wing is also providing consultancy and technical assistance for Gyesta Pondage Scheme of Bhutan and rehabilitation/ renovation of seven Mini/ Micro Hydel Power Projects of Bhutan.

Projects for development of water resources

CWC is very actively associated with investigation, planning and design of the various schemes for the development of water resources in the North Eastern region of the country. D&R wing is providing design consultancy for 24 projects out of which 9 are at construction stage. Detailed hydrological studies and design works in respect of these projects are in progress. The list of the projects is as follows:

Arunachal Pradesh

1. Debang Multipurpose Project
2. Dihang (Siang) Multipurpose Project
3. Kamlang Multipurpose Project
4. Lohit Multipurpose Project

5. Noa-Dihing Multipurpose Project
6. Ranganadi H. E. Project (Construction Stage)
7. Sissiri Multipurpose Project
8. Subansiri H.E. Project Assam

Assam

9. Harand Drainage Scheme (Construction Stage)
10. Kopili HE Project
11. Pagladia lrrigation Project

Manipur

12. Dolaitthabi Barrage (Construction Stage)
13. Jiri irrigation Project (Construction Stage)
14. Khuga Multipurpose Project (Construction Stage)
15. Thoubal Multipurpose Project (Construction Stage)
16. Tipaimukh Multipurpose Project

Meghalaya

17. Greater Shillong Water Supply Scheme (Construction Stage)
18. Rongai Irrigation Project (Construction Stage)

Mizoram

19. Bhairabhi Dam Project
20. Kolodyne HE Project
21. Mat Valley Multipurpose Project

Nagaland

22. Doyang HE Project (Construction Stage)
23. D-Zuza Multipurpose Project
24. T-Surang Irrigation Scheme

Hydrological studies

During technical appraisal of the project reports, the hydrological studies are examined and fresh studies are taken up wherever necessary. CWC also provides technical consultancy services to State Governments and other agencies for carrying out hydrological studies. Special studies on estimation of yield series and design flood etc. are also carried out by Hydrology Studies Organisation.

During 1998-99, detailed hydrological studies have been carried out in respect of 20 projects. Technical appraisal in respect of 22 water resources projects have been carried out. Replies to the comments/ observations and related studies in respect of 33 projects have also been examined. The revised Flood Estimation Report of Mahanadi sub-zone-3 (d) has been completed and printed for circulation. Studies for updating Flood Estimation Report of Krishna & Pennar sub-zone 3(h) have also been completed.

Planning of safety aspects of dams

Dam Safety Assurance and Rehabilitation Project was taken up by the Government of India with the assistance of World Bank with Central Water Commission (CWC) at the Centre and the States of Madhya Pradesh, Orissa, Rajasthan and Tamil Nadu as the beneficiaries. The objectives of the Project are to improve the safety status of 33 selected dams in the participating States through remedial works, installation of basic facilities and strengthening of the dam safety institutions in CWC and the four participating States. In addition, 22 dams were identified subsequently for rehabilitation by undertaking remedial works. The project was started during 1991 and was scheduled to be completed by September, 1997 but at the request of Government of India and the four State Governments, the project was initially extended up to

September, 1998 and has now been finally extended up to September, 1999. The revised cost of the restructured project as accepted by the World Bank is Rs. 4232 million against original cost of Rs. 45 5 9 million and the World Bank funding under IDA Credit has been reduced to SDR 68.8 million (US $ 93 million equivalent).

In the restructured project, during the first year of extension from October, 1997 to September, 1998, the number of dams identified for remedial works have been reduced from 55 to 28, with the addition of some facilities under institutional strengthening and basic dam safety facilities. Remedial works on 18 dams have since been completed.

Preparation of probable maximum precipitation atlas

One of the important activity under the Dam Safety Assurance and Rehabilitation Project (DSARP) is to take up studies for preparation of generalised Probable Maximum Precipitation (PMP) charts. PMP charts in respect of Mahanadi, Godavari, Cauvery and adjoining rivers and those of Sone, Betwa, Chambal and Mahi basins have since been completed, printed and circulated among user departments of the participating States. A Guideline for use of PMP Atlas has also been prepared and circulated to the user departments. A training course on "Use of Generalised PMP Atlases" was organised during August 25-28, 1998. Forty nine Officers from various State Governments, CWC and other Govt. of India Departments participated in the course. Proposal for awarding works for preparation of PMP Atlas under phase II are under active consideration.

National committee on dam safety (NCDS)

The National Committee on Dam Safety (NCDS) oversees dam safety activities in various States/ Organisations and suggests improvements to bring these in line with the latest state-of-the-art consistent with the Indian conditions. It acts as a forum for exchange of views on techniques adopted for remedial measures to old dams in distress. The Committee also monitors follow-up action on the recommendations of the report on Dam Safety Procedure circulated in July, 1986.

National committee on seismic design parameters (NCSDP)

The eighth meeting of National Committee on Seismic Design Parameters (NCSDP) was held on September 8, 1998. During the meeting, five projects were discussed for recommendation of seismic design parameters.

Research, development and training

Research schemes

Ministry of Water Resources provides funds for research and development schemes in the field of water resources development through various Indian National Committees. So far 188 research schemes have been sanctioned. One scheme costing Rs. 12 lakh has been sanctioned during this year. A number of new proposals are under active consideration.

Science & technology advisory committee (STAC-MOWR)

The STAC-MOWR meeting was held during January, 1999. The guidelines for implementation of R&D activities have been revised for effective physical and financial monitoring as well as dissemination of results and participation of NGOs in R&D Programme. Revised draft of guidelines are under examination in the Ministry of Water Resources.

Dam break studies

Dam Break Studies for 6 dams have been undertaken during the year 1998-99. Studies in respect of one dam have since been completed.

Water planning & projects wing

This Wing is responsible for overall planning and development of basinwise perspective plan for development and management of surface water, national perspective plan for the development of water resources in accordance with the National Water Policy, techno-economic appraisal of Water Resources Projects and assistance to the States in the formulation and implementation of projects, monitoring of selected projects for identification of bottlenecks to achieve the targeted benefits, preparation of projects for international assistance, environmental aspects, allocation of scarce construction material and machinery to the projects etc.

Project appraisal

One of the important activities assigned to CWC is techno-economic appraisal of irrigation, flood control and multipurpose projects proposed by State Governments. This task is performed and coordinated by Project Appraisal Organisation (PAO) and Project Preparation Organisation (PPO). The field units of Central Water Commission assist the headquarters in the appraisal of Medium Projects. After establishment of techno-economic feasibility of the project the Advisory Committee on Irrigation, Flood Control and Multipurpose Projects headed by Secretary, Ministry of Water Resources, considers projects for acceptance and thereafter recommends the projects for investment clearance by the Planning Commission. Besides, power projects proposed by State Electricity Boards/ Private Sector Organisations are scrutinised in CWC from hydrology, civil design, inter-state and cost angles in the case of hydro projects and for establishing water availability for cooling and other purposes in case of thermal projects. Technical aspects of water supply schemes are also appraised when referred to by the State Governments.

A similar function is discharged by the Project Preparation Organisation (PPO) under a Chief Engineer with a multi-disciplinary composition covering engineering, agronomy and economic disciplines in respect of Major, Medium Irrigation and Water Resources Consolidation Projects which are proposed for external assistance.

Meetings of technical advisory committee

During the year 1998-99, (up to January, 1999) the Advisory Committee met on 12.6.1998, 6.10.1998 and 27.1.1999 under the Chairmanship of Secretary (WR) and considered 18 projects comprising 1 multipurpose, 9 major and 8 medium irrigation project.

Project appraisal for external assistance

CWC has been providing technical assistance and guidance to the State Governments in the formulation and preparation of project reports according to the criteria laid down by the external aid agencies and also to conform to the guidelines of CWC and Planning Commission about investigation, planning, design, agro-economic and economic aspects. The project reports posed for external assistance are processed in CWC for techno-economic appraisal and acceptance of the Advisory Committee for Irrigation, Flood Control and Multipurpose projects for investment clearance by Planning Commission. Four more projects, Extension of Left Ayacut beyond the River Tel and Right ayacut beyond the River Sagde (Upper Indravati Irrigation Project, Orissa), Extension of Ayacut at 14.3 km of Jaypore Main canal (Upper Kolab Irrigation Project, Orissa), Lendi Irrigation Project (Maharashtra and A. P.) and Punasi Reservoir Project, Bihar are likely to be put up shortly to Advisory Committee for clearance which are also considered by the States for posing for external assistance.

Monitoring of projects

Intensive monitoring of some selected on-going major and medium Irrigation projects is being carried out by CWC to monitor the physical and financial progress of the projects, to identify bottlenecks causing delays in completion of projects and to suggest remedial measures for creation of the designed potential, as per schedule. Annual Reports on the status of monitored projects, highlighting critical issues needing attention are prepared and furnished to Planning Commission and the concerned State Governments etc. The externally aided/ Inter-State/ centrally sponsored major projects are monitored by the Project Monitoring Organisation (PMO), headed by a Chief Engineer, stationed at the Headquarters while the regional organisations of CWC, headed by respective Chief Engineers, take care of monitoring activities of other important major and medium irrigation projects. One hundred and thirty eight major projects (including ERM projects) and ninety six medium projects have been identified for monitoring during the IX Plan. Out of these, thirty four major projects are being monitored by PMO at CWC Headquarters.

Since 1996 Central Loan Assistance (CLA) is being provided to selected major and medium irrigation projects in the country under Accelerated Irrigation Benefit Programme. Central Water Commission (CWC) has been assigned the responsibility of monitoring the projects receiving CLA. The Field Monitoring Directorates of Central Water Commission are monitoring the physical and financial progress of AIBP components. Ninety one projects selected under this Programme are being monitored by CWC field monitoring organisations.

Environmental monitoring committee (EMC)

An Environmental Monitoring Committee (EMC) was

constituted in February, 1990 for monitoring the implementation of environmental safeguards of irrigation, multipurpose and flood control projects. The Committee has selected 85 projects for monitoring of which 17 are being closely monitored. Out of these 17 projects, the Committee has so far Visited 15 projects. Six of these projects have been visited twice.

Eight more projects out of the list of 85 projects have also been Visited. In order to monitor the progress of other projects, the Committee has advised various State Governments and project authorities to constitute State Level Environmental Monitoring Committee and Project Level Environmental Management Committee.

Sixteen State Level Environmental Monitoring Committees and 59 Project Level Environmental Management Committees have so far been constituted. Twenty six projects have yet to constitute the project Level Environmental Management Committee.

The progress achieved by the Environmental Monitoring Committees is being brought out annually in the shape of Annual Reports giving details of meetings, projects visited and directions given to various States/ Project authorities for implementing the safeguards stipulated at the time of clearance of the projects.

Environmental awareness

Efforts are being made to create awareness among the people about the environmental aspects of water resources development. To achieve this objective, papers and articles are being published in Bhagirath magazine published by Central Water Commission. Functions were organised on the World Environment Day during June, 1998 in the Headquarters and field offices of Central Water Commission.

Environmental impact assessment

Environmental Impact Assessment (EIA) of the proposed irrigation projects has been prescribed to study the beneficial as well as the adverse impacts of these projects. It is mandatory for any major project costing Rs. 50 crore and above to get environmental clearance from the Ministry of Environment and Forests (MOEF) before starting the work. The Expert Committee (EC) of MOEF for river valley and H. E. projects plays an important role in examining the EIA related aspects including the findings of the committee conducting public hearing in the project area. It deliberates on the merits and demerits of the project and conducts inspections for on the-spot assessment at the project sites, if felt necessary before recommending/rejecting the clearance of the project from environmental considerations. Chief Engineer (EMO) is a member of this committee and has participated in four meetings of the Expert Committee of MOEF. Chief Engineer (EMO) visited the project impact area of Dhamwari Sunda H.E. Project, H.P. as member of the subcommittee of EC. The EC cleared three projects which are Lower Suktel (Orissa), Lower Indra (Orissa) and Dhamwari Sunda (Himachal Pradesh) after considering 12 projects in all so far till 29.10.1998.

Rehabilitation and resettlement

Central Water Commission Is entrusted with the collection and compilation of data about rehabilitation measures being taken by the project authorities, norms/ acts/ policies adopted by the State Governments in respect of major and medium irrigation and multipurpose storage projects and preparation of draft of "National Rehabilitation and Resettlement Policy for affected persons of Reservoir Projects".

The draft National R&R Policy has been modified and included in the agenda prepared for getting the approval of National Water Board. R&R aspects of reservoir projects with details such as area under reservoir submergence, families/ persons affected and rehabilitation measures taken by the project authorities in respect of 162 existing and on-going projects (Major and Medium Irrigation/Hydroelectric projects) have been compiled on the basis of progress reports received from project authorities/status reports of Monitoring Organisations of CWC.

Application of remote sensing techniques

The Ministry of Water Resources' Standing Finance Committee approved the plan Scheme "Remote Sensing Applications in Water Resources Application and Development" to be taken up as continuation of VIII plan scheme, in the IX plan period at an estimated cost of Rs. 3 36. 11 lakh. The revised scheme includes new studies in various areas of application in addition to the continuing studies of the previous plan.

Following studies have been completed during 1998-99:

— Watershed prioritization of Mahi Bajaj Sagar Reservoir using Remote Sensing Techniques.

— Reservoir sedimentation of Kadana Reservoir using Remote Sensing Techniques.

— The studies on Flood Management and River Morphological study of River Yamuna, Reservoir Sedimentation studies of Ukai, Konar and Tilaya Reservoir are presently in advanced stage and are expected to be completed by March, 1999.

Studies on drainage problems in irrigates areas

The adverse effects of lack of drainage in irrigated areas include loss of land due to waterlogging, soil salinity and alkalinity and land degradation. Central Water Commission is presently engaged in the collection and compilation of data relating to water logging and soil salinity in irrigated commands. Collection of data of individual States is in progress. A State-wise status report on the drainage related problems is being prepared.

Monitoring of reservoir level and live storage capacity

Central Water Gommission has been monitoring Reservoir Levels and Live Storage Capacities in respect of 63 important reservoirs in India.

Hydrographic survey of important reservation in India

The scheme for taking hydrographic survey of important reservoirs has been sanctioned for an estimated cost of Rs. 5 79 lakh for the IX Plan period. Surveys in respect of two reservoirs (Konar and Tilaiya) have been completed and studies for five more reservoirs are likely to be commenced during the year (Kakki, Idukky in Kerala, Balemela in Orissa, Jayakwadi in Maharashtra and Linganamakki in Karnataka).

River management wing

This wing is responsible for technical matters relating to river morphology, flood management, techno-economic examination and acceptance of flood management schemes, collection of hydrological and hydrometeorological data, formulation of stage and inflow forecast in all the flood prone river basins, investigation and appraisal of medium projects/schemes ' monitoring of major and medium projects in which Command Area Development Programme is being implemented.

Hydrological data collection

The Central Water Commission at present operates a national network of 90 7 Hydrological Observation Stations. The basic data observed at field units are processed at various levels and the authenticated data is then transmitted to Central Data Bank of Central Water Commission for storage, processing and retrieval at the request of various user agencies. The hardware and software facilities available for storage of the data are being augmented continuously, incorporating various user requirements, and to carry out further improvements in the field of software development.

Water quality monitoring

In addition to observing the river flows, the Central Water Commission has been monitoring the water quality, covering all the major river basins of the country. At present, the Central Water Commission is maintaining a three tier system of laboratories for the analysis of various chemical parameters. The Level-I laboratories are located at 334 Field Water Quality Monitoring Stations on major rivers of India where physical parameters such as temperature, colour, odour, specific conductivity, total dissolved solids, PH and dissolved oxygen (DO) of river water are observed.

In addition, there are 21 level - II laboratories located at selected divisional headquarters to analyse the physio-chemical characteristics and biochemical oxygen demand of the water of the rivers. Level - III laboratories are functioning at Varanasi, Delhi and Hyderabad which are equipped with sophisticated equipments to analyse the traces of toxic elements, polyaromatic hydrocarbons, insecticides and micro biological inhabitants in the river water. The data generated is computerised in data base system and disseminated in the form of Hydrological Year Book, Status Reports and Bulletins. Twenty Water Quality Year Books are published annually and three Bulletins are issued each month.

Flood management

Out of the country's total geographical area of 32 mha, 40

mha has been assessed by the Rashtriya Barh Ayog to be flood prone, out of which 32 mha can be provided with a reasonable degree of protection. Up to March, 1998, an area of about 14.37 mha (tentative) has been provided with reasonable degree of flood protection through various flood management works.

The absolute control of flood and total protection from it is not possible due to techno-economic constraints. However, for the reasonable protection against floods, structural measures were adopted in the past. More emphasis is now being given to nonstructural measures such as Flood Plain Zoning, Flood Proofing and Flood Forecasting Techniques.

Flood plain zoning

Keeping in view the need for adopting non structural measures like regulation of economic and human activities in the flood plains, a model bill was circulated in 1975 to all the States for its enactment. So far, only the Government of Manipur have enacted a legislation for flood plain zoning.

Flood forecasting

CWC has 157 flood forecasting stations covering 62 river basins in India. During the flood season of 1998, 7110 flood forecasts including inflow forecasts were issued from 120 river flood forecasting stations, which were found to be useful for taking timely action to prevent the loss of human life, livestock and movable property.

Flood situation in 1998-99

The country as a whole received normal rainfall during the year 1998-99. However, there were floods of varying magnitude due to heavy rains in Andhra Pradesh, Arunachal Pradesh, Assam, Bihar, Gujarat, Himachal Pradesh, Karnataka, Kerala, Madhya Pradesh, Maharashtra, Meghalaya, NCT of Delhi, Orissa, Punjab,

Rajasthan, Sikkim, Tripura, Uttar Pradesh and West Bengal. According to the preliminary reports received from Assam, Bihar and Uttar Pradesh, an area of about 7.18 mha was affected by the floods during the monsoon season affecting a population of about 30.24 million in these States. Crops in an area of about 2.27 mha were also reported to have been damaged. During this year, North Bihar and Eastern Uttar Pradesh experienced unprecedented floods.

Considering the complexity and magnitude of flood management problem in Brahmaputra River system, Central Loan assistance outside the State Plan is being provided to the Government of Assam since 1974-75 for flood management works in the Brahmaputra Valley. Central assistance of Rs. 368.03 crore was provided to the State Government up to 1997-98 to undertake the flood control works. Of this, Rs. 357.94 crore has been provided as loan and Rs. 10.09 crore as grant. Now a proposal has been mooted to change the funding from loan assistance to Central Grant during the remaining four years of IX Plan.

River morphological studies

An Atlas of Eastern Rivers for taking up Morphological studies is being prepared by Central Water Commission since 1992. Volume I to Volume VII covering Brahmaputra and Barak basins were completed. In the year 1998-99, Volume VII I for river Ganga for the reach Allahabad to the Confluence of Gogra (Ghagra) With Ganga has been taken up. The Morphological Studies of river Krishna have also been taken up during the year.

Coastal protection works

The Coastal Protection and Development Advisory Committee (CPDAC) provides guidance to maritime States in protecting against coastal erosion by organising and co-ordinating programmes of collection, compilation, evaluation and publication of data relating to various natural phenomena and coastal processes which affect the coast line. It also prescribes the principles of designing and construction techniques for anti-sea erosion works. The Committee interim With the concerned agencies for transfer of technology in the field of coastal protection. The Committee had requested the maritime States to formulate proposals for protection of coastal reaches from sea erosion at vulnerable reaches in their respective States and send the proposals to Central Water Commission for preparing a consolidated National Coastal Protection Project (NCPP) for exploring the possibilities of getting for external assistance for the same.

Accordingly, the Governments of Kerala, Karnataka, Gujarat, West Bengal, Tamil Nadu, Andhra Pradesh, Maharashtra, Orissa and Goa have submitted their proposals for inclusion in the NCPP. These proposals were examined in Central Water Commission. The consolidated report of National Coastal Protection Project is being prepared in Central Water Commission.

Survey and investigation

The Central Water Commission has been carrying out detailed surveys and investigations including preparation of feasibility reports for the development of water resources in the country as well as in the neighbouring countries of Nepal and Bhutan.

Projects in Sikkim— The investigation of hydroelectric projects in the Teesta Basin for Cascade development has been taken up by Central Water Commission. The Investigations for the stages 111, IV and V have been completed and detailed project reports have been submitted. Investigation work for Teesta Hydel Project Stage-VI commenced during 1994-95 and all field works have been completed. The preparation of detailed project report is in progress. Field investigations of Teesta Hydel Project Stage-II were also taken up during 1997-98. Expert team from Central Water Commission and Geological Survey of India visited the project areas for finalization of dam and Power House sites for detailed investigation.

Projects in the North East— The Central Water Commission has been carrying out detailed surveys and investigations and preparing the project reports in the North Eastern States of the country. These projects are being investigated as deposit works from the North Eastern Council and the State Governments and various plan schemes of Government of India. Ten projects are at present in hand.

Detailed Project report of Kamlang Multipurpose project, Arunachal Pradesh has been completed and submitted to the sponsoring Agency. Detailed project report of 'D', Zuza Multipurpose project (Nagaland) is likely to be submitted by 1998-99. Survey and Investigation of one project in Arunachal Pradesh namely Nuranang chu has been taken up and Tawang chu is likely to be taken up during the year after the approval of Ministry of Water Resources.

Projects in the neighbouring countries -The Central Water Commission has been rendering assistance to the neighbouring countries In surveys and investigations and preparation of detailed project reports of water resources projects in the Himalayas. The projects, taken up as joint ventures of the Government of India With His Majesty's Government of Nepal and Royal Government of Bhutan areas under:

Pancheshwar multipurpose project

The Pancheshwar Multipurpose Project is a storage scheme proposed to exploit the potential of river

Mahakali. The project is located at about 2.5 km downstream of the confluence of the river Mahakali with Sarju. The river Mahakali drains a total catchment area of 12 100 sq. km of which 9720 sq. km lies in India and 23 80 sq. km in Nepal.

Pancheshwar Dam site was first identified in 1956 for a storage type scheme for power channel by erstwhile Central Water and Power Commission. In 19621 the Government of Uttar Pradesh carried out preliminary field investigations and a project report was prepared by WAPCOS in November, 1971.

Accordingly, field investigations were carried out independently on the Indian side and on the Nepalese side of the River between 1981 and 1991 by Central Water Commission and Government of Nepal. Based on these investigations, Government of India and Government of Nepal have prepared DPRs independently.

One joint Group of Experts (JGE) consisting of high level officials of both the countries has been assigned the job of preparing the joint DPR. For this purpose, 10 JGE meetings have been held. It has been decided to carry out some additional investigations for Pancheshwar Project (main dam) and for selection of regulating structure either at Purnagirl or at Rupaligad. However, further field investigations are held up decision regarding the modalities of investigations from His Majesty's Government of Nepal.

Sapta Kosi high dam multipurpose project

The second meeting of the joint team of experts of India and Nepal on Sapta Kosi High Dam Multipurpose Project was held in January, 1997 at Kathmandu (Nepal) in which both sides decided to take up the project jointly for detailed investigations and preparation of Detailed

Project Report. The Government of Nepal was requested to finalise the modalities of field investigations. However desired response is still awaited from the Government of Nepal.

Central Water Commission has been giving consultancy for rehabilitation of eight mini hydel projects in Bhutan. In addition Central Water Commission is also executing the following works as deposit works in Bhutan:

(i) Construction of River Training and Bank Protection works for the protection of permanent buildings in Paro Air field.

(ii) Execution of Permanent protection works for the Water Conductor System of Chenary M. H. Project, Stage-I.

(iii) Execution of civil works for rehabilitation and augmentation of Lhuntse M H Project.

(iv) Execution of civil works for rehabilitation of Chenary M.H. Project, Stage-II. Construction of about 700 metre long tunnel for carrying water conductor pipes is also part of this work.

(v) Execution of civil works for rehabilitation of Gyesta, Gidakom and Wangdi M. H. Project.

(vi) Exploratory core drilling works on behalf of WAPCOS for Tala project.

The agreements for the rehabilitation of Gidakom and Wangdue Mini Hydel Project have been signed between Central Water Commission and Department of Power, Royal Government of Bhutan.

Other projects

Manas-Sankosh-Teesta link canal project

The investigation work on the Manas-Sankosh-Teesta link canal was entrusted to the Central Water Commission by the Ministry of Water Resources. The work started in August, 1996 in consultation with the National Water Development Agency. Twenty per cent of the investigations were completed in the Eighth Plan period. Rest of the works will continue during the Ninth Plan. However, the work is held up at the moment because of non-availability of permission to continue survey works through the reserved forest areas of West Bengal and Assam.

Training of personnel

Training Directorate of CWC arranges training for in-service officers of CWC at all levels. These training programmes are held both within and outside the country. Officers of CWC are regularly deputed to various National and International seminars, conferences, workshops etc. Induction training for Assistant Directors is also being conducted by Training Directorate in addition to their training at the Central Training Unit, Pune.

This Directorate also arranges Apprenticeship training for fresh engineering graduates/ diploma holders/ vocational certificate holders in collaboration with Board of Apprenticeship training, Kanpur. A few students of Engineering degree courses are given practical training in CWC every year for a period of 4 to 8 weeks. Officers of CWC are also being trained in the latest technologies in the field of hydro-power generation through a World Bank assisted project being implemented by the Central Electricity Authority.

Central training unit

There is a Central Training Unit of Central Water Commission located in the premises of Central Water and Power Commission at Khadakwasala. It is now proposed to upgrade it to National Water Academy and build a separate complex for it in CW&PRS' premises.

Progressive use of Hindi

During the year, efforts were made in the Commission for implementation of the provisions contained in the Official Language Act, 1963 and the rules made thereunder. All documents falling under Section 3(3) of the above Act were issued bilingually. All letters received in Hindi were replied to in Hindi.

"Hindi Pakhwara' was organised from 14-25 September, 1998. Eight competitions in Hindi including Hindi Prashan Manch were organised. The winners were given cash prizes. Three Hindi workshops were also organised.

Vigilance/disciplinary cases

The vigilance/disciplinary cases and complaints received against officers and staff of CWC received proper and prompt attention. During the year 24 complaints were received and taken up for investigation. Investigation was completed in 3 4 cases and final decision was taken in respect of 17 cases, out of which in 6 cases, the officials found guilty were awarded major/minor penalties.

General ground water board

The Central Ground Water Board (CGWB) is a ;subordinate office of the Ministry of Water Resources. It is responsible for carrying out nationwide surveys and assessment of ground water resources and guiding the States appropriately in scientific and technical matters relating to ground water. The Board has generated valuable scientific and technical data through regional hydrogeological surveys, ground water exploration, resource and water quality monitoring and research and development. The Board also organises in-service training programmes for its own as well as other Central and State Government officials. It assists the States in developing broad policy guidelines for development and management of ground water resources including their conservation, augmentation and protection from pollution, regulation of extraction and conjunctive use of surface water and ground water resources.

The Board is headed by a Chairman, who is assisted by four Members, with four wings which are Surveys, Assessment and Monitoring (SAM) Wing; Sustainable Management and Liaison (SML) Wing; Exploratory Drilling and Materials Management (ED&MM) Wing and Training and Technology Transfer (T&TT) Wing.

The Board has 16 Regional Offices, each headed by a Regional Director with an equal number of supporting Engineering offices and Nine State Unit Offices for undertaking various field activities in the country.

Activities of the board reappraisal hydrological surveys

The ground water being replenishable and dynamic in nature, it becomes essential to conduct periodical surveys to assess the quality and quantitative changes in the ground water regimes in time and space. These surveys also help in measuring the impact on local ground water regime of various developmental activities like introduction of surface irrigation schemes, installation of industrial units and withdrawal of ground water.

During 1997-98, an area of 2.3 9 lakh sq. km was covered under these surveys and during 1998-99, against a target of 2.04 lakh sq. km, an area of 1.95 lakh sq. km has been covered in different States.

Exploration of ground water

The exploration of ground water to study the subsurface geological and hydrogeological setups and evaluate various aquifer parameters is carried out by the Board with a fleet of 99 drilling rigs (48 Direct Rotary, 36 Down the Hole and 12 Percussion and 3 Combination types).

Deep drilling for ground water exploration in ganga basin

It is proposed to explore and develop the ground water resources in unconsolidated formations in the Ganga Basin with the help of Geological Survey of India, National Geophysical Research Institute, Oil and Natural Gas Commission, Oil India Limited and Uttar Pradesh Remote Sensing Application Centre. As a part of the study, 15 deep resistivity soundings by the Geological Survey of India and 25 by the Central Ground Water Board, Northern Region were taken up In Lalkua-Haldwani area. A report has been prepared on remote sensing studies to delineate prospective recharge area in the Himalayan foothills by U. P. Remote Sensing Application Centre, Lucknow and Central Ground Water Board, Northern Region, Lucknow. The Oil India Limited drilled and logged their exploratory borehole at Bilkhedi, district Rampur, U.P. up to 1500 m depth and potential zones up to 1500 m depth have been inferred by them (OIL). The Board has obtained the broad exploratory information of the boreholes from OIL for further study. Interaction is underway with NGRI and BARC forage determination of ground water in deepest aquifers of western Uttar Pradesh.

Ground water studies in drought prone areas

The Board is carrying out intensive surveys and exploration programme in drought prone areas to delineate aquifers, which could provide sustainable supply of water during the periods of prolonged droughts. During 1998-99, Reappraisal Hydrogeological Surveys are being carried out in drought prone areas of 44395 sq. km in Rajasthan, Andhra Pradesh, Bihar, Karnataka, Madhya Pradesh and Kerala. Ground Water exploration is also underway in drought prone areas in Uttar Pradesh, Rajasthan, Maharashtra, Madhya Pradesh, Orissa, Karnataka and Gujarat.

Monitoring through the national hydrograph network stations

The Board is monitoring the ground water levels in the country four times a year through a network of 14769 National Stations. The water samples collected during the pre-monsoon monitoring are analysed for the purpose of ascertaining the changes in chemical quality of ground water.

Hydrology projects

The World Bank aided Hydrology Project for the peninsular State of India is being implemented in eight States. The project aims at improving the existing data collection network through construction of observation wells and replacement of some of the existing observation wells; setting up and upgradation of chemical laboratories; establishment of national and State data banks, integration and transmission of data; and providing training to the personnel engaged in the project activity. The Board is the nodal agency for the ground water sub-sector of the project.

Under the project, so far 2150 sites, spread over the eight beneficiary States, have been identified for construction of piezometers. Six hundred and five piezometers (194 in soft rock and 411 in hard rock terrain) had been constructed till March 1998 and 702 more (80 in soft rock and 622 in hard rock terrain) were constructed during the current year up to November, 1998. A total of 1415 piezometers are proposed to be constructed during 1998-99. Three Thousand Seven Hundred and Seventy Five Hydrograph Network Stations and 253 newly constructed Piezometers had been linked with GTS Bench mark till November, 1998.

The progress made in the other areas of the activities includes finalisation of specifications of automatic water level recorders (AWLRs) in consultation with the DHV consultants, World Bank Authorities and DGS&D (the procurement agency). Digital Water Level Recorders, Field Monitoring Kits, equipments needed for upgrading chemical laboratories and vehicles are being purchased. Reimbursement of a claim of Rs. 4,81,72,000.00 had been made till November, 1998. Base work for Hydrology Institutional Development Action Plan (HIDAP) Programme, and finalisation of specifications for procurement of various types of Computer packages by convening High Level Technical Group's meetings had been completed.

Data User Group (HDUG) comprising members representing various Government, NGO's and educational Institutions etc. was convened for ascertaining their data requirements. A two day National Seminar on Artificial Recharge of Ground Water was organised at New Delhi and one day workshops at Hyderabad, Nagpur, Bangalore and Kerala were organised to create awareness about the Hydrology Project. A two day workshop was also organised at Nagpur, Seventy eight Officers/ staff have been trained under various training programmes in Ground Water Hydrology and 28 chemists have been trained in various training courses in Ground Water Quality. The modification work of Regional Office Data Centres (RODC) and Chemical laboratory at Central Region, Nagpur and South Eastern Coastal Region, Chennai have been completed and at Kerala Region, Trivandrum is under progress.

Studies in group water exchange

The Board has taken up artificial- recharge studies under Central Sector Scheme in the Dark and Over exploited Blocks/ Taluks/ Watersheds of Maharashtra, Karnataka, Delhi, Punjab and Chandigarh U.T. These Studies aim to investigate the feasibility of undertaking various recharge measures suited for different hydrogeological setups by conducting field studies to operationalise the methodologies developed for augmenting ground water recharge and evolving sound guide lines for taking up artificial recharge projects in similar areas. Based on the studies undertaken, the Board will operationalise the artificial recharge schemes in cooperation with the respective State Governments.

During 1998-99, assessment of the impact of recharge through artificial recharge structures constructed in Amravatil and Jalgaon districts was carried out. In Karnataka, construction of one percolation Tank each at Erropotehenahalli and Manchiganahalli villages in Kolar district has been completed.

In Delhi, construction of Check Dam-III in JNU Campus and Check Dam IV in IIT Campus has been completed. Roof Top Rainwater Harvesting system in IIT has also been completed. A Brochure entitled "Artifical Recharge in Delhi" was also brought out in December, 1998.

Construction of Roof Top Rain Water Harvesting System was completed at CSIO complex, Chandigarh and assessment of recharge during monsoon was carried out. Construction of 7 subsurface dykes in Madhya Pradesh, Tamil Nadu, Kerala and West Bengal has also been completed. Water levels are monitored on continuing basis by establishing key observation wells in these areas to assess the positive impact of the artifical recharge schemes being implemented.

Technical examination of irrigation schemes

The Board scrutinises the proposals for medium and major irrigation projects, multipurpose projects and the proposals of power plants for use of ground water in order to determine their impact on ground water.

Report, Maps and atlases

The results of the investigations undertaken by the Board are suitably documented in the form of technical reports. These reports have been categorised as project reports, survey reports, district reports, state reports, basic data reports, maps and atlases. During 1997-98, 38 District reports were brought out by the Board. During 1998-99, 48 District Reports are proposed to be compiled.

The hydrogeological atlases of Maharashtra, Kerala, Bihar and Madhya Pradesh are currently under print. The atlases of Himachal Pradesh, Andhra Pradesh (Revised) and Tamil Nadu (Revised) are likely to be completed during 1998-99. The Board also brings out a publication on the ground water statistics annually.

Water quality analysis

The Board has set up water testing laboratories in the Regional Directorates to analyse water samples collected from hydrograph stations and those collected during surveys, explorations and other investigations. The Board has also set up a Hydrochemical MID Laboratory at Fariclabad.

Recently, a laboratory has been set up at Fariclabad. About 22,000 water samples are analysed annually for inorganic elements for determining and evaluating the ground water quality and its suitability for various uses.

The facilities for carrying out analysis of organic elements have also been created in some of the Regional Laboratories to monitor the impact of the use of fertilizers, pesticides and insecticides, oil spills, solid wastes and disposal dumps etc. The Board has acquired sophisticated equipment under the project "Improvement of Equipments for Water Quality Monitoring in India' with Japan's grant-in-aid programme.

Ground water authority

Central Ground Water Authority was constituted by the Government under the directions of the Supreme Court. The notification about the constitution of the Authority was issued on January 14, 1997. The Authority was earlier constituted for a period of one year which was later extended for five years through a notification on January 13, 1998.

As per the notification, the Central Ground Water Authority was created for the purposes of regulation and control of management and development of ground water. The following powers have been, given to the Authority to perform the following functions:

— exercise of powers under section 5 of the Environment (Protection) Act, 1986 for issuing directions and taking such measures in respect of all the matters referred to in Subsection (2) of section 3 of the said Act.

— to resort to the penal provisions contained in section 15 to 2 1 of the said Act.

— to regulate indiscriminate boring and withdrawal of ground water in the country and to issue necessary regulatory directions with a view to preserving/ protecting the ground water.

The Authority will function under the administrative control of the Ministry of Water Resources with its headquarters at Delhi and jurisdiction of the Authority will be the whole of India.

After its constitution in 1997, the Authority considered the following issues which required immediate regulatory measures:

— To conserve the ground water resources and ensure its prudent use.

— To control over-drawal of ground water in critical areas.

— To augment resource in areas of over-exploitation

— To achieve statutory quality standards for ground water set up by BIS and ICMR.

— To control discharges to ground water systems.

— To educate public about the adverse effects of decline in water levels and pollution of ground water through mass awareness programmes.

Action taken during 1998-99

— The Authority started mass-awareness campaign through notices in newspapers, programmes on television and radio and distribution of handbills.

— The first mass-contact programme 'Registration of tubewells/ borewells' was started in June' 1998 by setting up seven temporary camp offices in different parts of Delhi. About 24,545 ground water structures were registered in Delhi.

— Inventory of ground water structures was prepared in Najafgarh block of Delhi. More than 10,000 ground water structures were registered in this block.

— Microlevel surveys have been planned in vulnerable areas which include Najafgarh Block of Delhi, Fariclabad city, NOIDA, Gurgaon district, Ludhiana district, Diu and Pondicherry Union Territories.

— Central Ground Water Authority through CGWB and in collaboration with CPCB, organised ground water sampling in 300 different locations and identified areas where ground water was contaminated by concentrations of fluoride, nitrate and heavy metal in Delhi.

— The Authority has also conducted a special survey to assess the quality of ground water below Yamuna flood plain to see the risk factor of damage to ground water aquifer of Yamuna flood plains due to contaminated water of Yamuna.

— Central Ground Water Authority has notified Najafgarh Block of Delhi, Municipal Corporation area of Faridabad and Ballabgarh, Ludhiana City, Punjab and Diu Union Territory for prohibition and restriction of construction of any new ground water structure without the prior permission of the Authority.

— Public mass awareness functions were held in Najafgarh Block, Delhi, Faridabad city, Haryana and Ludhiana City, Punjab.

— Central Ground Water Authority is registering drilling companies which are in the business of drilling/constructing water wells.

— Draft of 'Environment Protection Rules for the Development and protection of Ground water' were circulated to all the States for their views/ comments.

Action to be taken

— The following action has been planned by Authority to be taken by end of March, 1999 to regulate over development and pollution of ground water resource:

— To notify Mehsana district, Gujarat; Gurgaon district, Haryana; Haldia and adjoining districts, West Bengal; Salem, Tamilnadu; Kanpur and NOIDA, Uttar Pradesh and Union Territory of Pondicherry.

— Arrangement of public mass awareness functions at Ludhiana, Gurgaon, Pondicherry, NOIDA Mehsana and Hadlia and adjoining districts of West Bengal.

— Completion of Registration of Ground Water abstraction structures at Delhi, Faridabad and Union Territory of Diu.

— Starting of Registration of Ground Water abstraction structures at Ludhiana city.

— Computerised database of ground water information for Delhi.

— Directives to industries/mining/commercial establishments for regulation of over-withdrawal of ground water in ground water vulnerable areas.

— Environmental impact analysis of industrial effluents on ground water regime in Faridabad.

— Preparation of material for public awareness for remedial procedures for contaminated and polluted ground water.

— Preparation of documentary film covering problems of decline and pollution of ground water in the areas notified by CGWA to create mass awareness about these problems.

Rajiv Gandhi National Ground Water Research and Training Institute, Raipur (Madhya Pradesh)

The Rajiv Gandhi National Ground Water Research and Training Institute (RGNGWR & TI) started functioning from Raipur (Madhya Pradesh) in May 1996. The construction of new Institute Building by NPCC Ltd. has been completed during this year.

It will be a premier institution for training of all the persons working in the field of ground water development and management and will also be a centre of research in this area.

Geographical studies

As an integral part of its activities, the Board undertakes

geophysical studies to support and supplement hydrogeological surveys, ground water exploration and short-term water supply investigations. Geophysical techniques are also employed to demarcate bedrock configuration, thickness of overburden and saline-fresh water interface. Central Geophysical cell, located at Faridabad, is entrusted with planning and programming of geophysical activities, acquisition and maintenance of equipment, organising geophysical training programmes and providing guidance in the filed surveys. A report on Geophysical investigation to demarcate the fresh and saline water interface of ground water along Najafgarh drain, New Delhi was issued by CGWB.

Short term water supply investigation

These investigations are carried out for locating sites for ground water structures and designing of tubewells and water lifting devices to provide a dependable water supply system in rural and urban areas, railway and industrial establishments with priority being given to Defence Organisations. During 1997-98, 223 short term investigations were carried out. During 1998-99, (up to November, 1998) 89 such investigations have been conducted.

Data storage and retrieval

The Central Ground Water Board and the State Ground Water organisations are collecting data on various aspects of investigation, development and management of ground water. The task of developing programmes required for handling of data with the use of computers and microprocessors has been initiated in the Board. The data of ground water levels from the Hydrograph Network Stations has been computersied. Storing of data of water quality and updating of personnel monitoring system have also been completed.

During 1998-99, a Local Area Network (LAN) is being established at the headquarters at Faridabad. Network nodes are being provided to all the sections. The Board is developing the required software. Pentium computers along With MS Office software have also been provided to the Regional, Divisional and Unit Offices of the Board.

Mathematical modelling studies

The Central Ground Water Board has conducted various studies on groundwater modelling. During 199798, mathematical model for part of Kachchh district was developed to simulate the aquifer and projections of water levels up to AD 2010 under various development options. The area simulated is 1000 Sq. Km around Anjar, Kachchh district of Gujarat. Data Collection, processing and calibration of the model has been completed. The validation and strategy generation for various development options has been at tempted on a trial basis. The modelling work is in progress.

BHUJAL NEWS

The Board publishes a quarterly journal, 'BHUJAL NEWS'. A number of scientific papers on relevant matters were contributed by scientists of CGWB and from other organisations. The journal contains various technical notes, news items, list of published papers and unpublished reports of the Board.

Application of remote sensing and GIS techniques to ground water studies

The real time use of satellite data from the Indian Remote Sensing Satellite and other satellites and aerial data and application of geographic information system being made by the Board for research and investigation for Ground Water have proved very useful. During 1997-98, Remote Sensing Studies in support of reappraisal hydrogeological surveys, ground water exploration and conjunctive use have been conducted by the Board in each Region. The exploratory sites have been selected in many districts with the help of remote sensing studies. The imageries for Kosi Canal Command area were visually interpreted and various hydrogeomorphic and hydrologic features have been delineated, based on the remote sensing studies. The areas for environmental studies in parts of Coimbatore and Erode district were identified for mapping of the protection zone of ground water depletion and pollution in Tamil Nạdu. Based on the aerial photo interpretation, hydrogeological, geomorphological and other structural features like lineaments were marked in Nanded and Akola districts and tentative sites for exploratory drilling were selected. Lineament map of Uts and Dadra and Nagar Haveli was made based on aerial photo interpretation or the preparation of hydrogeological atlas.

During 1998-99, (up to November, 1998) Remote Sensing Studies were taken up for demarcation of lineament to locate suitable sites for exploratory drilling in parts of Bhilwara district of Rajasthan, preparation of hydrogeological map in parts of Bardhman and Birbhum districts of West Bengal, mapping of protection zones of depletion of ground water and pollution for environmental studies in critical areas of Punjab. Image interpretation for hydrogeological mapping of Jalaun district of Uttar Pradesh state is under progress.

Ground water pollution studies

There has been considerable adverse impact on the quality of ground water due to the use of pesticides and fertilizers in agriculture and also due to industrial and urban wastes. Studies to monitor the effects of disposl of wastes on ground water regime are being carried out by the Board every year in different parts of the Country.

During 1998-99 (up to November, 1998) the ground water pollution studies have been completed in Lucknow, Allahabad and Varanasi districts of U.P. The studies of industrial wastes in Betwa river in Mandeep area of Raisen district of M. P., Asansol-Durgapur industrial belt of West Bengal, Digboi and Tinsukia of Assam and Jodhpur town in Rajasthan are under progress.

Studies on conjunctive use of water

Conjunctive use of surface and ground water is an essential aspect of developing ground water on sustainable basis. The Board has been taking up such studies regularly with the objective of ascertaining the hydrogeological conditions in the command areas to identify the areas affected by waterlogging and salinity, to assess the availability of ground water and to formulate action plans for co-ordinated use of surface and ground water. The Board has so far taken up such studies in ten major irrigation projects which are Sarda Sahayak Canal Command, Tungabhadra Canal Command, Hirakud Canal Command, Indira Gandhi Nehar Pariyojana (Stage I), Mahi Kadana Command, Nagarjuna Sagar Project, Indira Gandhi Nahar Pariyojana-II, Kosi Canal Command Area and Gandak Canal Command.

Progressive use of Hindi

Continued efforts are being made by the Central Ground Water Board for the promotion of progressive use of Hindi, which include compliance of Official Language Act, 1963, sending quarterly progress reports, holding of meetings of Official language Implementation Committee and imparting training to typists/ stenographers regularly. There is a scheme in force to encourage the use of Hindi in Official work. Hindi workshops were organised in the office. During the year 1998-99, Hindi books costing Rs. 18437.00 was purchased. Hindi Week was organised in Central Ground Water Board Office at Faridabad. On this Occasion Hindi essay, noting and drafting, Hindi stenography, Hindi typing and quiz competitions were organised. First, second and third winners in these competitions were given cash awards and certificates.

Central soil and materials research station

The Central Soil and Materials Research Station (CSMRS), New Delhi deals with field exploration/ laboratory investigations and basic and applied research in the field of geomechanics and construction materials concerning river valley projects. The Research Station primarily function as an advisor and consultant to various departments of the Government of India, State Governments and Government of India Undertakings. Broadly, the sphere of CSMRS activities is covered under the following three main disciplines:

— Soil Mechanics and Foundation Engineering including Soil Dynamics, Geotextiles, Technology and Soil Chemistry.

— Rock Mechanics including Instrumentation, Engineering Geophysics and Drilling Technology for Sub-surface Characterisation.

— Construction Materials and Concrete Technology including Chemistry of Concrete and Grout Technology.

Beginning as a Directorate of the erstwhile Central Water and Power Commission in 195 4, the CSMRS has today a staff of trained Engineers and Scientists specialising in the above fields. Further, the Research Station has been involved in the safety evaluation of existing hydraulic structures and quality control of construction works in various civil engineering structures in river valley projects. The CSMRS has also rendered consultancy for projects in the neighbouring and middle-east countries like Burma, Sri Lanka, Afghanistan, Bangladesh, Nepal, Bhutan, Iraq, Algeria etc. In addition, personnel from foreign countries have been trained in CSMRS in geomechanics and construction materials characterisation for civil engineering structures connected with river valley projects.

Technical activities during 1998-99

During 1998-99, investigations of a number of river valley projects were taken up and completed successfully. The Research Station also carried out a number of problem oriented applied research schemes. A number of training courses for scientists of State Governments and organisations of the Central Government were organised in geomechanics and characterisation of construction materials for river valley projects and connected civil engineering structures.

Client sponsored works

Investigation for as many as 61 river valley projects and other civil engineering structures have been handled successfully particularly for characterisation of foundation and borrow area materials. A large number of laboratory tests have been conducted for these by utilising the upgraded testing facilities and specialisation acquired through various UNDP assisted programmes. Based on an in-depth analysis of these tests, 51 detailed technical reports were finalised and forwarded to the respective project authorities.

Self sponsored basic/applied research works

The following self-sponsored basic and applied research works have been taken up/ continued:

— Prediction of Strength Characteristics of Soils Under Different Stress-Path Conditions.

— Strength Characteristics of Rockfill Materials Using Large Size Direct Shear Box.

— Effect of Fineness on Liquefaction Potential of Soils.

— Prediction of Consolidation Characteristics of Fine Grained Soils.

— Study of Filter Design Giteria.

— Characterisation of Rock fill Materials.

— Study on Dispersive Soils.

— Characterisation of Swelling Soils and Remedial Measures.

— Alkali Silica Reaction in Strained Quartz Bearing Aggregates.

— Development of Advanced Chemical method for Characterisation of Aggregates for Alkali Silica Reaction.

— Correlation between Compressive Strength and Ultrasonic Pulse Velocity Values of Concrete Cubes for Different Grades of Concrete.

— Preparation of State-of-the-Art Report of " Experimentation for Determination of Creep of Concrete".

— Updating the report on "Fibre Reinforced Shotcrete".

— Behaviour of Concrete Under Multiaxial States of Stress.

— Cation absorption capacity of Fly ash.

— Effect of P^H Value on Shear Strength of Black Cotton Soils.

— Silica Fumes/Micro Silica for High Strength/ Performance of Concrete.

— Role of Flyash in Minimising Corrosion in RCC Structures.

— FEM Analysis of Geotechnical Problems in River Valley Projects in the Himalayan Region.

— Rock Mass Classification Based on Physical Properties: Pwave, S wave and Resistivity.

— Correlation Between Uniaxial Compressive Strength and Point Load Strength Index.

— Interpretation of In-situ Stresses and Deformability Characteristics of Rock mass, Stress-Strain and Strength Characteristics of Rock Cores.

Significant achievements

Hot water spring at Nathpa Jhakri project, H.P.

A 27.3 km long Head Race Tunnel is under construction for generation of 1500 MW power at Jhakri. The ongoing tunnelling work has been hampered due to the presence of hot water seeping through 2.8 km long stretch from Wadal Portal. It is proposed to provide a 15 cm thick concrete liner along the inner face of the tunnel. Since the temperature is as high as 65 degree C, durability of the concrete liner is of utmost concern. After visiting the site by the senior officers of CSMRS, it was recommended to use Portland Slag Cement with a blend of 50/50 of slag and ordinary Portland cement. This recommendation has been adopted by the project authorities.

Bethali irrigation dam project, Rajasthan

The project envisages the construction of 18.75 m high and 2.79 km long earth-cum-masonry dam across the Bethali river. The main object of this project is to provide irrigation to an area of 43 16 ha. CSMRS carried out field and laboratory geotechnical investigations and collected undisturbed samples from different depths of the critical section along the dam axis and conducted the confirmatory tests. Based on the findings, it is inferred that the constructed dam section is safe.

Manas-sankosh-teesta link canal project

The proposed Manas-Sankosh Link Canal is a components of Manas-Sankosh-Teesta Ganga Link which envisages diversion of surplus water from the Manas-Sankosh river and intermediate major streams between Manas and Teesta like Ale, Rydonk, Torsen and Jaldhaka rivers. The work of field and laboratory geotechnical investigation of Manas-Sankosh Teesta Link Canal Project, West Bengal from Manas to Teesta was taken up. The present investigations were carried between RD 46 km to RD 118. 10 km for the characterisation of foundation and overburden materials. In situ permeability test was conducted. Various undisturbed and representative bulk soil samples were collected and tested in the laboratory. Based on the limited field and laboratory investigations, it was recommended that the foundation strata had to be treated by grouting, densification etc. so as to improve the impermeability of the strata.

Tala H.E. project, Bhutan

Geotechnical investigaitons for characterising foundation materials and evaluation of safe bearing capacity of various structures under construction viz. School Building, Administrative Building, General Manager/ Chief Engineer's residence, field hostel, staff quarters besides roads and bridges were undertaken. The investigations were carried on time bound and priority basis by deploying CSMRS' Mobile Field Laboratory at site. After completing field and laboratory investigation work, feasibility report was finalised at the site itself and handed over to the project authorities. This report includes computation of safe bearing capacity of foundation soil/ rock based on settlement criteria for the above structures for square, rectangular and raft footings. The project authorities were advised to adopt appropriate footings as per the requirement of safe soil pressure for the respective structures under reference.

Research/technical papers published during 1998-99

Fifty two research/technical papers were published in various journals and other publications by CSMRS.

Best Paper award was given to CSMRS in the seminar on High Performance Concrete (1998) held at Chennai organised by International Centre for Fibre Reinforced Concrete Composites (ICFRC) for the paper "Roller Compacted Concrete for Dam Construction - An Economically and Eco-friendly Alternative for Indian Conditions" authored by Rosy Ahuja, ARO, Chandrasekaran, CRO and Dr. K. Venkatachalam, Director.

IGS Best paper award on "Innovation in the field exploration" held at Chennai, organised by Indian Geotechnical Society for the Paper "Characterisation of Soil by Seismic Cone Penetration Test" authored by A. Roy, CRO and Dr. K. Venkatachalam, Director, CSMRS was also bagged by CSMRS.

CSMRS-NGI institutional co-operation programme

The Central Soil U Materials Research Station (CSMRS) and the Norwegian Geotechnical Institute (NGO have entered into an agreement for Institutional Co-operation Programme in the field of Environmental Geotechnology for a period of 3 years starting from April, 1997. The main emphasis in the Institutional Co-operation programme is on characterisation of landslides affecting water resources development projects.

Senior officers of CSMRS and Consultants from Norwegian Geotechnical Institute Visited the landslide prone areas in Gangtok, Sikkim and finalised the locations for installation of peizometers and also for construction of reference/ settlement blocks. An half-day workshop on landslides was also organised at Gangtok for the benefit of the irrigation engineers of Government of Sikkim.

Indian National Committees

There are two Committees Indian National Committee on Pock Mechanics and Tunnelling Technology (INCRMTT) and Indian National Committee on Construction Materials and Structures (INCCMS), which are the funding agencies for carrying out basic and applied research in the fields of :

- — Rock Mechanics and Tunnelling Technology
- — Soil Mechanics and Foundation Engineering
- — Construction Materials and Structures by providing financial support to various research/ educational institutions.

These two Committees have funded 41 and 18 projects for which Rs. 346.918 lakh and Rs. 169.334 lakh, respectively have been sanctioned.

Vigilance activities

During the year 1998-99, no departmental action has been initiated for minor/ major penalty against Group A, B, C & D officers of CSMRS. Major penalty proceedings initiated against 5 Group "B" officers and one Group "'C" official during the previous year remained under various stages of processing.

Progressive use of Hindi

Central Soil and Materials Research Station continued the implementation of the provisions of the Official Language Policy and rules, and the Official Language Act. A Hindi Pakhwara was organised from 1. 9.1998 to

15. 9.1998 to create consciousness amongst the staff and thus accelerate the use of Hindi as Official language. A half-day Hindi workshop on the use of Hindi in the day to day technical activities of the research station was organised. Annual Reports/ Newsletters were also published in English as well as in Hindi.

Central Water and Power Research Station

Central Water and Power Research Station (CWPRS) offers comprehensive R&D support to a variety of projects in the areas of development of water and energy resources and water-borne transport. The UNDP aid delivered through projects in selected disciplines such as ship hydrodynamics, photoelasticity, hydro-machinery, coastal engineering, hydraulic instrumentation, earth sciences, hydraulic structures and information technology, over the last four decades, has brought the Research Station at par with the leading hydraulic laboratories of the world. The infrastructure developed With these inputs over the successive Five Year Plans paved the way for further assistance by the UNDP in the areas of 'Mathematical Modelling of Fluvial and Ocean Hydromechanics' and 'Automated Operation of irrigation Canal Systems'.

CWPRS was recognised as the Regional Laboratory for the ESCAP in 1971. Nearly 90 per cent of the research effort is currently devoted to the study of government financed projects executed through various Central and State agencies. The capability of the Research Station has enhanced since then in the areas of thermal modelling, computational hydraulics, remote sensing, hydraulic instrumentation and field investigations.

During the year 1998-99 the Research Station has a target of recovery of about 450 lakh out of its non-plan expenditure of Rs. 1471 lakh through client sponsored applied studies.

Activities under plan projects comprise execution of five on going schemes, some of which are in advanced stage of completion. The total revised plan outlay for the year 1998-99 is Rs. 341 lakh, which includes Rs. 32 lakh towards transfer of title of equipment acquired through UN aided projects.

Research and development activities

Important R&D projects undertaken during the yea are as under:-

Hydrology and water resources analysis

The Hydrology and Water Resources Analysis Laboratory undertakes various water resources management studies such as those relating to simulation of probable maximum flood discharge, estimation of the flood levels, routing of the floods and reservoir operations, dam break flood analysis, design of the storm water drainage systems with the help of mathematical models, reservoir sedimentation, river channelisation,, back water effects, optimisation of water- resources utilisation, estimation of seepage, development of decision support systems, automated operation of irrigation canals, etc.

The important activities during the year are:

- Surface Water Resources studies for Markandeya river.
- Field measurements to study recirculation of hot water and vitiated water at intake of Kakrapar Atomic Power Station.
- Hydrologic and Hydraulic Routing Studies for NTPC Area of Simhadri Thermal Power Station, Andhra Pradesh.

River engineering

River Engineering Laboratory is responsible for studies

relating to flood protection works, bank protection measures, coffer dams and diversion works, barrages and weirs, bridge design, sediment control and exclusion devices, siting of cooling water intakes, vortex prevention at intakes, design of canals and canal structures, flood routing and flood forecasting, studies on transportation of river detritus and transportation of solids in conduits.

The important activities during the year are:

— Short term measures for the protection of left bank of Pavana river near Chinchwad, Pune, Maharashtra.

— Field studies for rating of Tungabhadra Right Bank Low level canal at KM251/8 50, Tungabhadra dam, Karnataka.

— Additional morphological studies for river Brahmaputra and Jinjiram at Phulbari town, Meghalaya for evolving training measures.

— Desk studies for raw water intake in river Kharsua for Neelachal Ispat Nigam Ltd. Duburi, Orissa.

— Hydraulic model studies for evolving Anti- erosion measures for the banks of river Brahmaputra at Gomi-Alikash Area.

— Model studies for evolving bank protection measures at Oakland-Nagaghuli-Maijan area up stream of Dibrugarh town along the left bank of river Brahmaputra.

— Model studies for protection of Gouranga setu near Nabadwip, West Bengal.

— Model studies for improving flow condition u/s of Farakka barrage by activating new channels developed near Bhutani Diara island and d/s of Rajmahal

— Studies for determination of schedule of Gate of Farakka Barrage during low flows.

— Morphological studies for training the river Sabarmati to stabilise its existing course at Golana, Gujarat.

Reservoir and appurtenant structures

Reservoir and Appurtenant Structures laboratory is responsible for efficient hydraulic designs of spillways, gates, water conducting systems and other structures appurtenant to dams and reservoirs; crest and spillway profiles, energy dissipators, protection works, high head gates, sluices and outlets, surge tanks, tunnels, penstocks and galleries, intake for pumps and power plants.

The important activities during the year are:

— Hydraulic model studies for the intake structure at Mhaisal, Stage 1 and at Takari, Stage 1 (Krishna Koyna Lift Irrigation Scheme, Maharashtra).

— Mathematical model studies of hydraulic transients in head race surge system of Koyna Hydro Electric Project, Stage - IV, Maharashtra.

— Model and Prototype studies in respect of Air demand, Hydrodynamic forces on the gate of River Sluice, Sardar Sarovar Project, Gujarat.

— Hydraulic model studies for double lake tappings, Koyna H.E. Project.

— Hydraulic model studies for irrigation sluice gates and airvents, Bansagar dam project, Madhya Pradesh.

— Hydraulic model studies with lowered stilling basin for Kurichu dam spillway, Bhutan.

— Studies for extension of right training wall of service spillway, Sardar Sarovar Project, Gujarat.

— Hydraulic model studies for downstream intake structure of Srisailam left bank H. E. Project, Andhra Pradesh.

— Hydraulic model studies for temporary crest profiles for the construction stage of Sardar Sarovar dam spillway, Gujarat.

— Hydraulic model studies for revised design of sluices and central overflow spillway, Nathpa Jhakri H.E. Project, Himachal Pradesh.

— Desk studies for Hydraulic Design of Spillway of Lower Mullamari Project, Karnataka.

Coastal and offshore engineering

The activities of the Offshore Engineering Group encompass: Design of ports and harbours; Design of maritime and off-shore structures including coastal protection works; Training of estuaries and tidal rivers; Evaluation of the effect of thermal discharge into the marine environment; Water quality and pollution, due to waste disposal; Inland water transport; Field data collection; Study of hulls and propellers, calibration of current meters; Navigation studies; Assessment of forces in mooring lines.

The important activities during the year are:

— Physical model studies for leading jetty and mathematical model studies for extension of port facilities at Pipavav port for M/s Gujarat Pipavav Port Ltd.

— Flow model studies for examining the effects on flow conditions due to tankers at virtual oil jetties of M/s IOCL and M/s HPCL and permanent jetties of M/s IFFCO and fourth oil berth of Kandla Port.

— Final technical report on depth studies for anti-sea erosion work: along North Chennai Coast.

— Mathematical model studies for training works of river inlet at Ponnani for fisheries and port development.

— Model studies for wet basin project at Mazagon Dock, Mumbai.

— Assessment of the effect of Farakka Barrage Water releases on the river Hugli - Bhagirathi from 1975 to 1994.

— Tranquility studies for the proposed extension of General Cargo berth in Visakhapatnam outer harbour.

— Hydraulic model studies for extension of Kandla Port jetty at Vadinar in Pathfinder creek.

— Water quality analysis for Kali river from Bommanhalli pickup dam, Karnataka.

— I -D Mathematical model studies to assess the effect of reduction in fresh water discharges on salinity intrusion in the river Hugli.

— Model studies for proposed cement jetty in Dharamtar creek by M/s Indo Rama Cement Ltd., Mumbai.

— Interim report on Hydraulic model studies for additional facilities at Mormugao port.

— Wave model studies to assess wave tranquility at the proposed LPG Jetty in Beypore port.

— I-D Mathematical model studies for development of reclamation of Mormugao port in Zuari-Cumbarjua estuary at Goa.

— Interim report on studies for hydraulic aspects for cofferdam in Mormugao bay for offshore stockyard berth of M/s MML.

— Hydraulic model studies for near field dilution aspects of Trans Thane Creek (TTC) Outfall, Mumbai.

— Field data collection and desk studies to examine coastal morphological changes in Muldwarka.

— Determination of wind and wave conditions and storm surge analysis for the cyclone of June, 1998 at the site of Sikka, Jamnagar.

— Hydraulic model studies for the proposed extension of existing rock bund for the development of Catamaran beach at the north side of fisheries harbour at Visakhapatnam.

— Wave flume studies for the design of island type breakwater at Tuticorin Port, Tamilnadu.

Hydraulic machinery

Hydraulic Machinery Laboratory caters to contractual tests on turbines, pumps (including submersible pumps), calibration of flow measuring devices etc. Measurement of critical performance parameters of large hydromachines like efficiency, flow rate etc. in the field. Evolution of remedial measures to mitigate operational problems of large hydromachines. Evolution of operational designs of pumping systems inclusive of remedial measures to mitigate water hammer in pumping mains. Evolution of hydraulic designs of pump intakes for thermal and nuclear power stations, large water supply systems, lift irrigation schemes etc.

The main activities during the year are:

— Desk studies for raw water intake in river Kharsua for Neelachal Ispat Nigam Ltd. Duburi, Orissa.

— Hydraulic model studies for pump sump of Takari State 1, Krishna Koyna Lift irrigation scheme, Maharashtra.

— Advice on selection of Anti-Surge Devices for Stage I and II Takari Lift Irrigation Scheme, Maharashtra.

Earth sciences

The Applied Earth Sciences Laboratory undertakes various studies involving different disciplines like Hydrogeology, Tracer Hydrology, Vibration Technology, Earthquake Engineering Research and Geophysics.

The important activities during the year are:

— Underwater seismic reflection survey for alpine industries at Okha, Saurashtra, Gujarat.

— Hydrogeological investigations in saddles 1 and 3 of Som-Kamla-Amba Project dam site, Aspur, Rajasthan

— Controlled Blast studies carried out during excavation of right bank canal for Karanja Project, Karnataka.

— Seismic Qualification tests on UPS manufactured by M/s. D.B. Power Electronics Ltd., Pune (Maharashtra).

— Underwater seismic reflection survey from Nariman point to Chowpaty, Mumbai.

— An Interim Note on Hydrogeological studies carried out for Augmentation of water supply at INS MANDOVI, Goa.

— Delineation of cavities and path of seepage at bay No. 1 of Ralli arm of Sir Arthur Cotton Barrage, Dowlaiwarm, A.P.

— Exploratory resonance search studies for a butterfly valve and actuator assembly from M/s Intervalve (India) Ltd., Pune.

— A report on controlled blast studies for Pentakali Project, Buldana, Maharashtra.

— A report on seismological studies at Almatti project (Karnataka State) for the period from 1. 1. 1990 to 31.12.1995.

— Interim report on underwater seismic reflection survey for Maroli port at Umargaon, Gujarat

— Evaluation of design seismic parameters for Tungabhadra Dam, Karnataka.

— Evaluation of site specific design earthquake ground motion for Teesta Hydel project, Stage VI, Sikkim.

— Interim report on ground water exploration carried out in two phases for Usha Ispat Ltd., Sawantwadi, Dist. Sindhudurg, Maharashtra.

Instrumentation and control engineering

Scientific analysis of natural processes, in nature or in the laboratory under simulated conditions, requires observation of various parameters of interest byway of measurements. The instrumentation and Control Engineering Laboratory at CWPRS is responsible for providing instruments for measurement of various hydraulic parameters data acquisition, analysis and control systems.

The Laboratory has equipped itself with sophisticated systems for measurement, data acquisition and analysis. The Laboratory undertakes field observations and data collection in these areas to provide essential and reliable data for use in physical/ mathematical models.

Mathematical modelling

Mathematical model studies for:

— Navigational aspects and assessment of maintenance dredging for development facilities at Kharo creek for M/s Sanghi Industries Ltd.

— Tidal current and siltation for development of ail weather port at Alewadi Dist. Thane Maharashtra.

— Evaluation of wave climate for development of landing facilities on the eastern side of Agatti, mini Chetlat Kadamat and Miltan Islands Lakshadweep.

— Wave tranquillity with the proposed island breakwater at Paradip Port, Orissa.

— Disposal of excess sea water from combined cycle power project of M/s L&T at Kovaya.

— Assessing the effect of proposed channel on flow circulation and salinity in Chilika Lake, Orissa.

— Hydrodynamic and siltation aspects for Beypore port, Kerala.

— Cooling Water discharge channel for Trombay Thermal Power Station.

— Wave tranquillity for development of an oil/ gas terminal at Tuticorin Port.

— Ship manoeuvring at the direct landing facility at Kavarathi, Lakshadweep.

— Outfall system of desalination plant at Kovaya near Pipavav port for M/s L&T.

— Hydrodynamic and siltation aspects for Beypore Port, Kerala.

— Determination of wave climate and orientation of jetty off Nagapattinam, Tamilnadu for M/s Madras Pefineries Ltd.

— Wave tranquillity for optimisation of harbour layout at Vadodara creek near Veraval, Gujarat for M/s Gujarat Sidhee Cement Ltd.

- Predicting Littoral Drift and Shoreline changes as a result of proposed port development at Beypore, Kerala.
- Deciding dredging strategy at IPCL jetty at Jageshwar for Improvement of Depth.
- Foundations and structures
- The Foundation Structures Group consists of six visions namely:
- Photoelasticity Division
- Model Engineering Division
- Rock Mechanics Division
- Soil and Concrete Division
- Hydraulic Structures Research Division
- Mathematics Division

The group undertakes model and prototype studies relating to foundation structural problems of dams, powerhouses, water conductor system, bridges, aqueducts, surge shafts, tunnels and rehabilitation of structures of national importance.

The important activities during the year are:

- Dynamic analysis for Tansa dam, Maharashtra.
- Crack monitoring studies of Hirakud Dam, Orissa.
- Evaluation of Design soil Parameters and Dynamic analysis of Jhuj Earthen Dam, Gujarat.
- Studies on sealing system API Sub & injecting system Adesivo HM sub referred by M/s Dr. Beck& Company, Pune to evaluate their suitability for underwater application.
- Rock mass characterisation - A geological appraisal

of rocks encountered in the excavation of Jewargi Branch Canal, Karnataka.

— Dynamic analysis of Warna masonry dam, Maharashtra.

— Studies for the evaluation of creep rate of mass concrete for Indira Sagar Dam, Madhya Pradesh.

— Rehabilitation of the distressed floor beams in the power house using epoxy compounds, Upper Indravati Hydroelectric Project, Orissa.

— Strengthening of scroll case and draft tube of four turbine units by epoxy grouting, Upper Indravati Hydroelectric Project, Orissa.

— Investigation on first span of Ralli Arm of Sir Arthur Cotton Barrage at Dowlaiswaram, Andhra Pradesh.

— Engineering properties of rock core samples from pressure shafts, Indira Sagar Project, Madhya Pradesh.

— Engineering properties of rock core samples from the dyke wan dam, Maharashtra.

— Assessment of the strength of the Distressed Beams in the Power house of Upper Indravati H. E. Project, Orissa by load test.

— Geological Appraisal and Pock Mass Characterisation in the excavation of Jewargi Branch Canal (Km 20 to Km 40), Karnataka.

Water and power information system

Water and Power Information System caters to collection, storage, analysis and retrieval of information in the broad areas of Water and Power.

United nations development programme schemes

Mathematical modelling centre for fluvial and ocean

hydromechanics

The UNDP assisted project of Mathematical Modelling Centre for Fluvial and Ocean Hydromechanics was executed at CWPRS during December, 1990 to June, 1997. Under this project~ the infrastructure for mathematical modelling in terms of hardware, software, field equipment for collection of prototype data and trained manpower were created at CWPRS. Due to this project, capability has been developed at CWPRS for solving different types of problems encountered in the area of Over engineering, port and harbour development, coastal zone management etc. using mathematical modelling techniques. This project was completed on June 30, 1997.

Automated operation of irrigation canal systems

— Baseline survey work was awarded to M/s Progressive Ptesearch Aids Pvt. Ltd., Pune.

— There are in all 3 5 distributaries in Chambal Division II covering 269 villages. Forty four villages catered by 11 distributaries were selected in the sample. Ten farmers and 3 landless labourers were selected from each village using systematic rand m sampling methods. Thus data on the following aspects were collected from 438 farmers and 123 landless labourers.

— Water delivery

— Efficiency of irrigation

— Operation of Irrigation canal system

— Agricultural pattern

— Socioeconomic conditions of the farmers

— Socioeconomic conditions of the labourers.

The work on Baseline survey was completed and the

draft final report had been submitted. It was reviewed and detailed discussions were held.

Construction of flumes at two sites in Sabalgarh Division has been completed for distributary flow measurement. A team of CWPRS engineers visited Chambal Canal site In April 1998. During the visit, water level and discharge data were collected for the last irrigation season. Uninterrupted Power Supply (UPS) system was Installed at the base station at Sabalgarh (M.P.).

Vigilance activities

In all, there were seventeen disciplinary cases and two vigilance cases against Group 'B', 'C' and 'D' employees. Out of these, three cases have been disposed off by awarding major penalties by disciplinary authority. In three cases, inquiry has been concluded and the inquiry reports are under consideration by the disciplinary authority.

Regular inspections are being carried out from time to time from vigilance angle. During the period April to October, 1998, six complaints in respect of Group A officers and one complaint in respect of Group B officer were received and investigated.

Use of Hindi

A programme of Hindi Kavi Sammelan was organised at CWPRS in March, 4 998. The fourth issue of the yearly Hindi Home Magazine "JALWANI" was published on this occasion. Articles of technical and nontechnical nature and other information of interest contributed by the staff-members have been included in this magazine. Summaries of 48 technical reports have been prepared in Hindi for inclusion in the forthcoming issue of Annual report of CWPRS. Four quarterly meetings of the Official Language Implementation Committee of CWPRS have been held during the period under report. A Hindi publication titled as "Nadi Abhiyantriki Patrika" covering technical articles based on the ongoing and completed technical assignments was brought out Two Hindi Workshops were also organised.

"Rajbhasha Protsahan Chal Shield' introduced by CWPRS for its technical divisions was awarded to the ""Hydraulic Analysis and Prototype Testing" Division based on the use of Hindi and participation in the activities concerning Hindi. CWPRS secured the second position and bagged the prestigious "'Chal Vaijayanti" Trophy of the Ministry of Water Resources for promoting the use of Hindi in official work during the year 1997-98.

Farakka barrage project

The Farakka Barrage Project is a subordinate office of the Ministry of Water Resources and is headed by a General Manager. The headquarters of the Project is at Farakka in West Bengal.

The Farakka Barrage Project is designed to serve the need of preservation and maintenance of Calcutta Port by improving the regime and navigability of the Bhagirathi-Hoogly river system. The increased upland supplies from Ganga at Farakka into Bhagirathi will also reduce salinity in the system and will ensure sweet water supply to Calcutta and surrounding areas.

The rail-cum-road bridge built across the river Ganga at Farakka establishes direct road and rail communication link to the North-Eastern States. The Bhagirathi, the Feeder Canal and the Navigation Lock at Farakka form part of the Haldia-Allahabad Inland Waterway (National Water Way No. 1). The principal components of the Project are:

— A 2245 metre long banrage across the River Ganga with rail-cum-road bridge, necessary river training works and a head Regulator on the right side.

— A 213 metre long barrage across the River Bhagirathi at Jangipur.

— Feeder Canal of 1133 cumec (4000 cusec) carrying capacity and 38.38 Km long, taken off the head regulator on the right of the Farakka Barrage.

— Navigation works such as Locks, Lock Channels, Shelter basin's; Control tower building, navigational lights and other infrastructure.

Progress of works

All the principal works connected with the two Barrages and Feeder Canal have been completed. The Farakka Barrage was inaugurated in 1975. Ancillary works like bridge at RD-29.50 of Feeder Canal, installation of lock gates at Kalindri etc., are in progress. The Farakka Barrage with rail-cum-road bridge over It has provided a communication link between North Bengal, North-Eastern States, Sikkim and Bhutan with the rest of the country.

The navigation lock at Farakka was substantially completed and Inugurated in November, 1987. The Navigation Control Tower has also been completed during 1996. This has opened a new era of inland navigation on the Haldia-Allahabad inland waterway (National Water Way No. 1). The navigation lock at Jangipur has been completed substantially except for some navigation aids and equipment.

The works like Road Bridge at RD.29.50 of Feeder Canal, permanent establishment and special repair works of residential and nonresidential buildings, roads, water supply, sanitation etc., of Farakka Barrage colonies at Farakka, Khejuriaghat and Ahiran, Kalindri, etc. continued during the year.

Special repair of head regulator and main barrage gates

Repair/rectification of eleven gates of Head Regulator gates including hoists, gantry crane, etc., were substantially completed at a cost of Rs. 2.45 crore.

Repair/rectification works of spillway gates, under sluice/river sluice gates, fish lock gates, gantry cranes with gantry rail, over hoist bridge, control panels, hoist system, etc., of Farakka Barrage were awarded to M/s. N. P. C. C. Ltd., and M/s. Jessop & Co., (both Government of India undertakling) on 50:50 basis, in April 1996. Progress of rectification works is being monitored closely to ensure its completion within a reasonable time.

Project works

The bank protection works at the tight bank of River Ganga downstream of Farakka Barrage for 6.0 km are in progress and a length of 3 km has been completed. The work from 5000 m to 5300 m for protection is nearing completion. Tendering action is under process for execution of protection work of further length of 200 m from 5300 m to 5 500 m.

The protection works against bank erosion on the right bank of River Ganga along Left Afflux Bandh of Jangipur Barrage covering a length of 3.25 km out of total length of 16.3 km have been completed. During the flood of 1998 the entire river side zone was fully inundated with an average depth of two metre water flowing with high velocity. Efforts were made to check the breach in the embankment by protecting the percolation and profuse flow through rat holes. As a result the embankment was saved. Remaining reach of the Left Afflux Bund of Jangipur Barrage is under observation.

Marginal embankment of the Left bank upstream of the river Ganga from the Guide bund of Barrage up to Manikchak Ghat is about 40 Km upstream of the barrage.

Out of this, 10 Km from Guide bund is under the jurisdiction of Farakka Barrage Authority. During the flood of 1998 discharge in the River Ganga exceeded all previous records with highest discharge recorded as 26,78,781 cusecs on 7.9.98. Due to high water level and highest discharge there were chances of breach near the junction of ninth and tenth marginal embankment. But due to timely execution of emergency protective measures and round the clock watch, the breach in the marginal embankment was avoided. The marginal embankment, however, suffered severe damages at different places. Action has been initiated by Farakka Barrage to take up protective measures. For the worst affected reach of about one kilometre as per approved drawing of C.W.C.

New schemes for the ninth plan

Keeping in view the excessive bank erosion of the River Ganga in the districts of Malda and Murshidabad, the Planning Commission had set up an expert Committee under the Chairmanship of Member (River Management),Central Water Commission, which recommended long term and short term measures costing Rs. 927 crore, out of which short term measures cost Rs. 315 crore and long term measures cost Rs. 612 crore. As suggested by the expert Committee, the Farakka Barrage Project Authority has prepared an estimate amounting to Rs. 160.84 crore for the work "'And Erosion., flood protection and river training measures" and submitted the same to the Ministry for approval.

Farakka hydroelectric project

The proposed Hydro-Electric Project at Farakka Barrage involves construction of a Power Station with installed capacity of 125 MW down stream of Barrage to generate hydroelectric Power. The Project Report has been prepared by the Central Water Commission and has been techno-economically apprised by the Central Electricity Authority. It has been decided to implement this Project through private entrepreneurs; on "Build, Own and Operate" (BOO) basis. Global tenders were invited for pre-qualification of prospective developers. Three firms which have shown interest to undertake the work have yet to submit their final offers.

A special Committee for environmental assessment of Farakka Hydro-Electric Project, constituted by the Ministry of Water Resources, visited the Project site in November! 1998. After inspection of sites the Committee suggested that the present cost of the Project including funds provided for environmental aspect should be worked out and preparation of an Action Plan for a forestation programme should be taken up.

Ganga flood control commission

Functions and organisational set-up

The Ganga Flood Control Commission, a subordinate office of the Ministry of Water Resources, was established in April 1972 with its headquarters at Patna. It serves as the executive limb of the Ganga Flood Control Board, which is headed by the Union Minister of Water Resources, and acts as the Secretariat of the Board.

The Commission is headed by a Chairman who is assisted by two full time Members, four Directors and supporting staff. The representatives of the concerned Central Ministries/Departments as well as the Chief Engineers of the basin States are either part time Members or permanent invitees of the Commission. The Commission has been mainly assigned the task of preparing comprehensive plans of flood management of various river systems in the Ganga sub-basin and drawing out a phased programme of implementation of various schemes from techno-economic angle, monitoring of important flood management schemes, assessment of the adequacy of waterways existing under the road and rail bridges and providing other technical guidance to the basin States.

Achievements during the year 1998-99

The Ganga sub-basin constitutes 23 river systems. Comprehensive Plans for flood management for all the 2 3 river systems were prepared by the end of the year 1990-91. Subsequently, the work of updating of Comprehensive Plans was taken up. Up to the end of March 1998 die updating of the Comprehensive Plans for ten river systems namely, Gomati (Twice), Mahananda (Twice), Ghaghra, Adhwara Group, Kamla-Balan, Bagmati, Burhi Gandak, Kiul-Harohar, Damodar and Punpun river systems was completed.

During the year 1998-99 updating of comprehensive plans for Mayurakshi, Ramganga, Jalangi and Ghaghra river systems remained under progress and out of these two are expected to be completed by the end of the year.

Assessment of adequacy of waterways under road

The reports on adequacy of waterways under the road and rail bridges in respect of 19 river systems including Punpun, Ajoy, Burhi Gandak, Mayurakshi, Bagmati, Mahananda, Damodar, Yamuna, Jalangi, Gandak, Gomati, Ghaghra, Ramganga, Rupnarain-HaldiR.asulpur, Tons, Kamla-Balan Adhwara group of rivers, Kiul-Harohar and Badua Chandan river systems were completed by the end of March, 1998. During the year 1998-99, preparation of similar report in respect of Sone river system is in progress and is expected to be completed by the end of the year.

Monitoring of important flood management schemes

In 1997-98, eight major ongoing flood management schemes were programmed to be monitored. Out of these, monitoring reports in respect of seven schemes including (i) Buxar-Koelwar embankment scheme in Bihar (ii) Badlaghat-Nagarpara embankment scheme in Bihar (iii) Punpun right embankment scheme (phase-1) in Bihar (iv) Ghea-Kunti basin drainage scheme in West Bengal (v) Tamluk drainage scheme in W. B. (vi) Tons Advance bund in U.P. and (vii) Baidula-Lakhanpur embankment scheme in Uttar Pradesh were completed and circulated to all concerned.

During 1998-99, monitoring reports in respect of (i) Punpun right embankment scheme (ii) Buxar-Koelwar embankment scheme (iii) Badiaghat-Nagarpara embankment scheme in Bihar and (iv) Ghea-Kund drainage scheme in W.B. were completed up to November, 1998. Collection of data/ information for preparation of monitoring report for the remaining schemes are under progress.

In addition to these, flood monitoring of Ganga river system during monsoon 1998 was done and 16 weekly flood reports were submitted to the Ministry. Annual flood report for the previous year 1997 was also prepared and circulated to all concerned. A report on the annual review of projects monitored by GFCC during 1997-98 was prepared and circulated to all concerned.

Performance evaluation of flood management schemes

Performance evaluation of six completed schemes namely (i) Lakhnauti bund scheme in U.P., (ii) Dubda basin drainage scheme in West Bengal, (iii) Kamla Balan embankment scheme in Bihar, (iv) Barhya-Kotha bund in U.P., (v) Mahananda embankment scheme in Bihar and (vi) East Mograhat basin drainage scheme in West Bengal were completed by the end of 1996-97.

Performance evaluation studies for Lucknow Town protection scheme in U.P. and Mahananda embankment scheme in West Bengal were taken up during 1997-98. The work on these schemes could not be started as terms of reference were required to be revised, based on experience gained from the previous works. The terms of reference were approved by the Ministry in 1998. The work will be awarded to consultants.

Technical examination of flood management schemes

Technical examination of flood management schemes is a continuing activity of this Commission. During the year 1997-98, 48 flood management schemes and 16 flood proofing schemes were technically examined.

During the year 1998-99 (up to November, 1998), 2 5 flood management schemes have been examined and comments sent to the concerned State Governments for compliance. The target for examination of flood management schemes and flood proofing schemes during the year was 30 and 40 respectively. It is expected that five more flood management schemes and 40 flood proofing schemes will be examined during the year. The progress on examination of these schemes depends upon the flow of schemes from the State Government concerned.

Meeting for presentation of comprehensive plans prepared by GFCC

Up to the end of March 1998 the Commission had organised meetings for presentation of the main points of Comprehensive plans of flood management prepared by it to the officials of the Government and non-officials for Sone, Punpun, Mayurakshi, Jalangi, Burhi-Gandak, Bagmati, Badua-Chandan, Gomati, Kiul-Harohar, Ramganga and Ajay river systems.

During the year 1998-99, action for organising the one day meeting for presenting the plans of Damodar, Adhwara group of rivers and Ghaghra river systems has been taken and is likely to be completed by the end of the year.

Maintenance of flood protection works of Kosi and Gandak project

Two High level Committees, one for Gandak and another for Kosi flood protection works have been constituted by the Government of India and Government of Bihar respectively, under the Chairmanship of Chairman GFCC. The Committees inspects the protection works every year and makes recommendations for protection works to be carried out before the onset of the next flood season. Kosi High Level Committee inspected the Kosi protection works in November. 1998 and made recommendations for protection works to be taken up before the flood of 1999. Gandak High Level Committee also inspected Gandak river In October 1998 and finalised the recommendations for works to be taken up before the flood of 1999. The concerned State Government executes the schemes as per the recommendations made by one of the committees subject to the availability of funds.

Appreciating the difficulties of the State Government and its crippled financial position as also the international implications involved in protection of Kosi and Gandak embankments in Nepal, the Ministry of Water Resources, have agreed to reimburse the cost of maintenance of Kosi/ Gandak embankments (Nepal portion only).

Extension of embankment of rivers Bagmati, Lalbakeya, Kamla and Khando

The Joint Committee for Embankment Construction from India and Nepal was constituted in the year 1991 to finalise the project report for extension of embankment on rivers Bagmati, Lalbakeya, Kamla and Khando. The Committee has since finalised the schemes for extension of embankment on Lalbakeya, Bagmati and Kamla rivers.

GFCC examined the pre-qualification and tender documents for Lalbakeya Embankment prepared by the Government of Nepal. The documents have to be approved by the Joint Committee on Embankment Construction.

In order to take up execution of Lalbakeya embankment, Ministry of Water Resources, has accorded approval for taking up the work of raising and strengthening of the existing embankment on the River Lalbakeya (Indian territory) which are required to be taken up prior to implementing the works of extension of Lalbakeya embankment in the Nepalese territory. The scheme was examined by GFCC and prioritisation of the work components was done. Rs. 200.00 lakh is provided in the budget of Ministry of Water Resources for the year 1998-99 for this purpose.

Tying up of flood protection embankment on right bank

In order to mitigate the miseries of the people of India and Bangladesh from inundation by River Teesta, both countries decided to tie up their embankments on the right bank In their respective territories and close the 1800 metre long gap in the embankment in 1997. The Government of West Bengal took up the construction work with Central funding. GFCC inspected the works in June and November, 4998 and provided necessary recommendations regarding the progress of works to Ministry of Water Resources for consideration for release of funds.

Contribution of technical papers

GFCC also contributes technical papers. Recentlya paper on "Role of flood forecasting in reducing flood damages" was presented by Member, GFCC in the National seminar on flood disaster management organised by the Institute for Resource Management and Economic Development.

Progressive use of Hindi

During the year all possible efforts were made in the Commission for implementation of the provisions contained in the Official Language Act, 1963 and the rules made thereunder. All documents falling under Section 3(3) of the above Act were issued bilingually. Hindi Fortnight was also celebrated enthusiastically.

Vigilance/disciplinary cases

The vigilance/disciplinary cases and the complaints concerning officers and staff of GFCC received proper and prompt attention.

5

Research and Development Organisations

Nuclear tests at Pokhran

India conducted five nuclear tests during the period May 11-13, 1998 at the Pokhran range in Rajasthan desert. The first three detonations took place simultaneously at 15.45 hrs. IST, on May 11. These included a thermonuclear device, a fission device and a sub-kiloton device. The fission device was much smaller in size and weight as compared to the one used for the May 18, 1974 explosion.

The thermonuclear device had two stages, the primary stage was a fusion-boosted fission device and the secondary was a thermonuclear device. The two nuclear devices, fired on May 13 at 12.21 hrs. IST, were in the subkiloton yield range. The detonations were very successful and predictions of the yield of the three devices were very accurate. The yield of the thermonuclear device was chosen to minimise the seismic damage to surrounding villages. The depths of emplacements were fixed so that the explosions were contained with no surface radioactivity after the tests and test sites. Detailed seismic analysis using 160 global stations and close-in acceleration measurements have since been carried out which confirms the estimated combined yield of May 11 tests to be around 60 KT.

Research reactors

Research reactors Apsara and Dhruva continued to be operated for production of radioisotopes and for providing facilities for neutron beam experiments and testing of neutron in-pile detectors. Their performance at required power levels was satisfactory. After extensive ageing studies, reactor CIRUS was taken up for refurbishing to extend its useful life.

Reactor design and development

Advanced heavy water reactor (AHWR)

Design, development, analytical and experimental activities were vigorously pursued. Fuel design and experimental studies to improve fuel performance were done. The prototype 52 pin fuel cluster was installed in the Flow Test Facility at Engineering Hall 7 for pressure drop and endurance testing. Vibration measurements on dummy fuel assembly were carried out to evaluate performance during high, moderate and low flows.

Thermal hydraulic studies

Experimental loops for carrying out tests on steady state thermosyphon and stability of two phase natural circulation were commissioned and preliminary test runs were started. Preliminary sub-channel analysis of fuel bundle was carried out. Steady state heat transfer analysis of the polycarbon blocks of AHWR moderator system was carried out. An experimental setup was fabricated to study 2-phase flow pattern transition using neutron beam radiography in APSARA reactor.

Component/systems design

Design of coolant channel was completed. A 3D model of AHWR building was completed. A detailed specification for pyrocarbon blocks was prepared. ECCS accumulator with fluidic device was designed using a specially developed computer code.

Reactor engineering

Integrated Garter Spring Repositioning system was

assembled and qualified for reactor work at MAPS-I site. Repositioning of the garter springs was taken up in five coolant channels. The design of Instrumented fuel pin for testing of PHWR fuel pin under Loss of Coolant Accident (LOCA) conditions was finalised. A diagnostic method for detection of turbine blade vibration was developed with data input from the reactor sites. Development of a passive hydrogen combiner device was completed and the system was commissioned.

All the operating facilities/loops *e.g.*, Integral Teat Facility, Flow Test Facility, 3MW boiling water loop, fuelling machine test facility were satisfactorily operated for conducting a variety of experiments, testing of components and data generation.

Reactor safety

Design and procurement related activities were carried out in respect of the Instrumentation and Control System for Containment Studies Facility (CSF). Quantification of human reliability based on Operator Action Tree Sequence and I-IRA Event Tree Model was done. Preliminary design of the PHT model vessel was carried out for the proposed Containment Studies Facility. Seismic re-qualification analysis for the identified structures and components of CIRUS was continued. The fatigue monitoring system at HWP, Kota was found to be working satisfactorily.

The data base development for implementing the same to HWP, Tuticorin has been completed. A facility, 'Nuclear Synergism Simulator' was set up and commissioned at PANBIT to test components under combined environmental conditions for studying the interaction effects of temperature, radiation, humidity and operating electrical stresses. A procedure for the qualification of components has been prepared. For life extension of Heavy Water Plant, Kota, a preliminary seismic re-evaluation of process tanks, dump tanks and their supporting structures was completed.

As a part of the cooperative contaminant research programme jointly sponsored by the USNRC and NUPEC, a pre-test analysis of 1:4 Scaled model of an existing Japanese pressurised water reactor (PWR) prestressed concrete containment vessel had begun and a set of preliminary results were obtained. The accident analysis of TAPSBWRs, for the case of recirculation Line Break and Main Stream Line Break was completed.

Reactor control instrumentation

The work on design and development of advanced computer/microprocessor based Instrumentation and Control (I&C) systems for forthcoming PHWRs at Kalga-1&2 and RAPP-3&4 was continued. Work was also carried out in other areas such as development of in-service inspection tools, design and development of software Verification and Validation (V&V) tools, hardware and systems reliability assessment and so on. An electrical supervisory Control and Data Acquisition (SCADA) was developed to monitor and c electrical equipment for RAPP-3.

The complete SCADA system was integrated and tested for the specific functions of monitoring, interlocks control and the system was installed site. The development of microcomputer based system for reactor power regulation for use in Kaiga- 1&2 and RAP 3&4 was completed. Reliability analysis of microcomputer based hardware circuit modules used in various safety and safety related I&C systems designed for 1&2 and RAPP-3&4 was completed.

The development of Coolant Channel Inspection System, BARCIS M III With special features to suit Fuel Machine vault layout at NAPS was completed. A four axis drive mechanism suitable for mounting on Fuelling Machine bridge was developed. A quad CCTV system for remotised alignment remotised calibration checking linear and rotary displacements inspection heads and surveillance Fuelling Machine vault was implemented.

A facility for on-line calibration checking of ultrasonic transducers was incorporated. The successful completion of this system has resulted substantial savings in foreign exchange. An on-line Fatigue Monitoring tern was developed to assess the structural degradation of components.

One such unit had been installed and commissioned at Heavy Water Plant, Kota. A computerised control system a KOMAGE hydraulic press for uranium oxide fuel pellet fabrication commissioned at Nuclear Fuel Complex and the field trials have been satisfactory. This will be a significant imp substitution.

As per MOU signed with IOC an Instrumented PIG for oil pi lines, was developed and trial progressed. The design, development, commissioning and testing of microprocessor based Traction Control System for 25 KV AC, 4200 HP, Locomotives of Indian Railways was concluded after successful full-load line trials of a retrofitted Locomotive at Bhusaval.

This project was a collaborative, effort among BARC, DOE and RDSO. The thyristor convertors were manufactured at ECIL as per design by BARC and RDSO. The hardware and software for the control system was jointly developed by BARC and RDSO. BARC has been actively involved in the FALCON RPV programme of DRDO and had designed and commissioned three tracking antenna control systems for the vehicle mounted 6' diameter antenna, in partnership with ECIL.

Refuelling technology

In-head calibration plug for BARCIS Mark-II has been successfully used in MAPS for calibration of ultra- sonic sensors. An automatic clamping mechanism was designed for wet INGRES delivery system. It will reduce time and men-rem consumption during garter spring repositioning in the reactor. Channel Isolating Plug for maintenance of end fitting seal face of PHWR has been developed and delivered to NAPS and successfully tested.

Nuclear fuels

Production of fuel pins with Mark II mixed carbide fuel composition for FBTR was recommenced. Fuel pins for sub- assemblies were fabricated and necessary DHRUVA fuel clusters were delivered Fabrication of fuel pins for the 11th&12th MOX subassemblies for TAPS were continued at Advanced Fuels Fabrication Facility (AFFF), Tarapur.

As a part of the development work on annular fuel pellet fabrication for PFBR a large number of acceptable quality annular pellets were fabricated at AFFF using a new tooling developed in-house. Work on the commissioning/operation of Computer Controlled Sol-Gel Plant was continued at AFFF, Tarapur. An indigenous microwave furnace designed and fabricated at the plant was commissioned for carrying out dry recycle work on MOX fuel pellet scrap.

Fuel reprocessing

Project KARP (Kalpakkam Reprocessing Plant), designed for reprocessing capacity of 100 Te per annum, was initiated into commissioning runs involving processing of spent fuel from MAPS on establishing satisfactory design safety case for regulatory authorisation by the Atomic Energy Regulatory Board. The Reprocessing Plant was dedicated to the Nation by the Prime Minister on the September 15, 1998.

The site clearance work for the on- going Project ROP, Tarapur was nearing completion. The process design has been put to peer review. Design Basis Reports for the primary containment storage tanks and secondary and tertiary barriers in stainless steel and the RCC vault housing the storage tanks for the IX Plan Project—AWTF, Tarapur were prepared. Investigations were also carried out on the applicability of dried banana pith (inner stem) for the sorption of various radionuclides which are generally present at trace level in Purex process waste effluents.

Nuclear waste management

BARC is responsible for safe management of all types and categories of radioactive liquid and solid wastes generated at Trombay, Tarapur, Rajasthan and Kalpakkam. During the year all the waste management facilities operated satisfactorily. The low and intermediate level liquid wastes were provided suitable treatment and bulk of the radioactivity was retained in the form of sludge concentrates.

The authorised limits for discharge of radioactivity through liquid route were reduced by AERB. However activity discharges to the environment were kept well below authorised limits. The solid wastes were collected, segregated, suitably treated and conditioned before disposal in engineered facilities. At Trombay, the organic liquid waste was transferred to newly augmented storage facility.

At Tarapur, the intermediate level liquid waste treatment plant was restarted after carrying out necessary modification and maintenance. Application was submitted to AERB for licensing the facility at Tarapur for storage of vitrified high level solid waste. Waste Immobilisation Plant at Trombay, was in the last phase of mechanical completion. For the first time in BARC, an indigenously developed and manufactured Servo Manipulator in collaboration with M/s.

HMT Bangalore was installed inside the vitrification cell and its performance was being evaluated for design intent. A Multi barrier design of active trench for safe transfer of high level liquid waste from source to the plant had been completed earlier, execution of this work was underway. Multi-zone medium frequency induction furnace for vitrification of high level waste, developed for the first time in the country was successfully commissioned.

A state-of- the-art Data Aquisition & Control System (DACS) was developed in collaboration with M/s. ECIL. The system was under installation at the plant site. Construction of main process building of Waste Immobilisation Project, Kalpakkam was nearing completion. Procurement of process equipment continued. Detailing of various systems and layouts was under progress. Studies on 'Recovery&Recycle of long lived actinides from high level liquid waste' and 'Vitrification of high level waste' were carried out as part of the process development for HLW management.

Management of spent solvent of reprocessing origin was demonstrated on a full scale. After successful runs based on 'alkaline hydrolysis' of TBP an active plant was in advanced stages of erection&commissioning. As an alternative to direct fixation in polymer matrix for spent lon-exchange resins, a strategy involving combination of oxidation process for complete destruction of spent organic lon- exchange resins were evolved and was under test on laboratory/pilot scale.

Vitrification studies were carried out on toxic waste streams arising during processing of beryllium from beryl ore. Based on these studies, details are being worked out for setting up of full scale vitrification facility at Beryllium Plant, Vashi. Development and use of specific sorbents/lon exchangers for removal of Cs, Sr and other radionuclides from different waste streams were carried out Repeated loading-elution-regeneration cycles carried out have established their successful performance. Preliminary work on the synthesis of magnetic sorbents for decontamination of low and intermediate liquid waste were initiated. Investigations were in progress for selection of suitable site for disposal of immobilised waste products in geological repositories in association with various national agencies.

Detailed geological and geophysical studies were completed at one site and were in progress at another site. Services were provided to all the units of DAE for *in situ* testing of air cleaning systems to minimise the release of gaseous activity to the environment. Special air filters for personal protection and air cleaning systems were designed, assembled and supplied to various users of DAE. Spent radiation sources from hospitals, educational institutes, industries and DAE units were collected and suitably stored/disposed in the engineered containment systems. Health, Safety&Environment Protection of plant personnel, public in general and environment against radiation continued to be the prime activity of BARC. Following were the activities:

Radiological safety and surveillance

Radiological safety support for nuclear power plants, research reactors other nuclear fuel cycle facilities, BRIT, VECC Calcutta and CAT Indore was provided on a routine basis. Environmental surveillance at nuclear power plant sites, fuel cycle facilities and Trombay was also provided. Personnel monitoring services were provided radiation workers from industrial, medical, research and DAE institutions Whole body counting of plant personnel for internal contamination was continued at the various Environmental Radiological Laboratories (ERLs) a other facilities.

Health physics coverage was provided to in-service Inspection (ISI) 66 coolant channels in MAPS-2; turbine overhauling work, shutdown MOV replacement, recirculation loop MOV stern replacement, core spray loop 11 and reactor clean up system return line replacement work and core shroud inspection work in TAPS-2; complete core unloading of CIRUS reactor and major refurbishing activity at PP, Trombay and PREFRE, Tarapur.

Environmental Radiological Laboratory at Kaiga was inaugurated on June 22, 1998 and a manual entitled "Environmental Radiological Laboratory Procedure Manual" and a brochure "Environmental Radiological Laboratory, Kaiga" was released. Kakrapar ERL was identified by the World Association of Nuclear Operators (WANO) Group as an area where good practices were being carried out and the Group expressed its desire to share the ERL experience.

Installation of new systems

A low cost Digital Pocket Radiation Dosimeter (DIGI DOSE) was developed based on semi conductor detector with continuous digital read out over a range of 1 Sv to 999999 Sv. Semi automatic TLD badge readers were developed and were put into use for Personnel Monitoring Service. PC add-on cards for ADC and data acquisition were designed and fabricated for aerial gamma spectrometer. Eight such systems are being developed for DAE and the Defence Services.

A compact wall mounted environmental dose monitor with LCD display and with an infrared trans-receiver based 1/0 communication facility was developed. High range gamma dose rate monitor was developed for mapping gamma radiation fields inside coolant channels of power reactors and these were used at RAPS and MAPS.

A software package was developed for the postal dose intercomparison of different radiotherapy centres in the country. A dose management software for personnel monitering programme was implemented. It was working successfully at KAPS, RAPS, MAPS& Dhruva reactions. A novel method of internal dose assessment based on the determination of thorium in the blood serum of occupational workers of a thorium Plant was developed and applied to estimate the internal dose to a few occupational workers at OSCOM.

The analysis of the samples and subsequent dose calculations showed that the annual committed effective dose due to thorium, to these subjects, was below the permissible limit. Individual values of fluence to ambient dose equivalent conversion factors were calculated for various radio active neutron sources used in calibration of radiation monitors.

Safety studies

Studies on "Leachability evaluation of Beryllium" from redmud and that stabilized with cement in different proportions using standard leachability protocols reveal that the effective diffusion coefficient of Be in the stabilized matrix was 7 to 8 orders of magnitude lower than the molecular diffusion coefficient of Be in the water, indicating the effectiveness of stabilisation. A probabilistic safety assessment model was developed for the long term safety assessment near surface radioactive disposal facilities. A comprehensive quality assurance protocol was developed to test various parameters that affect image quality in mammography.

A dosimetric protocol was established for the retirement of melanoma using eye plaque incorporating

1251 seeds. Dosimetric and safety studies on stents incorporating 32P/192Ir/188Re were carried out for evaluating their suitability for the treatment of resenosis following angioplasty.

Investigations on dosimetry of low energy electron beams were carried out thermoluminiscence phosphor was developed which is useful for environmental monitoring and studies in medical physics. Computerised glow curve deconvolution programme was developed for resolving complex TL glow curves. Comparative radiation safety evaluation of medical cyclotrons for selection of a unit for Radiation Medicine Centre (RMC), shielding requirement assessment of 500 keV, 20 mA electron beam accelerator at Vashi; Shield augmentation for storage ring Indus-I and biological shield design and ventilation requirements for the proposed POTON irradiator were carried out.

A complex model for generating wind fields was developed for application to non-homogenous terrains such as those in Trombay and Kaiga continued countrywide radon/thoron mapping. Studies on the daily human intake of heavy metals and their retention times in blood were carried out. Lead levels in human blood samples formed an indicator for lead levels in the atmosphere.

Services

Authorisations for movement of industrial radiography sources, no objection certificates for procurement and use of radioactive materials for industrial radiography and advisory services on safe transport of radioactive materials were provided on a routine basis. Safety analysis and type approval tests were carried out on colour and black&white TV monitors, X-ray baggage inspection systems, metal halide lamps incorporating 85

Kr and thorium frills, industrial radiography X ray machines, models of nucleonic gauges and a few consumer products incorporating radioisotopes, medical accelerators, a simulator, cobalt 60 radiotherapy units and remote afterloading units.

As a part of Accident Prevention Programme, a comprehensive safety status report was prepared and this contains information on accident statistics, special safety surveys, training on safety, first aid, fire fighting, medical examinations and emergency drills carried out. BARC won AERB safety shield for the fifth year in succession under the category of R&D Units. Analytical services for radiochemical analysis were provided to pharmaceutical companies. Passive monitoring for thoron and its daughters, in gas mantle industries, using SSNDT was carried out.

Isotope technology

The R&D activities at BARC were focused on development of processes for the production of isotopes, isotopic radiation sources and applications of radioisotopes and radiation which are of relevance to Indian industry and society. These activities include development of procedure for the production of fission produced molybdenum, 1251, 153Sm, 186Re, development of 32P and 1251 radiation sources for endovascular and eye brachytherapy, suitable radiopharmaceuticals for medical diagnosis, development of radiation process for cable polymer industry and utilization of isotopes and radiation sources for better harnessing of natural resources and as a diagnostic tool for industrial trouble shooting.

The development of trained professional for utilizing unique benefits of radioisotope applications in the industry and medicine forms another important activity.

In the field of nuclear medicine, development of therapeutic radiopharmaceuticals continued. A laboratory for monoclonal against Prostrate Specific Antigen (PSA) antibody production was set up. A polymer based on grafting of acrylic acid on carboxymethyl cellulose was prepared using Co-60 gamma irradiation.

Hydrogels were prepared by grafting acrylamide on carboxymethyl cellulose using Co-60 gamma radiation. These hydrogels are capable of selective absorption of basic dyes from aqueous solutions. Studies on radiation shielding integrity of thick multilayered components, made of lead, steel and concrete were carried out. In continuation of the isotope study in the Puma river basin in Maharashtra to understand the origin of salinity of the groundwater, samples collected from the area were analysed.

A series of radiotracer experiments were carried out in a trickle bed reactor with three different types of catalyst to understand liquid phase hydrodynamics. Electron Beam (EB) irradiation of diamonds was carried out at full beam power on commercial basis. An irradiation throughput of 40,000 ring was achieved by employing 17 spindles in the conveyor system. Radiation crosslinkable PE and P based EPR formulations for wire/ cab insulations in the form of sheets cables from Shriram Institute for Industrial Research, Delhi were irradiated various electron beam dose ranging from 25 kGy to 500 kGy. Twenty nos of nuclear explosion detectors used in battle tanks we gamma trigger tested in PANBIT Army based workshop, Pune.

Gamma scanning of Depropaniser column of M/s. Reliance Industrial Ltd., Hazira, was carried out for trouble shooting. The approval of radiation processing for several additional food items expected to provide the necessary impetus for commercialization of preservation process by the food industry. Water samples from Priyadarsh and other lakes in Antarctica which were collected during an earlier Indian expedition, in Jan-Feb. 1997, were analyse for environmental stable isotopes tritium.

Fuel and radiochemistry

Uranium-plutonium mixed oxide microspheres with 3% plutonium were prepared by the Sol-gel method. For the preparation of UO_2 fuel pellets Sol-gel microspheres pelletization Auto Sol-gel plant, an auto feeder vessel was designed and was in operation for the production of UO_2 microspheres.

To study fuel-clad and fission products interaction, use thermodynamic and X-ray data were obtained on certain alloys and compounds. Evaluation of extraction data PU(IV) using macroporous bifunctional phosphinic acid resin has shown feasibility of removal of plutonium from oxalate waste. Gamma ray spectrometric method was developed for the determination of plutonium content in the solid matrix and used routinely. Analytical services continued to be provided for the determination of metallic and nonmetallic constituents for the chemical quality control of Mark II FBTR fuel.

Work in the area of radiochemistry covered research in the field of nuclear fission, nuclear reactions, nuclear spectroscopy, development of NDA and neutron activation analysis. In the area of the actinide chemistry several new procedures were developed for the separation actinides and fission products. A large number of amides and diamides were studied with a view to their applications in separation of actinides from irradiated fuels (Th, U) as well as recovery of actinides from HLW.

In the area of spectroscopic analysis new methods were developed for determination of trace level impurities in ThO_2 matrix. The routine analysis of a large number of samples of fresh batch for FBTR fuel are being carried out. Use of EPR, PAS and fluorescence technique was done to understand some of the interesting solid state properties of actinide doped compounds.

Studies on fragment angular momentum in odd Z fissioning system 241Am (n,f) were carried out. Calibration of hull monitor set up at KARP based on fission product monitoring using HPGe detector was completed. Neutron activation analysis was used for determination of Au&Pd in samples of atomic minerals. Estimate of uranium in granite samples were carried out.

A procedure for the decontamination of alkaline intermediate level liquid wastes (ILLW) from plutonium and americium using hydrous iron oxide (HIO) was standardised. Analytical spectroscopy work was focussed on the ongoing efforts to find a suitable chemical separation procedure for determination of impurities in U/Pu by ICP-AES.

Chemical technology

Heavy water upgrading

All the tower internals for 1 4 sections of the 1050 mm diameter column of the upgrading plant for Kaiga-I were fabricated, activated, tested and dispatched to site. Fabrication of tower internals for Kaiga-II was completed and testing progressed. BARC successfully completed the analysis & certification work of heavy water exported to M/S Korean Electric Power Corporation, South Korea by Heavy Water Board. To meet the requirement of Neon-22 isotope of Defence Organisation, a thermal diffusion column was set up and operated. The results obtained were very encouraging.

Based on this data, a prototype column of suitable capacity was designed and was under fabrication. Another test assembly having five columns was set up to study the interstage flow -parameters. An advanced electrolyser plant for oxygen production was set up at BARC and successfully commissioned.

Desalination

6300 m3/d Combined MSF-RO Nuclear Desalination Demonstration Plant (NDDP), Kalpakkam : The detailed design of the MSF and RO plants were carried out and the proposal for taking steam, sea water and power from MAPS was prepared. The MSF and RO pilot plants set up at the BARC were operated to study the behaviour of high temperature operation of RO plant and the transient behaviour of the MSF plant. This data will be useful for coupling of the NDDP with MAPS. R&D work on synthesis of new polymers and membranes and development of compact spiral module system were successfully completed.

Chemical engineering

BARC has been engaged in developing specialised materials required the Atomic Energy Programme. The three pilot plants *viz.*, "Processing magnesium fluoride lining material "Facility for enrichment of Boron by ion exchange" and "Development 1500 Ampere prototype fluorine c and 5 tonnes/year sulphur hexafluoride" were set up. Setting up of the two plants under IX five year plan *viz.*

Development nuclear grade thorium oxide a Lithium metal pilot plant continued was vigorously pursued. The design of the plants was completed and procurement, infrastructure and other related matters were in progress. Specialised scintillation chemical and were being supplied to TIFR their Ooty project for gamma-rays detection and to other division in B for making scintillation counters. The other activities include development carbon anodes for fluorine cell, fused salt electrolysis for preparation of a metals and other R&D activities.

Materials science

This process was developed at optimised to obtain an adherent coating of boron on aluminium and stainless steel substrates, required for the fabrication of neutron sensing elements ion chambers and counters used reactor control. For hydrogen mitigation during accidental release of hydrogen gas a nuclear power station, a process was developed to fabricate a suitable catalyst using palladium and platinum coated alumina powder.

Technology development for YVO4: Eu3+ for high pressure metal vapour lamps and metal halide lamps was completed. At the request of IRE, investigation were carried out on the separation better than 99% pure neodymium permanent magnet applications and process was developed for the portion of pure neodymium. A process was optimised for the recovery of the heavy rare earths, in particular yttrium, from the indigenous xenotime concentrate. Over 99% leaching recovery was obtained by the sulphuric acid process. Separation of individual elements was carried out by dual cycle solvent extraction.

Production of uranium metal ingots was adequate to meet the complete requirements of research reactor fuel fabrication. Sustained in-house R&D efforts have led to the production of better quality ingots which has resulted in considerable improvements in fuel performance. Setting up of a plant for augmentation of uranium metal production has progressed considerably.

The technology for the synthesis of diethyl phosphoric acid (D2 EPHA), an important metal extractant in the organophosphorus series, was transferred to Heavy Water Board. Setting up of a pilot plant reached an advanced stage and the commercial production was scheduled to start in May/June, 1999 at HWP, Talcher.

The product from this plant will be able to meet the requirements for base metal industries, for uranium extraction from phosphoric acid and for separation of uranium from some ore bodies. A process for the separation and recovery of cobalt, nickel and other elements from the leach liquor of oceanic polymetallic nodules was developed at BARC for the Department of Ocean Development (DOD). Based on the processes developed at BARC for separation and at RRL, Bhubaneswar, for leaching, DOD and Hindustan Zinc Ltd., Udaipur, have planned to set up a pilot plant during the ninth plan to process about 500 kg of ocean nodules per day.

A development programme was initiated to prepare carbon shapes for use as scatterer in AHWR. Preliminary studies were carried out to fabricate carbon spheres in the size range of 10-25 mm diameter, followed by pyrolytic carbon coating. Development activities were continued on the preparation of refractory metals, alloys and intermetallic compounds. Pure vanadium metal was prepared by fused salt electro-refining using a vanadium-nitrogen alloy as a soluble anode.

A corrosion monitoring method, based on the analysis of electrochemical noise generated from corroding specimens was developed for laboratory and field use. The technique was undergoing test for use in monitoring the integrity of containers during long term storage of radioactive wastes. Alloy 718 will find extensive use in the KAVERI engine of the light combat aircraft (LCA). Following an understanding with Gas Turbine Research Establishment (GTRE), Bangalore, studies on some specific problems related to the fabrication of parts from this alloy were carried out and remedial measures suggested.

Aeronautical Development Agency (ADA), Bangalore, plans to use Ni-TiFe shape memory Alloy clips in the Agency's aircraft development project. A R&D programme has been undertaken to develop a tool for the expansion of the Ni-Ti-Fe clips and for characterization and eusability assessment of dimensionally recovered clips. An expansion tool that can carry out the deformation of the shape memory alloy component in a liquid nitrogen environment was designed and fabricated. A 29- kg ingot of Ni-Ti shape memory alloy of near equiatomic composition and good shape memory characteristics was prepared by double consumable vacuum arc melting at NFC. Several Ni-Ti-Fe alloys were prepared by non- consumable vacuum arc melting.

Kinetics of hydride blister growth was studied in relation to hydrogen concentration, cold spot/bulk specimen temperature and cold spot geometry. Specimens of aluminium, copper, porous nickel and titanium were successfully diffusion-bonded to stainless steel. A variety of advanced materials namely, intermetallics and composites were synthesized by the self-propagating high temperature synthesis (SHS) technique.

Single phase crystalline hematite (a-Fe_2O_3) particles of 0:.3 mm median diameter and a narrow size distribution (100% < 1 mm) were prepared by gel crystallization technique resulting powder was found accept for radioimmunoassay applications ANTARIKSHA which is a part Indian Space Research, Organisation

(ISRO), entered into an agreement M/s. Hughes Space and communication Centre, USA to supply 20 sets beryllium shafts and flange assemblies conforming to their design drawing and specifications. These assemblies were produced by precision machining at BARC. The final components were given a critical finishing touch.

Gadolinium is used as a "burnable" poison in the nuclear reactors to c the reactivity of fresh reactor fuel assembly. Preparation of $GdAlO_3$ carried out by citrate get route. The process is simple and recovery, other th handling losses, is highest.

Rare earths development

High purity neodymium oxide used for manufacture of neodymium (Nd) metal, which finds applications the making of neodymium/iron/boron alloy for permanent magnets. The process developed by REDS was successfully tested at IREL, Alwaye and tonnage quantities of product of internationally competitive quality were produced. IREL is further planning a joint venture for large scale neodyinium met plant. Pure Nd prepared by the BARC process was tested by Japanese users was found to be of high quality.

Ore dressing

Studies were carried out on Tummalapalle uranium ore using MGS with rougher tails as feed with the objective of improving recovery at the rougher stage. Mineralogical studies on uranium and associated metals along SSZ were continued.

Detrital and remobilized types of uraninite and brannerite formed by pronto-reaction are identified in Narwapahar ore samples. Autoradiographic studies were carried out to confirm the brannerite formation. Experiments were continued on the multi-metallic preconcentrate sample from Kyrgyzstan in order to improve grade and recovery of the tungsten and tin concentrates. Alkali roasting followed by leaching with water of the combined concentrate is being tried to evolve a generalized metallurgical flow-sheet to process the combined concentrate. Beneficiation studies were initiated on lead-zinc-copper ore samples from Sikkim.

In the Jaduguda Uranium ore, occurrence of detrital assemblage of chromite and uraninite was identified. Mineral chemistry and structural formula calculations on the tourmalines from Jaduguda indicated that they are Ai-poor belongings to Ca-poor metapelites and metapsamites with dravite compistion.

Remote handling and robotics

Research and development programme at BARC is oriented towards development of need-based and custom designed technologies in the areas of Intervention Robotics, Advanced Automation and Remotisation for beneficial substitution of manual tabour for a variety of task in nuclear facilities characterised by constraints such as hostile environment, limited work-space and inaccessible work areas limiting direct human intervention. The Bilateral Master Slave Servo manipulators which materialized through fruitful collaboration between BARC and HMT, Bangalore are under installation for field trials and commissioning at WIP, BARC site at Trombay.

With the completion of minor modifications in the mechanical subassemblies of the Co-60 Teletherapy unit and reassembly thereof, progressive integration of the control systems and interlocks was underway. Design of mechanical, electrical and control systems for the commercial scale irradiator (POTON) for sprout inhibition of onions and potatoes was finalised; fabrication of certain components and subsystems was underway.

Development of certain custom-made robotic/remote handling systems for power reactor maintenance progressed. Detailed design of the proposed inspection system for Moderator Heat Exchanger at NAPS reached the final stage and the necessary components are being procured.

Development of certain application oriented Robot configurations and mobile mechanisms was in progress. Based on the performance of the scaled down version of the Autonomous Guided Vehicle (AGV) for fuel rod handling, the basic design was under improvement to facilitate integration of the sensors and control system and direct scale up after final demonstration of the improved model.

Preliminary design of a Mobile Robot for inspection of PFBR main vessel was completed. Computer Aided Robot Programming (CARP) environment—an interactive graphic environment with several advanced features through multiple window GUI—was developed for the 6 DoF Robot and the functional system was demonstrated. Full 3D simulation of the robot motion under control was demonstrated. Methods were implemented for intelligent collision avoidance and robot locus generation from source to target objects for the 6DoF Robot. Necessary software and hardware were being developed for intelligent grasp control for the Robot Gripper. Other significant programmes currently under different stages of development include the 3 piece Mechanical Master Slave Manipulator, Power Manipulator for KARP, Periscope for FBTR and a comprehensive system for total automation of transfer package for BRIT.

Central workshops

Central Workshops of BARC continued to contribute towards design, development and manufacture of sophisticated equipment for R&D work as well as Power Reactor Programme. Assignments include manufacture of equipment for projects with international collaboration. Some of the major jobs undertaken included, AHWR Fuel Spacer Development, Replacement Tube Bundles for CIRUS, Seal & Sheild Plug Assemblies for DHRUVA, R.F. Cavity for superconducting Cyclotron, Steam Generators for FISBE, Detector frames for PHENIX, USA, Development of Roundway Bearing single &'V' type for 500 MWe PHWR, CRDM Components, Beam line equipment for 6.65 spectrometer, Antenna for Aditya Tokmak, Inclined Fuelling Transfer Machine, High temperature X-ray diffractometer, MACE Telescope, Hot neutron source, Liquid scintillator, Vacuum furnace for crystal, Universal calibration machine, Special purpose winch, Leak before break specimen, Laser based surface finish: measuring instrument and so on.

Electronics and instrumentation

Computer

Processing power available on 6-node ANUPAM Alpha Super Computer was further enhanced by adding another 4-node, thus presently giving a sustained performance of 1.5 giga flops for large scientific jobs, with a peak speed of 8 giga flops. An exercise was carried out to ascertain the feasibility of replacing dual CRAY-X/MP super computer, being used for medium range weather forecasting at National Centre for Medium Range Weather Forecasting (NCMRWF), DST, Delhi, with an ANUPAM Alpha super computer.

It was observed that an ANUPAM Alpha (1+4 node) can replace the presently operational dual CRAY-X/MP which is an obsolete machine and requires enormous resources for operation and maintenance. A new super computer ANUPAM PII using Pentium II personal computers and a fast 100 Mbps Ethernet switch, was developed. A 4 node ANUPAM PII, using Pentium II microprocessors @ 266 MHz gives a user performance of 248 MFLOPS, with a peak speed of I giga flop. ANUPAM PII can be easily scaled upto 128 nodes, giving a sustained speed of 14-15 giga flops. The image processing software being developed was further enhanced to support Shape Analysis, Adaptive thresholding and Fame processing. This software was used for evaluating hydride plated content in Zircaloy-2 pressure tubes, Analysis of Fracture Propagation in Materials and high temperature creep studies in Materials.

Electronics

Modernisation of the nuclear instrumentation of Fast Breeder Test Reactor at Kalpakkam was successfully commissioned and reactor attained criticality on June 25, 1998. As the core gamma at RAPS-2 during Ist approach to criticality was greater than 104 R/hr, elaborate tests were carried to measure the gamma tolerance the Boron-10 lined counters. Based on the results these detectors were replaced with Fission counters. The startup instrumentation was modified to interface with Fission counters

Prototype detectors were developed for neutron and gamma measurement in power reactors. A prototype boron- 10 lined proportional counter was developed for reactor start up instrumentation. An ion chamber was developed for Beam Spill Monitoring application at the synchrotron facility at CAT, Indore Seven neutron flux monitors incorporating 3He proportional counters were supplied to VEC, Calcutta for area neutron monitoring.

Eight numbers of "Rod Monitoring Units" were fabricated and tested by QS, NPCIL for shipment to RAPS 3 and 4 site. The sample unit was success fully subjected to seismic and climatic tests at ECIL. The on-line Turbine shaft expansion measurement unit for RAPS I & 2 are developed and supplied to site. These units are working satisfactorily. A battery operated portable MCA was designed around CHAMELEON (credit card PC) based CPU card with 8K nuclear ADC, programmable gain Pulse amplifier and programmable high voltage cards with ISA Bus.

Other significant achievements during 1998 included: Advanced Ultra sonic Imaging Systems (ULTIMA 100+) supplied to BHEL (Hyderabad); First model of Single Board PC Add on 200 MSPS Transient/ Repetitive waveform digitizer was developed. ADSP 2100 (DSP) based PC Add-on board was developed for high speed processing of ID/2D digital data such as digitized waveforms and images.

ANUGAMI-S because of entire dependence on host PC had low cost and hence had been accepted by IAEA for the Agency's Upgradation program. Eighty-one ANUGAMI-S cards were supplied to different countries under IAEA program. Second version of interface card ANUAGMI-P with on-board processor (TRANSPUTER) and memory is more versatile for acquisition of nuclear medicine imaging data and was installed at two institutes at Delhi—All India Institute of Medical Science (AIIMS) and at Institute of Nu clear Medicine and Allied Sciences (INMAS). MTMPS is a high performance PC-CAMAC data aquisition system developed by BARC for Accelerator based nuclear physics experiments.

Electronic systems

A computer based inspection system to highlight the internal disorders of mangoes has been developed and the installed in BARC. For fracture mechanics experiment, on piping components to carry out leak before-break studies, an image processing system with 4 CCD camera input was developed for simultaneously monitoring crack growth and crack mouth opening at specified displacement/load values. A PC based CCTV System with digital video storage facility was developed for video alarm assessment. A contact condition monitoring system to monitor up to sixteen door sensors and a micro-controller based distress alarm system were developed.

A dual channel acoustic emission analyse was developed to capture signals from piezoelectric sensors. The system was used successfully to detect simulated leaks in the seal plugs at fuelling machine test facility at BARC. A DSP card based Multi Frequency Eddy Current (MFEC) System hardware was commissioned at BARC. A compact pre-amplifier for direct mounting on the integral assembly of NaI(TI) scintillation detector coupled by photomultiplier tube was developed for use in linear profile scanner at RMC (BARC), Parel for detecting functional metastates of the thyroid patients.

Physical sciences

Nuclear physics

The 14 MV Pelletron accelerator was used to carry out a large variety of experimental studies using the medium energy heavy ion beams from the accelerator. Extensive Theoretical studies were carried out in Intermediate Energy Physics and Relativistic Heavy Ion Collision. Several features of absorptive tunnelling through complex potential barriers were investigated in relation to the heavy ion fusion process.

An exact statistical model code for the calculation of fission fragment angular distributions with inclusion of projectile, target spins and K-dependent transmission coefficients was developed for the analysis of the data of heavy ion induced fission reactions. The installation and commissioning of Folded Tandem Ion Accelerator

(FOTIA) continued. The gas handling system designed and fabricated was fully commissioned. The accelerator column section was raised to a voltage of 3.4 million volts. The pelletron machine was operated round the clock with an efficiency of 75% up-time, and was used by the experimental groups of BARC (NPD, Metallurgy, Radiochemistry), TIFF, SINP, VECC and IUC.

Superconducting LINAC booster project was progressing well. Detector parts for the muon tracking system of the PHENIX detector were fabricated in central workshops and delivered to LANL, USA. Further fabrication work was in progress for both the south and north arms of the muon detector. Collaboration experiments continued at the Legnaro National Laboratory, Italy and RIKEN, Japan. The experiment at RIKEN involves the study of giant dipole resonance in neutron rich nuclei using the radioactive ion beam facility.

Accelerator pulse

A 500 keV industrial electron accelerator developed indigenously by BARC was commissioned for its first phase of operation by the Hon'ble Prime Minister of India Shri Atal Bihari Vajpayee on August 10, 1998. Collective acceleration of Fluorine and Carbon ions to 28.5 MeV and 18 MeV respectively with ion current around 25 A peak was attained on KALI-200 generator. The KALI-5000 pulse power system having die ratings of I MV, 80 kA, 60 ns, was in the advanced stage of assembly.

NRL-HARL

BARC has a long-term programme of establishing a new astronomy facility, GRACE, in the country at Mt. Abu, Rajasthan, fat front-ranking research activities in the field of gamma-ray astrophysics. India's first imaging gamma-ray telescope, the principal component of the TACTIC telescope array, has already been successfully commissioned at Mt. Abu and was in use for regular observation campaigns. This year, the mechanical structures of three additional telescopes of the TACTIC array were installed at Mt. Abu and their special-design duplex cameras were fabricated.

Observations were carried out recently with an upgraded 169-pixel Imaging camera on several well-known gamma-ray sources, including 2 BL-Lac objects and a supernova remnant (the Crab Nebula). A path-breaking result was that Cerenkov images, produced by gamma-ray and cosmic-ray nuclear progenitors, exhibit a fractal character. This realization has resulted in a more robust event characterization scheme.

Another interesting investigation carried out concerns the utilization of the cognitive power of an Artificial Neural Network for real-time reconstruction of the arrival direction of a high energy primary seen by a wide-angle Cerenkov array. This result will have important consequences on the design of the MYSTIQUE telescope planned to be built at Mt. Abu during next few years. A highlight result in the area of theoretical astrophysics was the generation of a catalogue of potentially promising target sources of galactic and extragalactic genres for the experiments being set up at the GRACE facility.

Theoretical physics

BARC is engaged in the physics problems of reactor design, safety and operation. It also carries out research in many areas of physics and applied mathematics, such as transport theory, radiation hydodynamics, non-linear equations, numerical methods, classical and quantum chaos, and quantum optics. A new simulator code was developed for providing fuel management service to Boiling Water Reactors at Tarapur. For PHWRs, studies were conducted for the first approach to criticality for RAPS-2 reactor after shut down as a result of replacement of coolant channels. For Kaiga-1 & 2 reactors, reactivity devices were simulated for fuel bum up and cold and hot core conditions.

Physics design manual for Kaiga-1& 2, preliminary safety analysis report for RAPP-3 & 4 were reviewed. A core model based on modal kinetics method was developed for real time reactor simulator for 220 MWe PHWRs, to be used for training purpose. Design of AHWR/PHWR critical facility was worked out, especially for studying physics of 500 MWe PHWR lattices. Studies on efficient numerical methods used for the solution of neutron diffusion and transport equations were started.

Reasons for the failure of spherical harmonics expansion method for solving neutron transport problems in spherical geometry were identified. In the field of quantum optics, nonlinear optical properties of atoms in a laser cooled harmonic trap were studied. This problem is of interest in physics of trapped atoms and ions.

Laser and plasma technology

A variety of technically superior, cost effective plasma sprayed duplex structures consisting of a metallic undercoat and a, top ceramic coat was developed for in-house nuclear applications. During the year, air-operated, vortex-cum magnetically stabilized hollow electrode plasma torches with power capacities upto 100 KW were developed. An injection seeded, single longitudinal mode Neodymium: YAG laser has recently been installed.

Laser & Plasma Technology was working on gamma ray attenuation method for void fraction measurement in two phase liquid metal flows. Recently a seven detector system to receive gamma rays passing through various chords of the flow in a 75 mm circular pipe was installed on a rotating platform. This unique system was in use in collaboration with IIT Kanpur to develop and validate several scheme of tomographic algorithms and void fraction profiles.

Technical physics and protoope engineering

Several Ion-implanted Si detectors of varying sizes, developed, and a number of silicon surface barrier detectors for nuclear research were produced. Fabrication of improved direct reading dosimeters for the dose range 0-500 mR and showing natural charge leakage within 1% per d1ay was another significant indigenous achievement. The suitability of Pt/Pd thin films as catalysts for H_2 mitigation facility was studied and commendable progress was made on the development of ruggedised H_2S gas sensors, as well as H_2 gas sensors covering extended concentration range (0 - 8%).

Development of $CdWO_4$ crystal scintillator was carried out both for industrial computer tomography as well as dosimetry applications. BaB_2O_4 crystals were grown for non-linear optical applications and a detailed investigation on the effect of sodium doping was also performed. For a variety of applications, crystals of NaCl, KCI, LiF, CsI, CaF_2, BaF_2 and $CdWO_4$ were supplied in large numbers to users in BARC, NPC and DRDO. In the area of glass technology, preparation of silicate glass powder, arsenic chalcogenide glass windows was carried out. Another major activity was the development of packages for hybrid microcircuits in which Department of Space was involved.

Development work on building a compact RF generator capable of giving upto 2.5KW power at 27.12 MHz and its integration with inductively coupled plasma torch assembly was completed and this unit was also integrated with ICP-AES system developed for KARP. Precision magnet current regulators for particle accelerators were developed *viz.*, 50OAmp,75V for Folded Tandem Ion Accelerator (FOTIA), being commissioned at Trombay and 100Amp,40V for Beam Line Magnet being set up at Calicut University.

A special high voltage medium frequency power supply for electrochemical etching for CR-39 detector was fabricated. A variable temperature insert and a six tesla superconducting magnet were fabricated for magneto-resistance measurement and short sample test facility required for evaluating superconducting NbTi cable. In-house fabrication of UHV components and other mechanical assemblies/ subsystems required for the development of mass spectrometers, high resolution electron spectrometer and total gas analysers was carried out. Ascanning Auger electron spectrometer having spatial resolution of 5 mm was developed.

A needle valve based compact sample introduction system for D/H mass spectrometer was developed. In the area of superconductive basic investigations were carried out of the influence of disorder on the behaviour of flux line lattice under different magnetic histories, effect of surface barrier on magnetization relaxation and vortex lines in high temperature super conductors.

Condensed matter physics

A molecular dynamic (MD) simulation under pressure was carried out $MgAl_2O_4$ to clarify about disorder amorphisation and phase change. A modified Michelson interferometer was set up as VISAR. Radiation transport calculations ICF target designs need accurate opacity tables for a variety of materials a wide range of density and temperature.

Molecular dynamics studies of seismic wave velocities and density variations involving various phase transition of the geophysically important mine enstatite $Mg_2 Si_2O_6$ were undertake These are the first calculations of seismic velocity at high pressures and temperatures and have enabled an atom level interpretation of phase transition of mantle constituents and resultant seismic discontinuities.

Using a lattice dynamical approach, we have calculated the phonon frequencies and equation of state of $CasiO_3$ pervoskite at Earth's lowest mantle pressures. The calculated equation of state was in good agreement with experimental data. Neutron diffraction experiment were carried out on a number of compounds to study the atomic and magnetic ordering. A new technique of Three Dimensional Neutron CT scan (313 C Scam) has been developed. It is now possible to obtain not only conventional CT scan in slices but also to visualise the inner parts of any object in its three dimensional view by stacking of various CT scans one over the other. Two scientists from BARC were the first international users of any public beam line in SPRING-8, the third generation synchrotron facility in Japan. They collected diffraction data for a number of protein crystals.

Seismology

All routine monitoring channels at the Gauribidanur seismic array (GBA) and Delhi Seismic Unit (DSU) functioned satisfactorily without interruption. Enormous efforts were made to set up at various places including sites in the Pokhran region a host of on-line seismic monitoring systems operating round-the-clock with capability to acquire high-quality seismic data from probable underground nuclear test explosions.

Designed and developed indigenously, the seismic systems incorporated different types of triaxial ground motion sensors to provide digital data in high dynamic range covering a wide band of signal frequency from close-in to distant observations from source. All the above temporary as well as permanent seismic installations did indeed successfully record the Indian nuclear tests at Pokhran (POK-II) on May 11 and 13, 1998. Among the ongoing R&D activities, further work on seismicity investigations in the peninsular Indian shield, artificial neural network and parametric modelling of microseismic noise in the array space progressed well. The code duration magnitude scale developed earlier was re-examined and regression analysis performed on a much larger data set of regional earthquakes providing fresh inputs to the shield seismic study.

Spectroscopy

Highly efficient broad band anti-reflection coatings were designed, developed and optimised for Nd-Yag laser application. A high reflectivity intracavity for Ruby laser has been fabricated for ISRO. Several multilayer beam splatters were successfully developed for laser cooling experiment with R/T splitting ratio of 30/70 and 10/90 over the wavelength range 650 to 800nm.

Chemical sciences

Analytical chemistry

Analytical service support to various of BARC and other units of DAE were continued. The number of samples analysed during the year were about 3000 involving 7200 determinations. Different types of samples like metals and alloys, organic and inorganic compounds, biological and environment materials as well as solution sample were analysed using various technique like spectrochemical, electro-analytical chromatographic and nuclear analytical methods. Basic research in analytical chemistry was continued. Ion exchange behaviour of Nafion membrane for the removal of impurities from bulk Ga/Al solution or for the facilitated transport of alkali metal ions was investigate cyclic voltammetry of antimony and palladium was studied.

The reduction behaviour of lanthanum was studied us in various electrochemical techniques. Kinetic and thermo-chemical parameters for the reaction of the oxide and titanium dioxide were investigated. Thin layer activation techniques was employed for the study of surface wear in zircaloy. Analytical procedures were developed for the analysis of palladium antimony and selenium by electrochemical techniques. Trace impurities in high purity lead and of cadmium in uranium were analysed electrochemical procedures.

A method for the determination of trace level boron by spectrophotometry using both batch and flow injection was develop Charged particle activation analysis procedure for the determination of bulk hydrogen in nuclear materials was developed. Procedures were also developed or modified for the analysis mercury in zinc concentrates, arsenic in groundwater, high purity arsenic m and oxides, high purity reagents and various other materials.

Separation procedures were worked out for the determination of palladium and gold in geological materials using polyaniline as a novel ion exchange material. A gas chromatographic procedure for the determination of carbide carbon in inorganic materials was developed. Collaboration with CFSL, Hyderabad was continued in order to effectively use nuclear methods for forensic work. Irradiation facilities were offered to GSI and other academic institutions. An Ultra Trace Analysis

Facility (UTAF) was refurbished at HRDCentre for the analysis of high purity materials like arsenic and gallium.

Applied chemistry

Chemical decontamination of C/U system of TAPS Unit 2 was taken up. This consists of two phases. Phase-1 involved reaching a system temperature of 360-365 K and a dissolved oxygen content of < 120 ppb and this was accomplished. Preliminary experiments of Phase-2 involving actual decontamination were initiated. A modified feasibility report incorporating both the phases has been made ready.

Pulse radiolysis technique was used to find more stable Cr(II) complexes which have applications in LOMI decontamination technique. In connection with the Task Force constituted to look into thermodynamic and transport properties of thoria based fuels to be used in Advanced Heavy Water Reactors, bulk thermal expansion of pure ThO_2, $BaThO_3$ and $SrThO_3$ were investigated by Dilatometry from room temperature to 1073 K. The detailed phase relations in MF_2-YF_3 (M=Ba, Sr, Ca) were studied. Several new phases were reported for the first time.

A number of strategic materials, rare earth oxyfluorides, superconducting oxide $LaBa_2Cu_2CoO_{7+d}$ were investigated for bulk thermal expansion and volume thermal expansion by Dilatometry and High Temperature XRD from room temperature to 1073 K. Studies on the vaporization behaviour of alkaline earth thorates such as $BaThO_3$ $SrThO_3$, Cs_2ThO_3 Rb_2ThO_3 were initiated. The work on BaTh03 was completed and there was good agreement in the thermodynamic properties of this compound as derived from both transpiration and Knudsen method. A new experimental facility for the study of release behaviour of volatile and gaseous fission products from nuclear fuels was set up and will give useful data on their diffusion coefficients.

Bio-organic chemistry

The research activities are directed towards the border line between organic chemistry and life sciences. Both applied and basic aspects of bio-organic chemistry are undertaken. Antioxidants have aroused great interest in recent years because of their chemopreventive importance in many of the degenerative diseases and about 40 naturally occurring compounds belonging to different classes (flavanoids, xanthones, terpenes and so on) were screened for their lipoxygenase inhibitory activity.

The anti-lipoxygenase activities of ginger and garlic were evaluated and a bioactive compound was isolated from ginger. Immunomodulators have aroused recent interest as many of these are promising anti-cancer and radioprotecting agents. A new polysaccharide possessing immunomodulatory activity has been isolated from an Indian medicinal plant and its partial structure was established. Preliminary results show that it has radioprotective action as well. A provisional patent has been filed on its active.

Using a low valent titanium based protocol developed in BARC, synthesis of several vicinal diamines, was accomplished. The protocol was used for the preparation of compounds which may find application in nuclear medicine. A provisional patent has been filed for this novel low valent titanium reagent. Polypeptides are the emerging high-value chemicals which find applications as pharmaceuticals, food-additivies as well as radiopharmaceuticals. Using the available expertise, polypeptide ligands, were synthesised via a solid phase technique. The technique was being extended for the synthesis of somatostatin and its analogs.

The utility of the methodology was under development in making a combinatorial library of biomolecules. In continuation of the ongoing programme on Integrated Pest Management (IPM), work was targetted to some cash and agricultural crops. Using synthetic pheromones, mass trapping has been carried out in collaboration with Central Cotton Research Institute, Nagpur. The pheromone treated fields produced an enhanced yield (30%) of high-value marketable cotton. As a part of the MOU signed between BARC and Central Tuber Crop Research Institute (CTCRI), Thiruvananthapuram, field evaluation of the sweet potato weevil (SPW) pheromone was continued.

In view of very encouraging results, the pheromone treatments were incorporated for the All India Coordinated trials on SPW. The potentialities of the biological processes for the preparation of organic compounds are being increasingly realised. Biocatalysts (enzymes), the cornerstone of modem biotechnology are likely to contribute significantly it the future chemical industry. Towards this end, efforts were directed to design novel asymmetric synthesis of high-value, low-volume bioactive compounds such as pharmaceuticals and agrochemicals. As part of our efforts in the development of clean technology, effort were directed to design novel asymmetric synthesis of high-value, low-volume bioactive compounds such as pharmaceuticals and agrochemicals.

A plan based biosorption strategy was explore for the decontamination of some radionuclides. Encouraging results were obtained using the plant, Sesuvium portulacastrum. Good uptake of several metal ions *viz.*, Th, Eu, Cs, U and Sr present individually and as mixtures were observed with the biomass. Microbial biomass has also been used for bioremediation.

Chemistry

The other activities in the field of Chemistry were primarily in basic sciences in the thrust areas of radiation and photochemistry, chemical dynamics, catalysis, solid state chemistry, interfacial sciences, high Tc superconducting materials, nanoclusters of metals, inorganic and organometallic chemistry. BARC has also been actively engaged in R&D work on hydrogels, catalyst development, thin films, ultrapurification of materials, and so on. Some of the significant achievements of these investigations are highlighted below:

Research work was initiated on femto second transient absorption studies using the recently developed Femto Second Laser Spectrometer. Solvent effects on the relaxation of electronically excited laser dye LDS-821 and subsequent vibrational cooling, relaxation of excited benzil molecule, photoprocesses of fullerenes and their aggregation in solution phase were investigated.

The free radical intermediates resulting from a number of drug and antioxidant molecules and biomolecules were characterized by pulse radiolysis studies, and significant results were obtained. The reaction of NO and NO_2 with organic molecules, a thrust area in environmental research was being actively pursued. Metal nano-particles species of several systems were synthesized by radiolysis technique and their physical properties were established.

A new process for the preparation of polyvinyl alcohol-based hydrogen by irradiation was developed in collaboration between Chemistry and BRIT. The material was undergoing clinical trials for wound dressing on patients with bum injuries in local hospitals.

The commissioning and testing of Cluster Generation Machine set up earlier as part of the VIIIth plan project were completed. Multiphoton ionization studies were carried out on ketones. The clustering behaviour in bimetallic clusters was correlated with electronegativities of the constituent elements.

Transient electric bireffingence studies on micelles, and investigations on growth of micelles in cationic-anionic mixtures gave interesting results. Studies on self-assembled monolayers and surface activity were initiated. It was found that the poor selectivity of Amberlyst-15 ion exchange resin could be attributed to the state of water in the resin.

Heated Filament Chemical Vapour Deposition was scaled up and optimised for uniform diamond deposition on substrates covering up to 4.0 inch diameter, both planar as well as three dimensional. Diamond coated tungsten carbide tool inserts have shown more than a 100 fold improvement in high speed machining of aluminium based alloys, and a very good surface finish. Methodology was developed for making upto 1.0 inch diameter self- supporting diamond windows.

The metal and polymer-based catalysts developed for removal of hydrogen from the containment areas of nuclear reactors under postulated severe accident conditions were successfully tested in an engineering scale test reactor set up by Reactor Engineering. Advances were made in the chemistry of monomeric and binuclear palladium/platinum complexes with organochalcogenide ligands.

A mode-coupling theory based microscopic approach to the dielectric friction on an ion was developed to explain conductivity of electrolyte solutions, and for application to charge transfer reactions in solutions. A new perturbative density functional theory was formulated for the study of absorption of in homogeneous complex fluid mixtures on surfaces, and porous materials.

Water and steam chemistry laboratory

Analytical methods were developed for monitoring the chemical cleaning process. Decontamination studies were carried out on the failed HX of MAPSI and cut specimens from HX of MAPS-II. A new analytical method for the estimation of MPA and ETA was developed. Electrochemical corrosion studies on carbon steel in process cooling water were carried out. It was observed that >20 ppm N_2H_4 accelerates corrosion of CS in the presence of sea water.

Commissioning of high Temperature high pressure (HTHP) loop has reached an advanced stage. The carbon steel surge tank and the primary and secondary loops were commissioned and hot conditioned. The system parameters functioned as expected during the high temperature operation.

Investigation on the prevalence of Balanus reticulatus in the process water heat exchangers of MAPS was carried out. The effect of bacterial exopolysaccharide, alginic acid and agarose on Balanus reticulatus was studied. The results of acute thermal shock on barnacle larvae indicated that the response of larvae was dependent on the time and temperature of chlorination.

Bio-sciences

Nuclear agriculture and biotechnology

The pigeonpea culture TT97-48 was promoted to advanced yield trial (AVT) on the basis of its yield performance in the Southern zone by the All India Coordinated Research Project on Pigeonpea. Trombay groundnut cultures, TG 32, 33, 34 and 35 were promoted to AVT in different zones for different reasons. The possibility of using salt tolerant plants for phytoremediation of radio- cesium was studied using callus tissue and seedlings of Chenopodium.

The potential of the lactose utilising yeast Kluyveromyces fragilis biomass as a biosorbent for Cr (VI) was investigated. A process for the extraction of industrially important enzymes *viz.* catalase, invertase and alcohol dehydrogenase from yeast biomass was scaled up to treat over 10 kg of yeast. In signal transduction studies on potatoes, treatment with low concentration of jasmonic acid has shown enhanced expression of calmodulin indicating the importance of jasmonic acid as a signalling molecule in signal transduction.

Food technology

Based on the research and developmental work undertaken at BARC, the Government of India through a Gazette Notification in April 6, 1998 have cleared radiation processing of several additional food items for domestic marketing and consumption. These include rice, wheat products (atta, sooji, maida), dried fruits (raisins, dates, figs), mango, ginger, garlic, shallots, meat, chicken and its products. Earlier in August 1994 the Government had approved irradiation of onions, potatoes and spices. Additional clearances for irradiation of pulses and sea foods were recommended by the Central Committee for Food Standards, Ministry of health at its meeting held on 14th December 1998.

Application of radiation technology for preservation of food items can benefit both the farmer and consumer by reducing wastage. Recent laboratory Studies have shown that irradiation can extend the shelf-life of Mushrooms, strawberry, cakes and ensure microbial safety in traditional milk based sweet meats like 'Pedha'.

Irradiation enhanced the nutritional quality of legumes (pulses) by rapidly degrading the flatulence causing oligosaccharides (complex carbohydrates) into its constituent simple sugars during germination. BARC has taken steps to commercialize the technology. A commercial demonstration irradiator for the treatment of onions was under construction in Lasalgaon, Nashik district of Maharashtra. A commercial, demonstration irradiator for spices was nearing completion in Navi Mumbai.

Molecular biology and agriculture

Research in molecular biology and molecular agriculture emphasizes elucidation of basic mechanisms involved in cellular response to radiation and other stresses, genotyping in plants and humans, and introduction of the latest concepts and techniques in the biological research programme of BARC.

A multienzyme complex which can repair irradiated DNA in test tube was purified and characterized; specific site mutations in the human gene encoding carbonic anhydrase were made with a view to establishing the identity of the amino acids directly involved in the activity and folding of this protein; extensive computer analysis based on software developed in house led to an elegant Darwinian explanation of recently reported bacterial mutations with apparently Lamarckian characteristics; several image processing software useful in agricultural research were developed in collaboration with the Computer and Electronic Instrumentations; two bacterial proteins involved in regulation of cellular response to radiation and cold stress were purified for structural studies in collaboration with the X-ray crystallography group of CMPD; DNA-based techniques were used for diagnosis of genetic diseases and genotyping of human population groups; several new plant proteins induced by dessication were identified and cDNA encoding them was sequenced, and a new project for developing DNA markers for genotyping & genetic analysis of legumes was initiated.

Cell biology

The presence of oxygen is known to enhance radiation damage in several biological systems including cells in culture in vitro. Using rat liver and brain mitochondria, calf thymus DNA and plasmid pBR322 DNA, we have examined the mechanisms of damage induced by gamma-radiation in the presence and absence of oxygen as well as its modulation by these three compounds. Our results reveal that presence of oxygen greatly enhances damage in mitochondria as well as in plasmid DNA but not in calf thymus DNA and that caffeine has differential effects in the presence and absence of oxygen.

Studies were carried out to see the cytogenetic changes caused by in vitro treatment of human lymphocytes with 5-Azacytidine *in vitro*. Studies on the effect of low dose radiation exposure (LDR) on immune response were continued. Experimental conditions were standardised for the amplification of cDNA, representing DCNI(P22), the most basic protein of all the polypeptides that were investigated to be induced under conditions of prolonged desiccation in *Portulaca grandiflora.*

Work on Modulation of clastogenic activity of Mitomycin C (MMC) by absorbic acid was continued with human peripheral blood cultures. The result further confirmed that clastogenic effect of MMC in human lymphocytes was potentiated by Ascorbic acid. Analysis of chromosomal aberrations in peripheral blood lymphocytes of adult subjects of high background radiation areas of Kerala was done and metaphase spreads were analysed.

Radiation Medicine Centre (RMC)

Radiation Medicine Centre a involved in three major spheres of activity *i.e.*, research and development in health sciences primarily using radionuclides, patient related services involving diagnosis of many a disorder as well as treatment using radiopharmaceuticals and human resource development in nuclear medicine through formal teaching and training programmes for students..

Efforts were initiated to procure a state-of-the-art in-house medical cyclotron for the production of very short-lived radionuclides of physiological interest, *viz.*, ^{18}IF, ^{11}Cz, ^{13}IN, ^{15}O with half lives of 110, 20, 2 min. respectively during the IX Five Year Plan period. It was envisaged that associated computer-driven, remote-controlled, shielded and automated chemistry reaction modules would be installed for the rapid synthesis of large amounts of physiological active biomolecules like ^{18}F-2Fluorodeoxyglucose ^{11}C-methionine. ^{13}N-NH_4 + 15O substrates, and so on, employing the above radionuclides. The detection of the positron-emitting radionuclides in the human body would be achieved using Positron Emission Tomographic (PET) systems.

The use of these was likely to have a far reaching impact on patient management (diagnosis, prognosis and treatment) in the field of oncology, neurology, cardiology, infection, and so on. The facility would be first of its kind in the country and perhaps in S.E. Asia. The 'turn key' project was in an advanced stage of planing. A sophisticated dual-headed, variable angle SPECT gamma camera with fan beam collimator was acquired. The instrument has advanced capabilities, and would help to obtain two views of patients at one tune and thus speed up the throughput of patients. Further, it has a facility for networking, and would be a great boon to patients.

An old General Electric analog camera was upgraded to digital one by using indigenous P.C. based technology single layer acquisition card facility for on-line energy, linearity and uniformity correction, as well as SPECT acquisition and analysis. A Nude Mice Housing Facility was established at RMC. This would facilitate the development of experimental models of various types of tumours of human origin and would be useful for the study of agents that could be targetted to tissues, and help development of diagnostic/therapeutic agents.

Twelve batches of radio-therapeutic agent 1311-mIBG was prepared in-house for the treatment of patients of neuro- endocrine tumours like neuroblastoma, pheochromacytoma, and so on. In addition an equal number of diagnostic batches were also made. Presently this is the only laboratory in the country making this expensive, and relatively unstable radiopharmaceuticals. Aqueous kits of a variety of Sn(II) ligand and other kits were made indigenously using in-house developed technology, and stored at 45°C. These kits having superior properties were used to formulate radio pharmaceuticals for patients.

About 90,000 mCi amounts of 99mTc radiopharmaceuticals of various descriptions - for brain / cardiac/liver/ hepatobiliary/renal-glomerular filtration and anatomy/lungs/tyroid/salivary/thyroid and so on were formulated, dispensed and used. Procedures for coating antibodies to polystyrene tubes was validated. A RIA kit for microal-buminuria especially to detect diabetic nephropathy was extensively tested. A RIA kit for T_4 using antibody coated magnetic particle separation has been formulated for BRIT.

The therapeutic efficacy of Chlorin, a porphyrin derivative and a photosensitiser has been studied in mice with transplanted fibrosarcoma and mammary tumours. Following irradiation with Cu vapour + pumped dye laser (fibre optic needle based technique) it was found that there was necrosis in the respective tumours (proven by histopathology) study performed in collaboration with CAT, Indore.

Different types of tests for the diagnosis of tuberculosis at small health care centres/hospital based immunological assays/sensitive and specific PCR assays were validated. An I.A.E.A sponsored programme on molecular typing of mycobacterial strain in multi-drug resistant tuberculosis was under way. About 8000 radiodiagnostic investigations involving various organs / tissues/neoplams were carried out during the year.

Technical services

Apart from providing technical support and services to the R&D activities, major work for augmentation and upgradation of in-house services for BARC under IX Plan were taken up. A major upgradation programme which involves augmenting the capacity of central air-conditioning plant upgradation of major electrical works at Central Air-conditioning Plant, electrical substations, centralised supervisory control system (SCADA) for substations, interconnection of South and North Site substations, upgradation of South Site service water lines and so on was started. BARC continued with its energy conservation programme which resulted in considerable saving of power.

Indira Gandhi Centre for Atomic Research

The Indira Gandhi Centre for Atomic Research (IGCAR) at Kalpakkam, Tamil Nadu, is engaged in the development of sodium cooled fast breeder reactor technology, related fuel cycle and safety. The Fast Breeder Test Reactor (FBTR) is its major facility.

Advanced laboratories for carrying out research and development work in the fast breeder reactor technology have been set up. The Centre is developing a 500 MWe Prototype Fast Breeder Reactor (PFBR).

Fast reactor programme

Fast breeder test reactor (FBTR)

The reactor was operated successfully during the year, reaching a burn-up level of 45,000 MWd/t. The performance of the carbide fuel was found to be excellent. A major refurbishing was done to improve the plant availability and fire safety and a programme of irradiation of zirconium-niobium alloy, used in PHWRs was initiated.

KAMNI reactor

Regular operation of the reactor upto the rated power of 30 kW was continued. Irradiation of various samples and activation analysis of various structural and nuclear materials were carried out. Neutron radiography, an important application of this reactor, was also done. The reactor is ready for taking up the neutron radiography of FBTR fuel assembly. Prototype Fast Breeder Reactor (PFBR) The Site Evaluation Report was under review by AERB. Significant progress was made in the design components and systems of Nuclear Steam Supply System (NSSS) and conventional systems.

Preliminary Safety Analysis Report on reactor assembly, Heat transport system and on component handling were prepared and the first phase of the experiment project in this fields of core seismic design and main vessel integrity under hypothetical core disruptive accident were completed. The document for the material properties to be used in the design, was piled; the technology development the manufacture of the main vessel PFBR was completed; activity towards the technology development for Inclined Fuel Transfer Machir Grid Plate, Sodium Service Valves were initiated, and material specifications tube sheets of heat exchangers we prepared for initiating production.

FBR R&D and engineering

Engineering development

The operation of the Large Component Test Rig (LCTR) was continued heat transfer experiments. The fabrication of the full scale model of the control plug of PFBR was in an advanced stage of completion. The piping and the auxiliary for the experimental facility for sodium water reaction studies are expected be commissioned shortly. The experimental study on the likely sodium deposition in the narrow long annulus of Control and Safety Drive Mechanism (CSRDM) was up in a small sodium set up. A contract was concluded with M/s. KBL for the development of new hydraulic design, using 1/3 scale model, for a compact primary sodium pump.

The dynamic behaviour of the primary pump rotor was being studied experimentally in a full scale test section-in house. The initial results of the tests were satisfactory. A development contract was in progress at the Fluid Control Research Institute, Palghat for validation tests on slip joints of both primary and secondary sodium pumps. The former reached an advanced stage of fabrication and testing.

A DC conduction pump was designed and was under construction for use in failed fuel identification model of PFBR. The dash pot for the CSRDM was tested in full scale, and based on the test results, modifications continued. A high temperature electromagnet was assembled and its load carrying capacity and response time for the Diverse Safety Rod Mechanism (DSRDM) were verified. The results were encouraging.

A project for the development of Temperature Sensitive Magnetic Switch developed for measuring sodium flow in FBTR fuel subassemblies. The models for the study of the secondary flow distribution in intermediate heat exchanger were installed in FCRI, Palghat and the experiments progressed.

The experimental setup, for conducting the flow induced vibration studies on a prototype instrumented sub-assembly, was fabricated. A 1/5th scale model of the core outlet region of PFBR was constructed for the study of thermal striping near the control plug region and tests were in progress. The tests were carried out for the improvement of the performance of Sodium Ionisation Detectors (SID). Feasibility of using SID as a sodium leak detection system in the presence of flue gases from a fired heater was being explored.

Work on the Steam Generator Tests Facility (SGTF) progressed well. Detailed design of the sodium loop E components gained momentum and orders for the components were being placed. The detailed engineering design of the buildings was completed and the technical bids for the steam water system of the facility were progressed and recommendations were 4 finalised. The installation of the various components of the Isotope Separation Plant made significant progress and the contract for the plant piping works was awarded. The engineering experiments on pilot scale progressed.

Reactor physics

Periodic calibration of control rods, measurement of temperature coefficients of reactivity and monitoring of the reactivity loss due to burnup were carried out for FBTR. The probabilistic safety analysis for blockage of flow in FBTR fuel subassemblies and their detection were completed. The kinetic experiments for the verification of delayed neutron parameters and also the isothermal temperature coefficient measurements for KAMINI reactor, were completed. Experiments to irradiate various samples were conducted to fine tune the system. The PFBR core physics design was approved by the Project Design Safety Committee (PDSC). The document for safety analysis and shielding wen completed for approval of PDSC.

Materials chemistry

A radio-nuclide trap made of Reticulated Vitreous Carbon (RVC) for removal of radioactive cesium from sodium was successfully tested and found suitable for reactor application, Studies were conducted on the compatibility of zircaloy with sodium. A sophisticated direct reading spectrometer was commissioned for qualitative determination of the constituents of stainless steels, ferritic steels and incoloy used in nuclear applications. Fundamental studies for understanding the role of diluents in the solvent extraction process in fuel reprocessing were carried out.

Thermal ionisation mass spectrometric studies were conducted on dissolver solution of the spent fuel pallet of FBTR to assess the burn-up level. Electrochemcial hydrogen meters and carbon meters were designed, developed and installed in FBTR secondary sodium circuit. A meter based on diffusion of hydrogen through nickel coil and detection by thermal conductivity detector, was installed and commissioned for monitoring hydrogen in FBTR cover gas (argon). Various experiments to enhance the sensitivity of SnO, based sensors for detection of hydrogen were carried out.

Fuel chemistry

One of the samples of FBTR fuel pin was dissolved in nitric acid and the bumup of the fuel was measured by determining the concentrations of uranium, plutonium and selected rareearths in the dissolver solution. The feasibility of using the indigenously developed bifunctional phosphinic acid resin for recovering uranium from raffinate streams was successfully demonstrated, at NFC, Hyderabad, The synthesis of the resin on large scale was taken up with a local manufacturer. The resin was also found to extract zirconium and hafnium.

Basic studies on solvent extraction were continued. A commercially available aminophosphonic type resin was evaluated for actinide recovery. It was found to extract uranium from a variety of acid media. Studies were undertaken to develop inorganic sorbents for extraction of Cesium from high active waste solution. A new combustion synthesis route was established for the preparation of thoria powder, which could be sintered to theoretical densities more than 95% at relatively low temperatures. This method using citric acid as the fuel was found to have many advantages over the conventional route.

Electronics and instrumentation

Client-server based Maintenance Management Information System was developed for FBTR to take into account the maintenance schedule, performance history, spares and and so on, a Mobile Data Acquisition system for MAPS, PLC based control system for Structural Mechanics Laboratory of IGCAR and Distributed Data Acquisition System for RAPS-II were developed and implemented.

Metallurgy and materials technology

Low Cycle Fatigue (LCF) properties of indigenously developed modified 9 Cr-I Mo steel was characterised over a temperature range of 773 to 873 K to assess its suitability for PFBR Steam Generator (SG) applications. Detailed investigations on LCF behaviour of austenitic steel 316 L(N) weld metal and 316 L(N)/316 L(N) weld joints and creep fatigue tests on 15 Cr- 15 Ni-2.2 Mo titanium modified austenitic stainless steel (D9 alloy) with titanium to carbon ratio of 4 in solution annealed and cold worked conditions were carried out for PFBR.

Alternative technology was developed for aluminising of inconel 718 and its welding for PFBR SG. 316 L electrodes with controlled nitrogen content was developed in collaboration with an Indian firm. A technique based on ultrasonic velocity measurement was standardised to characterise the annealing behaviour of D9 alloy. Theoretical and experimental works were carried out to determine the temperature distribution in plates during welding by Shielded Metal Arc Welding process and a correlation was established, for predicting the residual stresses in weldments.

Investigations on stress corrosion cracking of 316 LN samples in sodium hydroxide were carried out to assess the behaviour of the components during cleaning, after their exposure to liquid sodium in a fast reactor. A novel method of "heat correction' was used to develop multiple heat stress, rupture correlations for a large number of ferritic and austenitic structural steels. Repair welding procedure for type 410 stainless steel for low pressure turbine blades of KAPS was established using 316L electrodes.

Materials research

A facility installed for laser treatment of surfaces was used in the systematic study of microstructural changes in 2–1/4 Cr –1 Mo steel on laser treatment. Precise and accurate vapour pressure measurements were made and enthalpy of sublimation was estimated in cesium iodide by horizontal thermal analyser as a transpiration apparatus. Studies on depth profiling of defects were conducted in thin film interfaces and colossal magneto resistance films by using the indigenously built Low Energy Positron Beam (LEPB) Facility.

An ultra-high vacuum compatible facility commissioned for analysis of mass spectra of evolved gas at high temperatures, was used to characterise the structural and stoichiometric transformation in nuclear fuel cycle materials. An integrated flux locked loop electronics for linearising the output of the indigenously built SQUID was designed, fabricated and tested successfully.

Post-Irradiation Examination (PIE) The PIE was carried out on three experimental subassemblies irradiated in FBTR showed that no appreciable amount of swelling had taken place and the reduction in the gap between the fuel and the clad was only marginal. Further, no changes in the microstructure were observed in the fuel after irradiation and there was no effect of fuel-clad interaction. Experiments on irradiation of pressurised capsules made of zircaloy tube and zirconium - niobium alloy, to study the in-reactor creep rate, were started and the first two capsules were discharged from FBTR and PIE progressed. This will help in determining the useful life of the coolant tubes and planning of their replacement in PHWRs. Non-destructive Testing and Evaluation A MOBile SCANner (MOBSCAN), having a travel of 15 metres and a stroke of 500 mm, with a provision for mounting a camera, was designed and developed for non-destructive examination of large plates.

A Remotely Operated Power MANipulator (ROPMAN) provided with six degrees of freedom and with a gripper, was designed for hot cell applications. It is capable of upgradation to a full-fledged robotic arm. The design and development of a walking robot for in-service inspection of steam generators was completed.

The system can automatically deploy ultrasonic, eddy current and vision probes. It is adaptable to various types of heat exchanger configurations and can also scan large plates. This can also be modified to carry a manipulator arm, a closed circuit TV camera and so on, for maintenance/surveillance applications. Experimental studies were carried out to characterise the secondary phases in cold worked AISI 304 SS specimens using SQUID. These measurements were successful even with 10 % volume fraction as compared with 20 to 27 % for other methods.

The technique ot laser scattering was developed and successfully applied for the study of corrosion pits in stainless steel, monitoring the roughness of machined surfaces and the characterisation of laser induced surface modification. A laser based etching technique was also established for non-contact etching of metallic and ceramic specimens. An impact echo test method was developed for reliable examination concrete structures.

This method overcomes the limitations in the non-destructive examination of thick structures by using low frequency ultrasonics. IGCAR extended its expertise in the areas of NDT and failure analysis to other DAE units and also to a large number of strategic / core sectors of Indian industry.

Computing facilities

Enhancing the computing facilitied at IGCAR continued. Work progressed for establishing an ATM Optical Fibre backbone for networking of their various facilities of IGCAR. Commissioning of the Firewall system was on hand for improving the network security for the internet facility. Various modules for the computerisation of IGCAR administration and the Hospital Management System were developed and their testing progressed.

Health and safety

A bubble detector was indigenously developed and calibrated. It was used for evaluation of neutron shielding properties of borated compressed wood and also for evaluation of neutron dose to patients undergoing high energy X-ray and electron radiotherapy. Design of major components of a Compton profile spectrometer and the development work on the Intense Pulsed Neutron Facility had made significant progress. An Electron Cyclotron Resonance X-ray source was designed and constructed for use as a portable medical imaging unit.

A miniature pocket dosimeter, with audible alarm for every preset cumulative dose increase and overall cumulative dose was designed and fabricated. A continuous gamma dose logger for site environmental monitoring was also developed as an import substitution. An indigenous modelling code for the estimation of the activity release, transport and deposition of corrosion products as a function of time and distance in the primary sodium circuit of FBTR, was developed and validated successfully.

A 2-dimensional numeric code, handling the hydrodynamics of a simulated Core Disruptive Accident was developed. Stress-strain correlation under dynamic pressure loading was studied at room temperature. Efforts were on hand to correlate the shock energy and strain energy of the deformed specimen. A 100 U condenser bank was set up to generate transient pressures. This will be used in fast reactor safety studies related to containment capability.

A programme to model the fuel behaviour in reactor accidental situations was initiated. To assess the consequences of damage suffered by concrete in contact with sodium, experiments were conducted. Two experimental trials were carried out to study the air-cleaning of sodium fire containments. The aerosol trapping efficiency of the beds was found to be above 95 %. Fabrication of some of the components for the sodium fire test facility was started.

Safety surveillance inspections were carried out at all the facilities at Kalpakkam. Safety educational programmes and first aid training were also conducted, as a part of industrial safety. All incidents and occurrences were investigated in detail and a database software for the same was developed.

Coastal Atmospheric dispersion studies by employing tethered balloon, tower and mini-sodar were continued at Kalpakkam. A new thermo-luminescent phosphor, capable of measuring radiation dose of 5 mR was developed. Criticality safety evaluation of the process vessel for RAPS, shielding calculations for beam port of KAMINI reactor and testing of the shielding integrity of blisters, shield doors and hot cells of KARP were carried out. A LAN for the safety related activities was established.

Fuel reprocessing

FBTR fuel reprocessing

The Safety Report for the Lead Mini Cell (LMC) was cleared by Safety Committee and is under the scrutiny of SARCOP. The installation of the facility reached an advanced stage of completion. The cold commissioning of LMC, for reprocessing FBTR fuel on laboratory scale, is targeted for July 1999.

Fast reactor fuel processing plan

The site works for the air-conditioning and ventilation and service piping were completed. Tender for the fabrication of the process vessel was issued. Specifications for the cell piping works were prepared and the drawings for one of the cells were taken up. Most of the reconversion boxes were received at site. Preliminary design of radiation shielding glass frames was worked out for the radiation shielding windows received at site. U-233 refurbishing of system for recovery from thorium rods

Commissioning tests for the second campaign of uranium-233 recovery from irradiated thorium rods, were completed. With the clearance obtained from Safety Committee, the hot operations were continued.

R and D activities

A solvent extraction method was developed from acetic acid medium was employed in the recovery of U-233. Methods were also developed which will replace the use of hazardous formaldehyde, resulting in lesser waste volume. Extracto-spectro-photometric determination of uranium and plutonium was developed for fuel reprocessing application.

Engineering and technical services

Civil engineering

The civil engineering group handled all aspects of civil engineering., services right from conceptual, structural, architectural and public health, designs, estimates and contracts, quality control and construction of all projects in IGCAR, CWMF, KARP," WIP and also preliminary design work connected with PFBR. Design and construction of the housing, other public buildings and so on, in DAE Township were, also carried out. Consultancy services: for architectural and structural designs: were rendered to MAPS, BARC some of the aided institutions.

The extension building for the Fuel Reprocessing Development Laboratory was completed. Towards the infrastructure development in IGCAR, civil works related to the construction of security building, compound wall, widening of roads at IGCAR entrance and so on, were taken up.

The civil works for the IX plan projects such as mechanical maintenance and vibration building, substation building for steam generator test facility, structural mechanics lab., electronics and instrumentation laboratory and Quality assurance building and so on, were taken up. The construction of 112 quarters in the new township at Anupuram was progressing well and will be completed shortly. The IX plan works related to housing and infrastructure development were initiated at Aunpuram.

Construction of sixth battery of 49 tile holes for CWMF, inflammable stores building for KARP and main process building of WIP were completed. Special investigation works to assess the static and dynamic parameters and liquefaction potential of PFBR site were completed.

The bore hole studies for 90 metres depth for soil investigation made progress. The contract on the studies related to shore line stability for Kalpakkam was awarded to National Institute of Oceanography and the work progressed. Studies towards the development of special concretes for PFBR commenced.

Engineering services

Operation and maintenance of electrical, air-conditioning and ventilation and communication systems continued. Various energy saving measures were implemented for the electrical distribution and lighting systems in the Township. Specification for procurement of energy efficient 500 TR centrifugal chillers were finalised, and procurement of substation equipment for SGTF progressed. Internal electrification works made progress for various quarters at Anupuram. Technical support was provided to other organisations.

Quality engineering

Quality Assurance and NDT services were provided for various projects such as FRFRP, Technology Development works related to PFBR, Boron Enrichment Plant and others, and Quality surveillance, pre-service and in-service inspection support were extended to Heavy Water Plants at Manuguru and Kota, TAPS, IAF and so on. A development study to evaluate the influence of welding parameters on impact and fatigue properties of weld joints of boiler materials for PFBR was completed.

Management services

Significant progress was made in the implementation of the Phase I of the Purchase Management System at Madras Regional Purchase Unit, Chennai. A system for the feedback information to the indenters in respect of various tenders and purchase orders was developed and introduced.

A sophisticated system for monitoring the expenditure of all the capital projects of the Centre was implemented successfully. A system for preparation of budget proposals for capital projects was designed & developed and the same was under release. Procurement of the servers and client nodes for the LAN for interconnecting the Project Monitoring/Purchase Manage-ment Systems progressed.

Central workshop

Central Workshop caters to the manufacturing and R&D needs of various facilities and projects at Kalpakkam. It also serves for the technology and process development for the manufacture of nuclear components, which will be transferred to the Indian industries for execution. The Workshop developed a sleek miniature TIG welding torch. A mockup study for the development of high temperature brazing for joining copper conductor with SS 316 LN duct was in the final stage of adoption for the DC conduction pump for PFBR.

Technologies under evaluation for transfer included production of Yttrium Vanadate phosphor for use in mercury lamps, and technology for Lascan Dia Gauge. For NPCIL, development of ISI equipment for Moderator Heat Exchanger and RAPS type steam generator continued.

Pateninglcopyright activity

Three patents were given in acceptance and five patents were filed with the Patent Office, Mumbai.

Exoprts

BARC supplied Second lot of 500 Thoria buttons to General Electric, USA; Bulk reagents for Radio-immunoassay (RIA) to EGYPT; Liquid injection system and gas apparatus for radio-tracer experiments to Bangladesh; TLD Badges with provision of TLD badge reader services to Saudi Arabia; Gamma-Camera-Interface-Cards to Latin American, Asian & African countries through IAEA.

Management services

Project monitoring: The project coordination activities for all projects for which financial sanction was received, continued. Databases containing information on all the projects under R&D, I&M, and Power Sectors in BARC were created for project monitoring. Action was initiated for procurement of a variety of items. A statistical report on the retirement profile of scientific and technical staff for the period 1998-2002 was prepared to define future recruitment policy.

6

Water Resources Authority Advisory Board

National Institute of Hydrology

The National Institute of Hydrology was established in December 1978 with its headquarters at Roorkee by the Government of India as an autonomous society, fully aided by the Ministry of Water Resources.

The Union Minister of Water Resources is the President of the NIH Society and the Union Minister of State of Water Resources is its Vice-President. The Ministers-in-Charge of Irrigation in the States, the Secretaries of different Ministries in the Government of India concerned with water and related areas and experts in hydrology and water resources are members of the Society.

The Secretary, Ministry of Water Resources, Government of India, is the Chairman of the Governing Body. The Institute's research and other technical activities are monitored and guided by Technical Advisory Committee (TAC) headed by the Chairman, Central Water Commission. The Director of the Institute is appointed by the Government of India and he is the Principal Executive Officer of the Society.

In order to deal with the specific hydrological problems of different regions of the country and for providing effective interaction with the States, the Institute has set up regional centres for Hard Rock region, North-Eastern region, Western Himalayan region, Ganga Plains, Deltaic and East Coast region and for Ganga Plains (South) at Belgaum, Guwahati, Jammu, Patna, Kakinada and Sagar respectively. The Regional Co-ordination Committees have been constituted for each of the six regional centres to ensure effective coordination with various academic and field organisations and to advise on programme of studies and research.

Studies and research

The studies and research in the Institute are being conducted under eighteen scientific divisions at Roorkee and six regional centres. The studies and research are carried out broadly under the following major categories:

— Basic studies and research

— Applied studies and research

— Software development

— Field and laboratory oriented studies

— Sponsored and consultancy research

During 1998-99, work on studies involving 70 reports was carried out. Scientists and scientific staff of the Institute at its headquarter and six regional centres have published more than 80 papers in national and international journals and proceedings of national and International Conferences/Seminars and Symposia.

Software development

During this year, an interactive software package for Flood Frequency Analysis was developed which is useful for determining estimates of extreme flood corresponding to different return periods using different frequency distributions as applicable to the time series of data. Another software has also been developed for flood control operation of a multi-reservoir system consisting of a number of reservoirs either with or without gates.

Since the inception of the institute, besides carrying out regular basic and applied research and development studies, the Institute and its regional centres have also taken up a few problems with emphasis on research content, which are specifically referred to it by Central and State Government Organisations and Public Sector undertakings. Also a number of Central and State Ministries are sponsoring research projects taken up by scientists of the Institute. During 1998-99 four ongoing projects were continued. Studies on seven projects were completed and final reports submitted.

Indian National Committee on Hydrology (INCOH)

The Indian National Committee on Hydrology (I NCOH) was constituted by the Ministry of Water Resources in the year 1982. It is an apex body with the responsibility of co-ordinating the various activities concerning hydrology in the country. The Chairman, Central Water Commissions is the Chairman of the Committee with members drawn from Central and State Governments as well as experts from academic and research organisations besides a few members drawn from non-governmental professional associations. The Committee gets a feed back from States and co-ordinates activities of state level through state co-ordinators. The Secretariat of INCOH is with NIH. The Committee has successfully fulfilled its role and made important contributions for hydrological activities in the country during the past 16 years.

The main activities of the Committee includes preparation of state-of-the-art reports, providing technical and financial assistance to various organisations for organising seminars, symposia etc., organisation of national symposium of hydrology, every year providing sponsorship to research schemes in hydrology which are funded by Ministry of Water Resources and assisting various States in the constitution of their State level hydrology committees. The Committee brings out a bi-yearly journal entitled "Jal Vigyan Sameeksha" and also co-ordinates the International Hydrology programme of UNESCO in India.

During the year, the Committee provided sponsorship to nine conferences, seminars, etc. The Committee also provided technical and financial support for organisation of Ninth National Symposium on Hydrology which was held at Amritsar. During the year, two R & D projects sponsored by INCOH were completed and presently 18 projects are in progress. Work on completion of 7 state-of-the-art reports has been taken up during the year. Two issues of Jal Vigyan Sameeksha are expected to be published by the end of the year. India is actively participating in the Fifth phase of I HP of UNESCO. Initial preparations for India's participation in IHP-VI have also been started.

UNDP Project

A project worth US $3.00 million titled "Developing Capabilities for Hydrological Studies' assisted by UNDP under the Third Country Programme was in operation in the Institute since November, 1991 in order to achieve the following objectives:

(a) To develop capabilities and facilities at the Institute for undertaking hydrological studies for optimal utilisation of water resources in order to meet the growing demands of rising population of the country; and

(b) To establish capacity and capability in NIH Regional Centres, to undertake water balance studies in catchments with different water balance characteristics in three identified regions.

The following areas of hydrology have been developed through the project:-

— Hydrological Instrumentation
— Deltaic Hydrology
— Nuclear Hydrology
— Hydrometeorology
— Lake Hydrology
— Catchment Hydrology
— Data Processing Analysis
— Snow Hydrology
— Mountain Hydrology
— Remote Sensing Applications
— Environmental Hydrology
— Forest Hydrology

The project has been successfully completed in December 1997. A number of scientists have been trained abroad under this project

Hydrology project

Hydrological data of right quantity and quality Is an essential pre-requisite for rational and efficient water resources planning, development and management. To improve the overall technical capabilities of data collection, data processing and development of data Bank and analysis technique, the World Bank funded Hydrology Project was started in September 1995. The World Bank Supervision mission held discussions with NIH and other Central and State Organisations during July, 1998. The performance of NIH has been rated as 'satisfactory.' The following three training courses were organised during the year under the Hydrology Project:

— "Ground Water Hydrology with special reference to Coastal Areas" at NI H Regional Centre, Kakinada.

— "Computer Applications in Hydrology" at NIH, Roorkee.

— Water Quality Monitoring and Modelling" at NIH, Roorkee.

The DHV consultants organised a training course on HYMOS - 4 Windows version at NIH for training NIH scientists, who, in turn, will train Engineers of the State Govemments.

Under the Hydrology Project work on the following demand driven Research and Development Projects has been started during the year in collaboration with concerned state organisations:

— Fresh Water- Saline Water Inter Relationships in Multi-aquifer System of Krishna Delta In Andhra Pradesh.

— Estimation of Irrigation return flow In Lokapavani Area of K R Sagar Command in Karnataka.

— Artificial Measures for Ground Water recharge in Alluvial and Hard Rock areas of Maharastra.

— Joint Reservoir Operation Studies for Bhima River in Maharastra.

— Three packages of computers and their peripherals have been procured and installed.

Award

The Institute has instituted two awards. Bharat singh Award is given biennially In recognition of significant research contributions in the area of hydrology. The National Hydrology Award is also given biennially for stimulating original research, organisation and promotion of research activities in operational hydrology. During 1998-99, the Bharat Singh Award for the year 1997 and National Hydrology Award for 1996 have been decided.

Dr.K.D.Sharma of CAZRI,Jodhpur was selected for the National Hydrology Award (Rs. 1 0,000/-) for 1996 and Prof. P.B.S.Sharma of New Delhi and Prof. S.Vedula of HSC, Bangalore have been jointly chosen for the Bharat Singh award of Rs.20,000/- (Rs. 10,000/- each) for 1997.

Finances and budget

The Institute receives funds from the Ministry of Water Resources as grants-in-aid. The revised budget for Hydrology Project for the year 1998-99 was 66.00 lakh.

Use of hindi

All efforts for promoting the use of Hindi not only in the administrative works but also in the technical and scientific activities have been made. A number of original research papers in Hindi have been published in reputed journals. The work on Hydrology Terminology of about 600 terms in eight Indian Languages is in the final stage of completion.

Vigilance

During the year, there was no vigilance case requiring major or minor penalties. Departmental enquiries were conducted whenever required and necessary follow up action taken.

Narmada control authority

Constitution, functions and composition

In pursuance of the decision of the Narmada Water Disputes Tribunal under Clause XIV of its final order, the Government of India framed the Narmada Water Scheme, which, inter-alia, constituted the Narmada Control Authority and Review Committee in 1980 for proper implementation of the decisions and directions of the Tribunal. The Narmada Control Authority has been vested with the powers for the implementation of the orders of the Tribunal with respect to the storage, apportionment, regulation and control of the Narmada Waters, sharing of power benefits from Sardar Sarovar Project (SSP) regulated release of water by Madhya Pradesh, acquisition of land likely to be submerged under the Sardar Sarovar Project by the concerned States, compensation, resettlement and rehabilitation of the oustees, sharing of costs and implementation of the environmental safeguard measures.

The Authority is headed by the Secretary, Ministry of Water Resources, Government of India, as its Chairman, with Secretaries of the Union Ministries of Power, Environment and Forests, Social Justice and Empowerment, Chief Secretaries of the four party States, one Executive Member and three full-time Members appointed by the Central Government, and four part time Engineering Member's nominated by the party States, as Members.

The Review Committee of the Narmada Control Authority (RCNCA) may suo-motu or on the application of any party State or Secretary to the Government of India, Ministry of Environment and Forests, review any decision of the Authority.

In urgent cases, the Chairman of the Review Committee may, on application of the Government of any party State, or Secretary to the Government of India, Ministry of Environment and Forests, grant stay of any order of the Authority pending final decision or review.

Meeting of narmada control authority

The Authority held two meetings during the year on July 1, 1998 and December 18, 1998 in which Issues relating to resettlement and rehabilitation, environment and procurement of TG Sets for the river bed power house of Sardar Sarovar Project.

Sub-groups/sub-committees

The Authority has constituted the following discipline based Sub-groups:

1. Resettlement and Rehabilitation Sub-group under the Chairmanship-of Secretary, Union Ministry of Social Justice and Empowerment.
2. Environment sub-group under the Chairmanship of Secretary, Union Ministry of Environment and Forests.
3. Rehabilitation Committee under the Chairmanship of Secretary, Union Ministry of Social Justice and Empowerment.
4. Narmada Main Canal Sub-committee under the Chairmanship of Executive Member, Narmada Control Authority.
5. Hydromet Sub-group under the Chairmanship of Executive Member, Narmada Control Authority.
6. Power Sub-committee under the Chairmanship of Member (Power), Narmada Control Authority.

Two meetings of the Resettlement and Rehabilitation Sub-group, two field visits of the Rehabilitation Committee, one meeting of the Narmada Main Canal Subcommittee, one meeting of the Power Sub-committee and one meeting of the Hydromet Sub-group were held during the year.

Publications

The NCA has been publishing a quarterly journal Narmada Ghati Vikas Patrika in Hindi and English in which the objectives and planning of water resources projects in the basin, details of progress of construction, benefits from these projects and other important issues are furnished briefly for the benefit of the readers.

Resettlement and rehabilitation activities

The Resettlement and Rehabilitation policy for the affected persons of Sardar Sarovar Project is based on the decisions and the final orders of the Narmada Water Disputes Tribunal (NWDT) Award. Considering the socio-economic and cultural background of the population being displaced and with a view to improving the living conditions of these people, all the three participating States have formulated their own policies which contain more liberal provisions than those envisaged in the Narmada Water Disputes Tribunal Award.

The construction programme of the dam is now linked with the progress of Resettlement and Rehabilitation to ensure successful rehabilitation pari-passu with the implementation of the project out of a total of 40,727 project affected families, house plots have been allotted to 9,970 families and agricultural land has been allotted to 9,634 families up to September 30, 1998. The project affected families are also provided subsistence allowance, rehabilitation grant, ex-gratia productive assets and civic amenities like primary schools, wells, hand-pumps, transit sheds, Insurance cover, electrification and employment to some of them.

Environmental safeguard measures

All studies relating to the clearance of Sardar Sarovar Project and Indira Sagar Project have been completed. Further studies to firm up the mitigative measures are continuing. The studies so far conducted have shown that the positive impacts on environment will be many. The negative impacts., if any, can be managed with the help of safeguards being implemented. Relevant environmental action plans are also in place and under advance stage of implementation. Draft guidelines for conservation and development of Fisheries in the reservoir, streams and rivulets are on the anvil. A management information system using computer network with participating States and coordinating Ministries of Government of India is being developed in NCA.

In Sardar Sarovar Project, out of the total targeted area of 1,79,180 ha for catchment area treatment of directly draining sub-watersheds, an area of 1,21,161 ha has been treated up to September, 1998. Compensatory afforestation work has been carried out in an area of 45,270 ha against a total target of 46,358 ha. This work is being done in lieu of 17,943 ha taken by the Sardar Sarovar Project for submergence and resettlement and rehabilitation in Maharastra. Baseline data have been collected, action plan has been prepared and preventive and curative measures are being implemented in project and command areas and at rehabilitation sites as far as the health related issues are concerned. Epidemiological surveillance studies are also making progress.

In Indira Sagar Project, out of a total targeted area of 62,975 ha for catchment area treatment of directly draining sub-watersheds, an area of 40,818 ha has been treated up to September, 1998. Compensatory afforestation work has been carded out in an Area of 67,183 ha against a total target of 80,945 ha. This work is being done in lieu of 41,420 ha used by the Indira Sagar Project for submergence, residential colony, power house complex, dam, saddle dam and approach roads.

Energy management centre and hydromet network

The Narmada Control Authority has planned the setting up of Energy Management Centre at Indore at a cost of Rs. 36.9 million for monitoring the sharing of power produced at Sardar Sarovar Project by the party States. The total work was divided into four packages. Packages-I and II comprising Micro Computer based

Remote Terminal Units and Personal Computer based Data Acquisition System have been awarded to M/s. BHEL. Package-III, comprising allied equipment for the Energy Management Centre like diesel generating set, air-conditioning, multi-channel voice logging recorder etc., has been awarded to M/s. NELCO. Package-IV, comprising time of day metering system has been awarded to M/s. INTRAX. The supplies of equipments under various packages has been completed and the work of installation of equipment is under progress.

A contract was signed with M/s. ECIL in September, 1996 for an amount of Rs. 12.85 crore for implementation of Real Time Data Acquisition System (RTDAS) Network comprising 26 Remote Stations with Sensors to communicate Real Time Data on water level and other hydro-meteorological aspects to a Master Control Centre at Indore for forecasting of floods at major projects like Sardar Sarovar Project. The Project is now planned to be implemented by December, 1999.

Budget and finance

The expenditure incurred by the Authority on Office Expenses, construction of buildings for staff quarters/ office complex and setting up of Energy Management Centre is to be bome out of the Narmada Control Authority fund, contributions to which are made by the participating States of Gujarat, Madhya Pradesh, Maharastra and Rajasthan equally. The share contribution for establishment of Hydromet Network is given presently on the basis of ad-hoc formula till the issue is finally resolved by RCNCA.

Sardar sarovar construction advisory committee

The Sardar Sarovar Construction Advisory Committee (SSCAC) was constituted in 1980 by the Government of India in accordance with the directions of the Narmada

Water Dispute Tribunal (NWDT) with a view to ensuring efficient, economical and early execution of Unit-I (Dam and Appurtenant works) and Unit-III (Hydro Power works) of the Sardar Sarovar Project.

The functions of the Committee include scrutiny of estimates, technical features, design, specifications, contracts and monitoring of the progress of construction. The Secretary, Government of India, Ministry of Water Resources, is the Chairman of the Committee. The Officers of the concerned departments of Irrigation, Power, Revenue, Welfare etc. of the four party States of Gujarat, Maharashtra, Rajasthan and Madhya Pradesh and Narmada Control Authority are Members of the Committee. The Committee has a Secretary of the rank of the Chief Engineer. The Secretariat of the SSCAC is located at Vadodara.

Permanent standing committee

The SSCAC has a Permanent Standing Committee (PSC) with the Executive Member, Narmada Control Authority as the Chairman and representatives from Ministry of Water Resources, Central Water Commission, Central Electricity Authority and Sardar Sarovar Narmada Nigam Ltd. and all the four party States as Members. The Secretary, SSCAC is the Member Secretary of the PSC.

Important decision taken by the SSCAC/PSC

The following important decisions were take during 1998-99 :-

— The draft proposals for Ninth Five Year Plan (1997-2002) amounting to Rs. 14,000 crore and Annual Development Plan 1998-99 for Rs. 2 100 crore for the Sardar Sarovar Project were discussed by the PSC and recommended for approval.

— The issue of payment of Share Cost by the Party

States of Maharashtra, Rajasthan and Madhya Pradesh to Gujarat towards the expenditure on Sardar Sarovar Project was discussed to work out a strategy for early payment of arrears of share cost.

— The extension of time limit sought by M/s. ECIL for implementing Real Time Data Acquisition System (RTDAS) project in the Narmada Basin was approved.

— Claim for extra item rate of Rs. 635 RM for providing 12m long 32 mm dia rock bolts in Power House Cavern was approved.

— The claim of the contractor for the work of controlling excessive flow of water through the construction sluices at EL 18 m in Dam blocks No. 35 and 36 of main dam was discussed and finalised.

Progress of works sardar sarovar dam

The Sardar Sarovar Dam was programmed to be raised to a minimum elevation of 110 m during the year 1997-98 for achieving partial benefits of irrigation and power as decided by the SSCAC in its sixty-second meeting. However, this could not be achieved due to the objections by Madhya Pradesh about the final height of the dam and the constraints of the Resettlement and Rehabilitation of the Project Affected Families. There has been no significant progress in the raising of the concrete dam during the year.

The raising of the power dam and right non over flow blocks No. 51 to 64 from EL 133 m to EL 146.5 m (top of dam) was approved by the SSCAC in its sixty-third meeting held in December, 1997. The minimum level of spillway blocks No. 30-46 is maintained at EL 80.3 m only in view of the restrictions imposed by the Supreme Court judgement dated May 5, 1996.

Canal head power house

The Civil and Electrical works of Canal Head Power House have been completed and all the five units each of 50 MW capacity are ready for commissioning.

River bed power house

The work in the River Bed Power House had been held up due to development of stress zone in the power house cavern and non receipt of embedded parts for the T.G. Sets because of some contractual problems.

The issue has now been settled and an agreement has been reached with M/s. Sumitomo Corporation, Japan (Supplier of T.G. Sets). The Works in the River Bed Power House are likely to be resumed soon along with the installation of T.G. Sets.

National projects construction cooperation limited

Organisation

National Projects Construction Corporation Limited (NPCC) was established in the year 1957 as a Construction Company to provide the necessary manpower and know-how for construction of canal system, irrigation and river valley projects, dam and barrages, hydro-electric, thermal power, Industrial structure, surface transport, bridges and fly-overs, building and townships and air-fields etc. In its existence of over 42 years, the Corporation has been associated with over 120 projects of national Importance all over the country involving some at the most remote and hazardous locations. The Corporation has also successfully executed several overseas projects in the Middle-East countries, Nepal and Bhutan etc.

Orderbook position

The Order Book Position as on 30.10.98 was Rs.274.09 Crore. In order to enhance the Order Book Position, the

Corporation has diversified its activities. In this direction, Memorandum of Understanding have been entered into with other Organisations/firms. MOU has been signed with M/s. TCIL in the field of trenchless technologies and other work of this Organisation. To further activate the marketing, MOUs have been signed with reputed companies.

A thrust has been made in the field of Interior works of the buildings for which offers are being called from NPCC by various clients. This being a new field of activity for Corporation, MOUs have been signed with experienced architectural firms.

Projects completed

The following projects were completed by NPCC Ltd. during 1998-99:

— Head Race Channel for Indira Sagar Project, Khandwa

— IOCL work at PAGUTHAN and AMOD

— Site levelling and Reservoir works for Faridabad Gas Power Project

— Construction of buildings for South Campus, Delhi

— IOCL work of Gidha

Works under execution

At present, the Corporation is working on 83 projects spread all over the country. These include, 14 Irrigation and river valley projects, 7 hydro-electric projects, 12 thermal projects, 9 industrial projects and 41 other miscellaneous projects. Some of the projects in hand are as follows:-

Irrigation and river valley projects

Manu Barrage (Tripura), Khuga Dam and Spillway

(Manipur), Rajghat Dam (Uttar Pradesh), Indira Sagar Aqueduct-cum-bridge at Rani Avantibai Canal, Gotegaon (Madhya Pradesh), Maharani Tunnel (Tripura), Sharada Sahayak Canal (Uttar Pradesh), Dolaithabi Barrage (Manipur), Bakreshwar Dam (West Bengal) and Thamileru Earth Dam, Eluru (Andhra Pradesh.).

Thermal projects

Bokaro Thermal Power Project (Bihar), CHP for Vindhyachal T.P.P. (Madhya Pradesh), Coal Handling Plant and General Civil Works of Unchahar T.P.S. (Uttar Pradesh), Kahalgaon Super Thermal Power Project (Bihar), Mejia T.P.S. (West Bengal), Talcher Super Thermal Power Project (Orissa), Korba S.T.P.P. (Madhya Pradesh), Anpara T.P.S. (Uttar Pradesh), Faridabad Gas Power Project (Harayana), BHEL Karaikal (Pondicherry), and Farakka S.T.T.P. (West Bengal).

Industrial projects

Miscellaneous Works for Rourkela Steel Plant (Orissa), Water Treatment Plant at Bangalore (Karnataka), BPCL Works at Cheppad (Kerala) Indian Oil Corporation Limited at Taloja (Maharastra), IOCL Works at Cheralapally (A.P.), Integrated Water Supply Scheme at Talcher (Orissa), Trivandrum Sewerage Work at Thiruvananthapuram (Kerala), Coke Oven and Power House Complex for KMCL (Orissa) and Structural works for NALCO at Damanjodi (Orissa).

Miscellaneous projects

The Corporation undertook several construction assignments relating to buildings, roads, hospitals, bridges, flyovers and loco sheds etc. These include TNUDP Bridge at Chennai (Tamil Nadu), Nuclear Fuel Complex, Hyderabad (Andhra Pradesh), Central Ground Water Training and Research Institute at Raipur (Madhya Pradesh), Tungabhadra Bridge at Kurnool (Andhra

Pradesh), Damodar Valley Corporation Buildings at Maithon (West Bengal), Hospitals at Raichur and Renubenur (Karnataka) and Fisheries College at Agartala (Tripura).

Training

In order to give a boost to the training functions, the training cell of the Corporation was reorganised. During the year, a training course was organised in-house in which training was imparted to 18 engineers drawn from NPCC and P & T Department. Further, 21 officers/staff were deputed for relevant external training courses upto December, 1998.

Working of VRS scheme

During the period from 1.04.98 to 30.11.98,.a total of 154 employees had exercised option, under Voluntary Retirement Scheme. Out of them, 125 employees have been. relieved from the services of the Corporation and remaining 29 employees have yet to be relieved. They will be relieved on receipt of allocation by Government of India from the National Renewal Fund. A sum of Rs.2566.63 lakh has been spent so far on extending Voluntary Retirement benefit to 1778 employees upto 30.11.98 since the introduction of Scheme in the year 1991.

Water and Power Consultancy Services (India) Limited, New Delhi, provides technical consultancy services in the water and power sectors. The services cover prefeasibility studies, investigations, designs, tender-documentation and evaluation, construction management, operation and maintenance as well as training. The fields of activity encompass irrigation and drainage, flood control and reclamation, ground water exploration and development, water supply and sewerage, hydro and thermal power, ports and harbours, inland waterways, environmental engineering, dam and reservoir engineering and integrated agriculture development.

Financial achievements

The year 1997-98 had been a momentous one both from the point of view of performance as well as in respect of significant policy orientation for the Company's growth. The Company had been able not only to sustain the growth of business but could significantly improve upon the same. The consultancy income reached an all-time high of Rs. 2581.67 lakh, the highest growth rate in recent past. In the foreign exchange earnings front also in spite of constraints and difficulties in the foreign market being faced currently as a global phenomenon, the Company has been able to post net foreign exchange earnings equivalent to US$ 4.69 lakh. The Company paid a dividend of Rs. 60 lakh which is 30 per cent on its paid up capital of Rs. 200 lakh. The Company, since its inception, has been able to manage its business operations from its own resources and has not taken recourse to borrowings. The Company bagged the export promotion award of EEPC for 1996-97.

Irrigation and multipurpose projects

Major projects undertaken in various states include:

Andhra Pradesh: Kurnool-Cuddapah Canal Modernisation Project in association with Nippon Koei Company Limited, Japan.

Assam: Feasibility Report for Deopani and Amreng Medium Irrigation Projects.

Orissa: Survey, planning and design of micro-canalisation and drainage network for Upper Kolab Project; survey, planning and design of micro-irrigation and drainage system for ayacut of

16,500 ha of LMC in Upper Indravati Irrigation Project Reach - 1.

Punjab: Data computerisation for water resources management; review of hydrological and hydro-meteorological observation station, water quality testing facilities and institutional arrangement.

Rajasthan: Command area chakbandi and preparation of final L-section of Indira Gandhi Canal System; topographical survey for pipeline alignment from Bilaspur Dam to Hagiwala Headworks; sub rectangulation surveys of Gadra road sub-branch system of IGMC; sub-rectangulation survey of life scheme area of IGNP; command area survey of flow area of IGNP Staged- II water-shed management project; flood moderation study of, Bharatpur and Alwar districts.

West Bengal: Micro planning for a pilot project in the command of Teesta Barrage Project Performance evaluation of system analysis of Mayurakshi Reservoir Project.

Other assignments

— Back-water effects studies on main river Wainganga u/s of Gosikhurd Dam.

— Bhima-Sina Link Canal Project-Ph-II work for construction supervision of irrigation and canal structures.

— Master plan for Flood Protection works on river Chenab, J&K.

— Master plan for Flood Protection works on river Tawi (Two branches), J&K.

— Study on assessment of ground water in Dark Blocks of Punjab - NABARD.

— Dutch-aided Five year Operational Pilot Project (OPP) for reclamation of saline and waterlogged areas in Haryana.

— World Bank aided "Special Study on Efficiency of Shallow Tubewells in 14 districts of U.P."

— Artificial Ground water Recharge and Reuse of waste water for Jaipur city, as sub-consultant to ANTEA International.

Socio-economic studies and soil survey

— Socio-Economic Survey of villages under submergence of Gosikhurd Project, for Vidarbha Irrigation Development Corporation, Nagpur.

— Semi-Detailed Soil Survey in the Command Area of Pagladiya Dam Project in Assam - for Brahmaputra Board.

Training

— Seventeen National level and 15 State level training programme on CAD, PIM and Waterlogging were conducted.

— Five Study tours on "Development of Water Control system for diversification of crops in Maharashtra State", funded by European Community for the Engineers of Irrigation Department Maharashtra were undertaken.

— Training and Documentation Centre has been set up for National Level Training Programme on Modular Training Approach in Irrigation Management, produced and developed by the Indo-Dutch Production Management Unit (PMU) of Netherlands' Embassy, under Indo-Dutch Bilateral Cooperation.

Water supply and allied projects

— Preparation of detailed project report for sewage

treatment plant adopting UASB technology in four towns of Tamilnadu.

— Augmentation of water supply from Manali Pumped Storage, Tamilnadu.

— Leak detection, assessment and supervision of repair works for Bangalore, PHED.

— Pre-delivery Inspection of pipes and Materials on behalf of Tamilnadu Water Supply and Drainage Board, Chennai.

Important studies/assignments overseas

— Punjab Integrated Rural Water Supply and Environmental Sanitation Project funded by World Bank.

— Komering Project Stage-III (Phase-I) in Indonesia.

Information technology

— Consultancy for Upper Kolab and Upper Indravati Irrigation Project, Government of Orissa.

— Pilot Water Resources Study of Godavari basin upto Paithan Dam, Government of Maharashtra.

— Integrated Simulation Studies and Real Time Operation of SMP Project, Government of Orissa.

— Technical Assistance for Planning and implementation of Rural Development in Karnataka and Rajasthan, World Flood Programme.

— Monitoring and Evaluation Study of Rural Water Supply Schemes in Maharashtra and Karnataka for Rajiv Gandhi National Drinking Water Mission.

— Preparation of Pictorial Book and Film on Water Resources Development on the occasion of 50 years of India's Independence for the Ministry of Water Resources.

— Modernisation of Sukla Irrigation Project, Government of Assam.

— Water Management and Water Harvesting Study in U.T. of Dadra and Nagar Haveli.

— Development of Project Financial Management system for the Eighth India Population Project (I PP), Municipal Corporation of India.

Dam safety

— Consultancy Services to review and appraise the proposed design solution for strengthening of Tansa Dam (Maharashtra)

— Investigations into the remedial measures against deterioration of Civil Hydraulic structures inChiplima Power House - II, (Orissa).

INCID activities

During the year, WAPCOS continued to provide secretarial assistance to INCID. A three member delegation consisting S/Shri B.S. Ahuja, Commissioner (PP), MOWR and Team Leader, R. Jeyaseelan, Chief Engineer (Monitoring - Central), CWC and P.B. Parabrahmam, Member- Secretary, INCID participated in forty ninth IEC Meeting and Tenth Afro-Asian Regional Conference held at Sanur, Bali, Indonesia from 1925 July, 1998. Shri P.L. Diwan, Chairman and Managing Director, WAPCOS (India) Limited presented his paper on "Saline and Brackish Water in Irrigation -Implications to the Management of Irrigation, Drainage and Crops".

Ministry of Water Resources is sponsoring the ICID eighth International Drainage Workshop from January 31 to February 4,2000 in New Delhi and has sanctioned a grant of Rs. 62 lakh. M/s WAPCOS (India) Ltd. will organise the Workshop on behalf of INCID. Chairman, INCID has constituted the Organising Committee and the

Technical Committee for organising the Workshop. The First Information Bulletin and Call for papers for the Workshop will be issued shortly. The Second Information Bulletin is to be issued before March, 1999.

INCID published the Status Report on "Sprinkler Irrigation in India"' and the State-of-the art paper on "Pipe Distribution Systems on Irrigation and Drainage" is in the press. An updated detailed study on "Participatory Irrigation Management in India" and the Eighth Annual Report of INCID for 1997-98 are under compilation and are expected to be published during the current financial year.

INCID has co-sponsored two National Seminars on "Water Management for Sustainable Agriculture-Problems and perspectives of 21st Century", held at New Delhi from 15-17 April, 1998 and "National Seminar on Socio- Economic Aspects of Sub-Surface Drainage and Water Management", held at Jaipur, Rajasthan from 22-23 May, 1998. In addition to the above, INCID and CSSRI, Karnal will organise a Special workshop for 10 experts from the Aral Basin States on "Drainage and Water for Agriculture and Agro-Forestry in Salt-affected Soils" during the first week of March, 1999. The proposal is in advanced stage of processing.

INCID officials have actively participated in: (1) Interactive meet on Bio-Drainage; (ii) Water Management for Sustainable Agricultural Production; (iii) Water Management in Flood-Prone Areas in connection with the Forty-eighth ICID Foundation Day Celebrations; and (iv) Workshop on NICNET-based Irrigation, Water Management for Senior Managers.

INCID continued monitoring of 62 on-going research schemes. Ministry of Water Resources released a grant of Rs. 30.20 lakh for these schemes. The four Sub-Committees of INCID held one meeting each during the year ii i which various completed schemes and new proposals besides monitoring of on-going projects were approved. INCID has recommended two new research schemes to MOWR for funding during the current financial year.

Three issues of "INCID NEWS" Quarterly Newsletter Volume No. 5 have been released.

Ports and harbours

— EIA study for breakwater at Pawas Bay, near Ratnagiri, Maharashtra for M/s Finolex Industries Ltd.

— Detailed Project Report for development of port at Maroli for M/s National Telecom of India Ltd.

— Development of fishing harbour at Harnai and Sakhrinate in Ratnagiri for Government of Maharashtra.

— Rehabilitation of damaged breakwater at Porbandar for M/s Gujarat Maritime Board.

— Techno Feasibility Study for Development of Fresh Water Lake at Port Blair (A&N Island) for M/s Andaman Lakshdweep Harbours Works under Ministry of Surface Transport.

— Cooling water system at Sikka Thermal Power Station for M/s Gujarat Electricity Board.

— Review of proposed Modification/ Strengthening of existing jetty in Kranja Creek at Khopta for M/s Essar Steel Ltd.

— Detailed Engineering for Cement terminal at Vasai Creek for M/s Saurashtra Cement Ltd. (SCL).

— Detailed Engineering for Shore Protection Works at, Balagarh Char for M/s Calcutta Electric Supply Company Ltd.

— Technical Evaluation of proposals for development of Vijayadurg Port for Zoom Developers.

— Planning and Design of jetty/ Wharf including approach at Thangaserry for M/s Gujarat Ambuja Cement Ltd.

Power

— Detailed design and engineering work of Purulia Pumped Storage Project (4× 225 MW), West Bengal in association With EPDC (Japan).

— Review of design and engineering of World Bank funded Nathpa Jhakri H.E. Project (6 × 250 MW) in Himachal Pradesh.

— Detailed design and engineering for Hirakud— `B' (4× 52 MW) and Chiplima 'B'(4 × 50 MW) H.E. Project, Orissa.

— Design of Gates and Bridges for Bisalpur Dam, Rajasthan has been completed.

— Planning and Design of Construction of Pump House for Command Tank—4, Dwaraka project has been completed.

— Planning and Design of Construction of Pump House for Command Tank—2, Dwaraka project has been completed.

— Design of Ash slurry disposal system for Anpara Thermal Power Project, U. P.

— Review of DPR and providing assistance in finalisation of Power Purchase Agreement and Water Supply and Management Agreement of Upper Krishna Project (4× 7O MW + 1× 17 MW), Karnataka.

— Review of detailed design of Harangi H.E. Project (2× 4.5 MW), Karnataka.

— Consultancy for third stage tailings dam and dyke at Jaduguda mines, Singhbhum, Bihar.

— Preparation of document (PQD and RFP) for Anjunem H.E. Project, Goa.

Environment

— EIA of a jetty, at Vasai Creek, near Bhayander, Mumbai for Saurashtra Cements Ltd.

— EIA of Hydro-Electric Project, district Kinnaur, H.P. for NJPC.

— Dam break Analysis study for Umrong Dam, Meghalaya for NEEPCO.

— Environmental studies for Purulia Pumped Storage Project, West Bengal.

— Environmental Audit Study for four sites at Karnataka and Maharashtra for Geraghty and Miller, U.K.

— Environmental Audit Study for one site at Ghaziabad, U.P. for G&M, U.K.

— EIA of a breakwater at Pawas Bay, Near Ratnagiri Maharashtra for Finolex Industries Ltd.

— EIA of a jetty at Krishnapatnam, District Nellore, A.P. for GVK Power Ltd., Hyderabad.

Overseas activities

Power

— Three WAPCOS advisors are working with Zimbabwe Electricity Supply Authority (ZESA) in the field of operation and maintenance of two thermal power stations in Zimbabwe.

— Engineering project management and supervision of completion of World Bank funded Hwange Power

Station Phase- II Upgrade Project (4120 MW + 2 × 220 MW), Zimbabwe. Three WAPCOS experts are working in the field providing requisite services for the project.

— Infrastructure development, detailed design and engineering and construction, supervision, and monitoring for Tala H. E. Project (6 × 170 MW).

— Detailed design and engineering for the development of 132 KV Transmission Grid in Eastern Bhutan, involving 200 km line and 7 substations.

— Review of basic designs, drawings and specifications, construction methodology and assisting the Kurichu Project Authority in monitoring programme and planning of the project for Kurichu H.E. Project (3 × 15 MW + 1× 15 MW), Bhutan.

Water supply

— Laboos Area Water Supply project (Contract -III) funded by OPEC of Arab Fund in the Republic of Yemen.

— Water Supply and Sewerage Scheme for Gedu Township at Tala H.E. Project, Bhutan.

Progressive use of Hindi

To create an awareness about the use of official language Hindi in official work and to speed up progressive use of Hindi, Hindi Fortnight from September first to September 15, 1998 was observed in WAPCOS. All officers/ employees of WAPCOS were requested to do their maximum official work in Hindi. During the Hindi fortnight, Hindi essay writing, Hindi stenography and Hindi Typewriting competitions were organised and a special short-duration official language cash award scheme was also implemented to encourage officers/ employees to do their maximum official work in Hindi.

Participants were given prizes on the basis of quantum of work in Hindi done by them. In these competitions as many as 85 officers/ employees actively participated.

Five officials actively participated in the Annual incentive scheme of noting and drafting in Hindi and they were given cash prizes. One of them was Chief Engineer (Commercial) whose mother tongue is Tamil.

Emphasis was laid on ensuring compliance of the provisions of Section 3 (3) of the Official Language Act and on increasing correspondence in Hindi. Efforts were also made to persuade, motivate and encourage officers and employees to do their maximum official work in Hindi. To facilitate the use of Hindi in official work, several standard drafts and notes were made available for day-to-day use either in Hindi or in bilingual form.

Meetings of Departmental Official Language Implementation Committee were held regularly and progress made in the implementation of the annual and other orders/ instructions of the Government of India. relating to the use of Hindi in official work was reviewed in these meetings.

Two Hindi workshops were organised during the year for imparting practical training in noting/ drafting in Hindi. Thirty two Officers/ Employees participated in these workshops.

WAPCOS' efforts were recognised through award of the rolling shield for best performance in the use of Hindi by the Ministry of Water Resources for the year 1997-98 also. This award was presented by the Secretary for Water Resources to CMD, WAPCOS at a function held in the Ministry on 15.9.1998.

To promote progressive use of Hindi in the Company including its Technical Wings and to create interest in the use of Hindi in official work, the bi-monthly in-house Magazine in Hindi continued to be brought out regularly during the year covering all activities/ achievements of the Company and other items of news value.

Appointment of weaker sections

The Company follows Government guidelines/ instructions on reservation policy for SCs/ STs/ OBCs/ Physically Handicapped/ Ex-Servicemen etc. Relevant rosters, as prescribed by the Government, are maintained for plotting the reservation for these categories of candidates. Due consideration has been given to the recruitment of minorities and their representation on the Selection Committees. The instructions given by the Government under 15-point programmes for minorities are being followed by the Company in recruitment process.

Under the Special Recruitment Drive launched in 1996-97 to fill up the backlog of vacancies reserved for SCs/ STs, the Company had identified 10 vacancies (2 for SCs and 8 for STs) in various categories of posts both in Technical and Non-Technical sides. The Company has been successful in Filling up the above reserved vacancies except three for which action is in hand to fill up the same soon.

The Company had also launched a Recruitment drive for Physically Handicapped in 1996-97. Under this drive, two vacancies were identified. The Company has been successful in filling up both these vacancies.

The Brahmaputra board

This, an autonomous statutory body, was set up under Brahmaputra Board Act, (46 of 1980). The jurisdiction of the Board covers the Brahmaputra and Barak Valley, encompassing the States of the North Eastern Region either in full or in part. The Board started functioning from 11th January, 1982 with headquarters at Guwahati. The main functions of the Board are as under

(i) To carry out surveys and investigations in the Brahmaputra valley and prepare Master Plans for control of floods, bank erosion and improvement of drainage in the valley.

(ii) To prepare the Master Plans on development and utilisation of water resources of the Brahmaputra valley for irrigation, hydro-power, navigation and other beneficial purposes.

(iii) To prepare detailed project reports and estimates in respect of the dams and other projects in the Master Plan as approved by the Central Government, along with the cost attributable to different purposes or uses.

(iv) To construct, with the approval of the Central Government, multipurpose dams and works connected therewith proposed in the Master Plans as approved by the Central Government, and also maintain and operate such dams and works.

(v) To prepare, in consultation with the concerned State Government, a phased programme for construction by the State Government of all dams and other projects proposed in the Master Plan as approved by the Central Government.

(vi) The Board may maintain and operate any dam or project as long as it deems necessary so to do.

(vii) To perform such other functions as are supplemental, incidental or consequential to functions specified above.

Brahmaputra Board during its existence of more than 17 years has generated voluminous data base in the form of Master Plan of Brahmaputra and its tributaries and 8 rivers of Tripura. This information would be of immense utility for selection of various Multipurpose projects, drainage development schemes and anti erosion schemes. These Master Plans are periodically updated. Brahmaputra Board is also closely associated with the monitoring of the schemes taken up by the Flood Control Departments in the North Eastern Region.

The status of preparation of Master Plans, DPR for Multipurpose projects and drainage schemes is giver, below

Preparation of master plan

The Master Plan has been taken up in three parts under

- Main stem of Brahmaputra i.e. Master Plan Part-I
- The Barak and its tributaries i.e. Master Plan Part-II
- Thirty nine tributaries (39) of the Brahmaputra and eight (8) rivers of Tripura i.e. Master Plan Part-III

The Master Plan Part-I for Brahmaputra mainstem and the Master Plan Part-II for Barak and its tributaries, prepared in five volumes each were also approved by Ministry of Water Resources, Government of India, in July, 1997. The formulation of draft Master Plan Part-III comprising 39 tributaries of the river Brahmaputra and 8 rivers of Tripura was started during 1989-90 and on the basis of the comments/suggestion received from various State Government and Central Government Departments, Master Plans for 13 tributaries have been modified and approved by the Brahmaputra Board so far. These Master Plans are Buri-Dehing, Dikhow, Dhansiri (S), Kopili-Kollong, Puthimari, Ranganadi, Gumti, Pagladiya, Dikrong, Manu, Muhuri, Jia-Bharali and Noa-Nadi.

The Board has undertaken the preparation of Master Plan for Lohit sub-basin, an important tributary of Brahmaputra and Dhaleshwari river in Mizoram. Survey and Investigation of these Master plans are presently under progress.

Master plan for majuli island

Majuli is an island in the river Brahmaputra with an area of 900 sqkms. In order to find out a long term solution as well as sustainable short term measures for protecting the Majuli Island from acute erosion problem, Brahmaputra Board has undertaken preparation of Master Plan for Majuli Island. Survey and investigation is presently going on.

Preparation of detailed project

Pagladiya dam project (Assam)

The project involves construction of an earthen dam of about 26 m high. The detailed project report at an estimated cost of Rs. 472.00 crore (1997 price level) was approved from techno-economic angle by the Technical Advisory Committee (TAC) of the Ministry of Water Resources in August, 1995. The cost has been updated to Rs. 522 crore at price level of 1998. The project has also been cleared from environmental angle by the Ministry of Environment and Forest, Government of India, in September 1996. Clearance of the Ministry of Social Justice and Empowerment has also been received. Investment clearance is under active consideration of the Ministry of Water Resources, Government of India.

The Project envisages flood moderation and irrigation benefits With incidental power generation as given below:

Flood control	40,000 ha.
Irrigation	54,160 ha. (Annually)
Incidental Power	3.0 MW (50% load factor)

The Board has already initiated action on pre-construction survey. A public awareness programme has been launched to educate the people likely to be effected with necessary rehabilitation/resettlement package for the oustees of the project. Fresh socio-economic bench mark survey in the catchment area in the Vicinity of the reservoir, command area, flood protected area and survey for rehabilitation and resettlement of the persons affected by the Project is under progress. The Board has constituted a high level committee comprising officers from CSMRS, CWC, GSI and Brahmaputra Board to list, review and study the requirement of additional data for works required for designing and construction of Pagladiya Project. The Committee so constituted is also to recommend additional investigation works if any, required to be carried out after the study. The Committee has visited Pagladiya Project on 07.4.98 and recommended a few studies to be carried out by the Board for investigation of the foundation of the project.

Tipaimukh dam project (Manipur - Mizoram)

The detailed Project report was approved from techno-economic angle by the Technical Advisory Committee (TAC) of Ministry of Water Resources in August, 1995 for an estimated cost of Rs.2899 crore (1995 price level). It envisages construction of a 162 metre high rockfill dam with an installed capacity of 1500 mw. It will also provide flood protection to 1.43 lakh ha of land located in the downstream areas in the Barak Valley of Assam. The Ministry of Social Justice and Empowerment has cleared the project. The Ministry of Environment and Forest suggested specific interstate clearance which is being pursued by Brahmaputra Board and Ministry of Water Resources with the three states of Manipur, Mizoram and Assam for obtaining their concurrence from all aspects.

Siang (Dihing) dam project (Arunachal Pradesh)

The original proposal of Siang Dam Project of 1984 has been modified into three Dams at (i) Yingkiong (near Pugging village) on the river Siang, (ii) at 15 Km. Upstream of Kaying on the river Siyom and (iii) at old site Rotung. Submergence of important towns like Yingkiong, Along and pangin have now been eliminated. Survey and investigations at the new sites are in progress. The Arunachal Pradesh Government have also given clearance for dams of lower height without submerging the important towns and limited valley lands used by local tribal communities for agricultural purposes.

The estimated power potential of three dams mentioned above is 11000 MW, 700 MW and 2000 MW respectively.

Subansiri dam project (Arunachal Pradesh)

The original proposal of Subansiri Dam Project of 1984 has also been modified into three dams (i) Upstream of Daporijo near Menga on Subansiri river, (ii) on kamala river upstream of Tamen and (iii) old site at Gerukamukh. Survey and investigation have been initiated at the new sites. Clearance of Arunanchal Government for dams of lower height, avoiding submergence of important towns, has been obtained. The estimated power potential of these three dams is 2500 MW, 200 MW and 600 MW respectively.

Lohit dam project (Arunachal pradesh)

Alternative site at Mompani downstream of Hayuliang has been selected by a joint inspection team comprising officers from Brahmaputra Board, GSI, CWC and representative from Government of Arunachal Pradesh. The estimated power potential of the dam Is 3000MW.

Kameng dam project (Arunachal Pradesh)

In accordance with the request of Government of Arunachal Pradesh, Kameng Dam Project near Bhalukpong is under investigation. The Project envisages construction of a rock fill dam with a height of 200 metre near Tipi. The project Is likely to generate 1500 MW (Installed capacity) of power besides other benefits like flood control, irrigation, navigation and recreation etc.

The proposal is being studied to avoid submergence of Pakui wild life sanctuary and examine its feasibility along with the proposal for Bichhum - Tenga link dam Investigated earlier by CWC and NEEPCO. Brahmaputra Board has discussed the matter with Forest Department of Government of Arunachal -Pradesh. It seems that the construction of the project will not affect the wild life sanctuary.

Jadukata dam project (Meghalaya)

The project envisages construction of a 117 m high concrete dam at 9 krn south west of Nongstain township in Meghalaya over the river Jadukata (Kaynshi). The proposed installed capacity of the project is 450 MW. Feasibility stage is in progress.

Someswari dam project (Meghalaya)

The project envisages construction of a 62 m high rock fill dam 6 km upstream of Nanhgalbibra township in Meghalaya over the river Someshwari (Simsange). The proposed installed capacity of the project is 130 mw Preliminary investigation work is under progress.

UM-N-Got (Meghalaya)

The project envisages construction of 120 m concrete dam over the river UM-N-Got (Meghalaya). The proposed installed capacity of power is 710 mw Preliminary stage investigation works are in Progress.

Debang dam project (Arunachal Pradesh)

The Project envisages construction of 165 m high rock fill dam over the river Debang (Arunachal Pradesh). The installed capacity of hydropower from this project will be 2500 mw The preliminary investigation works are in progress.

Kulsi dam project (Meghalaya -Assam)

The project envisages construction of 60 m high rock fill dam with an installed capacity of 36 MW. The preliminary stage investigation works is in progress.

Bairabi dam project (Mizoram)

The project envisages construction of 60 m high rock fill dam on Dhaleswari river with an installed capacity of 75 mw of hydropower. The survey and other investigation works is in progress.

With the implementation of all these projects in phased manner, an estimated hydropower potential of the order 28,829 MW is proposed to be created. These projects will also provide considerable flood relief in Assam Valley.

Preparation of project report for drainage development

The number of drainage congested areas so far identified in the Master Plans are 22 in Brahmaputra Valley, 8 in Barak Valley and 3 in Tripura. The problem is mostly flood induced.

Harang drainage development scheme

The Ministry of Water Resources have cleared the scheme for execution at an estimated cost of Its. 10.81 crore by Brahmaputra Board during the Ninth Plan. Pre-construction Survey and other works are in progress. The Brahmaputra Board has initiated necessary action with the Government of Assam for acquisition of land required for construction of sluices, embanks and resectioning of the drains. A pre-qualification bid was floated for shortlisting of contractors for construction of sluices. Tender documents for these works is being issued.

Status of other scheme

The Brahmaputra Board has handed over five Drainage Development Schemes to Flood Control Department Government of Assam, for taking necessary action according to the request of the Government of Assam. These schemes are Amjur, Barbhang, Deroi, Ghagra and Pola.

The other drainage development schemes viz. Jakaichuk, East of Barpeta and Jengrai have been cleared by CWC for estimated cost of Rs.2.69 crore, Rs. 1.34 crore and Rs. 1.49 crore respectively. "No Objection" from Government of Assam is awaited for the execution of the schemes.

Two schemes - Joysagar and West of Barpeta have been submitted to CWC an d presently being examined by them for necessary clearance. Rudrasagar drainage development scheme in Tripura had been discussed with the State Government and is being modified to cover pisciculture and tourism aspect as well.

North eastern hydraulic and allied research institute (Nehari)

In accordance with clause 7 of the Assam Accord, the Brahmaputra Board was entrusted with a task of establishing the North Eastern Hydraulic and Allied Research Institute (NEHARI) in September, 1985.

The Institute located in an area of 47 ha at Rudreswar, North Guwahati was taken up for implementation in 1988-89 for establishing a hydraulic laboratory with three model trays, one flume and construction material testing facilities for rock, concrete and soil.

The hydraulic model testing facilities and the laboratories for testing materials have been operationalised in December, 1996. Hydraulic model for Jiadhal river was constructed in 1997 and studies carried out as a part of the research programme.

The studies reveal that morphological changes occur in the river due to high sediment load and debris contributed both due to high rainfall and geologically fragile hills in Arunachal Pradesh. As suggested by the Expert Team in its visit during September 1997 to Majuli Island, a rigid bed model covering entire Majuli Island of Brahmaputra reach is under progress for which necessary survey and investigation are in the final stages.

During the last one and a half year, about seventy five soil samples collected from different locations of N.E. Region were tested. Twelve out of these samples were from proposed project sites of NEEPCO.

Rest of the samples have been collected from the sites of different drainage development schemes which have been proposed as well as from the locations of the projects proposed by the Brahmaputra Board. During this period, seventy two samples of rocks were tested. Out of these nine samples are from Turial and Kopili lower stage projects of NEEPCO. Apart from this, cement and aggregates were also tested in the laboratory.

Betwa river board

In accordance with the Inter-State agreement of July 1972 between Madhya Pradesh and Uttar Pradesh, a decision was taken to constitute a Control Board for the execution of the Rajghat Dam Project, a joint venture of these States. Accordingly, the Betwa River Board was constituted by enactment of the Betwa River Board Act, 1976 by the Ministry of Water Resources for efficient, economical and early execution of the Project. The headquarters of the Board is at Jhansi in Uttar Pradesh.

The Union Minister of Water Resources is the Chairman of the Board with Union Minister of Power, Chief Ministers and Ministers-in-charge of Finance, Irrigation and Power of the two States as its Members. The activities of the Board are managed by the Executive Committee of the Board under the Chairmanship of the Chairman, Central Water Commission. The last meeting of the Executive Committee was held on 23rd October, 1998.

Rajghat dam project

Rajghat Dam Project is an Inter-State project of the Governments of Madhya Pradesh and Uttar Pradesh, being constructed on River Betwa about 22 km from Lalitpur. The project includes construction of 43.8 m high and 562.5 m long masonry dam across the River Betwa flanked by an earthen dam having a maximum height of 29.5 m and a total length of 10.79 km. On completion, the project will provide irrigation to 1.38 lakh ha of land in Uttar Pradesh and 1.21 lakh ha of land in Madhya Pradesh. The system of water distribution in both the States has to be devised by the respective States. The power generated from this Project will be 45mw (3x15 mw).

The cost and benefits of the project are to be shared by these two States equally. The projects existing on the downstream, are Matatila Dam Project, Dhukwan Weir and Parichha Weir. Thus, Rajghat Dam Project will serve as the mother storage for irrigation in Uttar Pradesh and Madhya Pradesh through cascade of hydraulic structures in the downstream of River Betwa.

On completion of the project, the regulation of reservoir shall be carried out by the Betwa River Board, whereas operation and maintenance of Rajghat Hydro-Electric Power House shall be done by the Madhya Pradesh Electricity Board (M.P.E.B.).

The estimated cost of Rajghat Dam at March 1995 price level is Rs. 266.16 crore and that of the Power House at March 1997 price level is Rs. 131.00 crore. Approximately more than 98 per cent of the physical work of Dam has been completed. The remaining works of raising of four piers out of 19, erection of remaining 15 gates out 18, and laying of deck slabs are in progress. Ninety percent of the civil work of the Power House has also been completed. The electrical and mechanical work is in advanced stage of execution. The Rajghat Dam Project is scheduled to be completed by June, 1999.

Bansagar control board

Organisation and composition

In pursuance of an Inter-State agreement among the States of Madhya Pradesh , Uttar Pradesh and Bihar, the Bansagar Control Board was constituted in January, 1976 for efficient, economical and early execution of Bansagar Dam and connected works. The headquarters of the Board is at Rewa in Madhya Pradesh.

The Union Minister of Water Resources is die Chairman of the Board and Union Minister of Power, Chief Ministers, Ministers-in-charge of Irrigation and Finance of the three States, and Minister-in-charge of Electricity of Madhya Pradesh are its Members. The day-to-day affairs of the Board are managed by the Executive Committee set up under the Chairmanship of the Chairman, Central Water Commission. The expenditure on the office of the Board is initially met out of the budget grants of the Union Ministry of Water Resources and subsequently reimbursed in equal proportion by the three States of Madhya Pradesh, Uttar Pradesh and Bihar.

During the last five years, Bihar has contributed only Rs. 6.5 crore out of which Rs. 3.5 crore was paid in the current financial year. The expenditure during 1998-99 upto December, 1998 is Rs. 25.03 crore and cumulative expenditure upto December, 1998 is Rs. 556.10 crore. Government of Bihar has yet to pay arrears of Rs. 77.825 crore towards their share cost.

Budget

The budget approved by the Executive Committee for 1997-98 and 1998-99, share due from each State and the contribution received upto December, 1998, are given below:-

(Rs. in Crore)

	1997-98	1998-99
Budget approved by the Executive Committee	85.00	87.85
Share of the States		
Madhya Pradesh	42.50	43.925
Uttar Pradesh	21.25	21.962
Bihar	21.25	21.962
Actual Contribution		
Madhya Pradesh	(-) 0.76	(-) 12.515
Uttar Pradesh	17.00	(+) 6.257
Bihar	(+) 3.00	(+) 6.257

Tungabhadra board

Tungabhadra Board was constituted by the President of India in exercise of the powers vested under section 66(4) of the Andhra State Act, for completion, operation and maintenance of Tungabhadra Project. The Board controls of the common portion of the Tungabhadra Project. The Krishna Water Disputes Tribunal has made specific provision in the Award for the use of Tungabhadra waters by the States of Karnataka and Andhra Pradesh. The responsibility for carrying out this specific provision relating to the use of Tungabhadra waters has been entrusted to the Tungabhadra Board by the Tribunal. The Board is regulating the water for irrigation, hydro-power generation and other uses from the reservoir.

At present, the Board consists of a Chairman appointed by Government of India, a Member representing Government of India and two Members, one each representing Andhra Pradesh and Kanataka, on a part-time basis. The funds for the functioning of the Board are provided by the two State Governments.

The working table for canal-wise distribution of water among the States is prepared every year by the Tungabhadra Board in consultation with the State Governments and reviewed from time to time during the water year. The regulation of water is carried out in accordance With this working table.

The utilisation of water by the two States during the water year 1998-99 till the end of December, 1998 was 70.429 TMC ft. for Karnataka and 40.908 TMC ft. for Andhra Pradesh as against the assessed quantum of 179 TMC ft. as on December 31, 1998 for the entire water year 1998-99. The evaporation losses during the current year from June 1998 to December 1998 were 7.341 TMC ft. to be shared by Karnataka and Andhra Pradesh in the ratio of 12.5 :5.5.